*This work is dedicated to the memory of*

# Eleanor Tufts

*who opened up*
*art history*
*to great women artists*

# *Art, Myths, and Rituals:*

## *Visual Language for the New Reality*

Kyra Belán

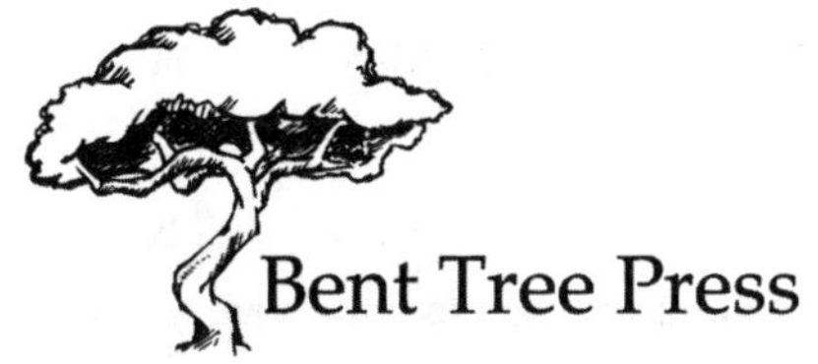

Cover design by Kyra Belán and Charles Martin.
Front cover art by Kyra Belán.
Back Cover Photo: Elegant Photographics.



Printed in the United States of America.

ISBN: 1-933005-69-6

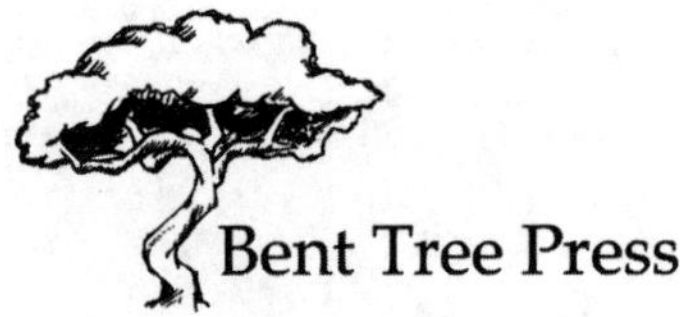


59 Damonte Ranch Parkway, #B-284 • Reno, NV 89521 • (800) 970-1883

www.benttreepress.com

Address all correspondence and order information to the above address.

# Contents

# *Preface*

Mythology, as expressed through visual images, has been with us since the beginning of prehistory. Myths change through time whenever a society or culture, together with its value systems, undergoes a structural change. Myths must remain relevant to each particular social paradigm that has engendered them. Current mythology is struggling to keep up with the new social reality. Therefore, I have chosen to look carefully at the mythological, symbolic, and archetypal content in the visual arts of the past and present and to use those sources for my inspiration. The artworks in this book are intended to provide images for the contemporary interpretations of world mythology.

This book has been written for the college-level audience and the general public with the intent of offering new options in visual language that relate to the rapid social change that our society is now undergoing. The original version of this book was published in 1996 under the title *Earth, Spirit, and Gender: Visual Language for the New Reality*. For the convenience of the reader, I have included notes and a bibliography of the books that were sources of my information. The readers should be able to access these texts in order to further broaden their knowledge of art history, mythology, or related subjects. The illustrations of the artworks in this book are organized and numbered for easy reference.

My special thanks to Betty Owen, who encouraged me to pursue this subject. I also wish to thank my husband, Charles Martin, for his patience, understanding and emotional support. My sincere thanks to Alessandra Comini for her belief in the timeliness of this manuscript and to my editor Jon Hughes Fuller, who was open to my ideas. This is my opportunity to acknowledge my gratitude to the hundreds of people who have participated in one or more of my performances, many spontaneously joining a performance in progress. I also thank Terry Bergamo for making some of my performance costumes. My sincere thanks to Ronnie Rotschild, Vicki Hendricks, GL Sullivan, Anjal Soler, Bill Taylor, Toni Montesi, Greg Eisman, Marie Canaves, Alicia Sanches, Patti McDounough, Janice Hartwell, and Ray Burggraf for their assistance or support.

# *Foreword*

My interest in world mythologies began in early childhood. Life has always offered me many opportunities to travel, and so it was that I found myself in a city park in northeastern China when I was four years old. A giant bronze statue of Kwan Yin or Guan Yin, the Chinese Goddess of Compassion, stood with her head tilted slightly downward. It was as if she looked directly at me. Her face was enigmatic, yet calm and beautiful. Appearing to emerge from a lotus flower, she stood as a majestic embodiment of the divine feminine.

As a schoolgirl in Argentina, I was impressed by the love and reverence that people felt for Nuestra Señora de Lujan, the protective and caring mother of Argentina, representing the *marianismo* of all South America. During my studies in that country's public schools, I learned about the myths and religions of numerous South American and Central American native cultures, all of which worshiped the divine feminine as much as they did the masculine. Visits to the library and my teachers' lectures allowed me to discover the rich heritage of the goddesses and gods of ancient Egypt, Greece, and Rome.

Being brought up with archetypes of the Great Mother helped me to develop self-confidence and a belief in my own potential as a human being. This early self-assurance was followed later by a conviction that I had the choice to express my personal point of view, philosophy, and value system through art. Because of my early exposure to many cultures, my art and my ideas about the meaning of art are influenced by a global, rather than exclusively Western, paradigm. I see myself as a citizen of the world.

At the beginning of my career as an artist, this belief in freedom of expression was almost subconscious. I just assumed that the social system would allow me to exercise this freedom. I produced art without being conscious of the fact that what I was doing was not supported or condoned by the current social order. It required numerous encounters with censorship, with the labeling of my work as controversial, and with extensive rejection of my exhibit proposals for me to realize that I was venturing into forbidden territory. Now I have the perspective of over two decades of being a professional artist in an androcentric society. I am now more than familiar with the reaction of much of society to my artworks that represent images of spirituality or sensuality from the female point of view. And I still believe that including matristic elements and the concept of the female gaze in our culture is important. It motivates me to continue this journey into the realms of spirit, ecology, sensuality, and aesthetics.

Along with the realization that positive female archetypes and myths have had on my self-esteem, self-assurance, and self-worth came the desire to share this experience with others, male and female. A society that projects itself as a single-gendered structure cannot achieve or maintain a healthy balance within itself or with the original Great Mother, our planet Earth. At this time of political and ecological crises it is essential to re-integrate the myths and archetypes of patriarchy with the rich heritage of the old matristic societies. Consequently, a future social paradigm is beginning to emerge: a global culture of spiritual and material balance.

The arts perform an important function within any social transition. My work clearly reflects the re-introduction of the female principle into contemporary society. Visual images have always been used to represent and to interpret myths, symbols, and archetypes; the power of an image is immense as human beings visualize their concepts. Images take root and populate our dreams and visions of past, present, and future realities.

I believe that matriarchal and multi-cultural mythologies must be reintegrated, re-created, reinvented, and re-embedded into the human mind to pave the way for a gender-balanced, multi-cultural future; I am dedicated to this process. The presence of these images in our culture enriches the psyches of both genders, accelerating the change in the individual mind-set. This new mental construct is a society that values harmony, balance, multi-culturalism, and natural environment.

# 1

# *The Issue of Gender Identified Art*

Getting a visual message out into the world is a formidable problem for any artist. For an eco-feminist artist to get her message across is immensely more difficult, as the audience is often unable to receive the full impact of the intended message. Contemporary society is often unaware of the meanings of myths, archetypes, and symbols that constitute extensive but little known history of matriarchal civilizations. Current patriarchal structure often does not permit or encourage the inclusion of female achievements, symbols, archetypes, and points of view in its history of culture. Women in the visual arts are especially vulnerable: exclusion of their artworks from art museums and art texts was practiced routinely for many centuries, and this situation is just beginning to change today. The spectator, therefore, when faced with my art, is able to perceive through the lens of andro-centric values only the formal aspect of the work, and perhaps a portion of the message.

Like other women artists and writers, I exist within a social structure that ignores or minimizes the achievements of my gender. Female achievement was routinely left out of history texts, generation after generation. The remaining information is often ignored today, and excluded from the majority of the school and college textbooks. During the two thousand years of rigid one-gendered orientation, outstanding women in every field of human accomplishment believed themselves to be the first ones to break through the male-dominant structures and to achieve in their field. Often they had no knowledge of female role models. Today some women may know of a few great women, since the process of reinserting women into the history of humanity has just begun. Even in the new millennium, personal achievement by a woman is often perceived as exceptional rather than normal behavior for her gender. Because of this belief, some women do not feel at ease with their success in their fields of expertise. The patriarchal orientation of most educational systems conditions many women to believe that they are less important than men.

Since the decade of the seventies, which was a period of significant social change, ground-breaking worldwide feminist research has been taking place in all areas of human knowledge and cultures. These studies corroborate the enormity of female contributions within all types of societies, but in particular within the matriarchies. However, this knowledge is only beginning to trickle down into the pool of human consciousness. This new knowledge is disseminated in our culture mainly through the printed word. The feminization of our one-gendered culture, which includes the arts, is gradually taking shape. Yet humanity can become whole only through integrating female visions and values into the patriarchal paradigm. The new integrated social system will redirect the future of the planet away from ruthless self destruction. Neither wars, the decimation of our natural resources, or prejudice against race or gender will be able to survive this social change.

Artistic visions have served a prominent function within all social structures. My goal is to provide new visual images that can better reflect a changing society. These visual images are about a search for a peaceful coexistence of humans and nature, and a power balance between the genders and races. They offer a glimpse into a social system of the future that recognizes and values the fact that all human beings are evolving into a higher level of consciousness.

All of the world's religions, myths, and archetypes are inventions of human minds. Since the deepest recesses of prehistory, humans have been spinning tales that subsequently evolved into their religions. These original mythologies were gradually transformed through the millennia, providing humanity with new forms of belief and archetypes that reflected the many changes in its social structures. In the past, each socio-religious shift was mirrored by a change in the visual images that those cultures produced. As new images were created, they reflected all the changes within the social structures. These transformations continue today in order to give birth to the new gender-balanced and multi-cultural social order.

As most societies changed from matriarchal to patriarchal paradigms, their religious mythologies and archetypes increasingly projected the masculine, while obscuring or obliterating the feminine. This slow and gradual process took thousands of years. The first matristic civilizations were many thousands of years old, and most scholars date them beyond 35,000 BCE. The conversion to patriarchy began about 5,000 years ago. This time span is comparatively short within the context of the totality of human history, and current social changes indicate that we are witnessing the development of yet another social model.

During this period of transition, planet Earth is experiencing a dawning of the new possible future—that of a *partnership society*, a term first used by Riane Eisler in her book, *The Chalice and the Blade*. Within this new culture, female visions, myths, archetypes, and values will be allowed to coexist with the surviving components of patriarchal culture. We are already beginning to experience an accelerated shift in consciousness and spirituality. My artworks attempt to describe and predict this shift.

This transformation within our society is both physical and spiritual, and it is deeply affecting all human beings. It is bringing into focus the need for inclusion of submerged female values that lie dormant under the layers of the dominator model's militaristic and hierarchical society. Historically feminine values, which many men and women are now beginning to adopt, regard world peace as essential. They also promote reverence for all ecosystems, advocate love and compassion as cardinal functions of a civilized society, accept the belief in the interconnectedness of earthly and spiritual realms, and respect the inherent rights of each human being to pursue his or her freedom. All these issues are visually and symbolically represented in my artworks, and the text of this book is an extension and explication of my visual statements.

The main source of inspiration for my art is drawn from prehistoric, ancient, Native American, and other cultures that, in part, are predecessors of a new world that is now forming. These cultures provide me with an unlimited number of myths, archetypes, and symbols to recreate, recombine, revise, and incorporate into my art. I do not feel an obligation or desire to conform to prescribed rules of the old model of society, which subdivides all human life into boxes, files, or drawers. A postmodern approach to art-making allows me to use many aspects of the creative process to achieve a particular artistic outcome.

My knowledge and use of mythology is translated into an artistic production of work that promotes the empowerment of women in our society and a re-interpretation of female and male archetypes and symbols of an earth-based spirituality. This work is a projection of a changing society that is undergoing a process of self re-evaluation and self re-creation. My art attempts to explain and predict how the current value systems are shifting into the realm of a peaceful, non-hierarchical, and connected society.

This artistic journey includes an exploration of sensuality and sexuality, attempting a new inroad into the beginning of the development of erotic and sensual images from the female perspective. This experience is a celebration of the emerging female gaze. These images of the male nude form are an adventure into human sensuality from a female viewpoint. They herald the beginning of the development of visual sensuality inherent in the female gender, but yet largely unexplored.

Visual sensuality has been developed in the male gender, but is often lacking in women. This lack of visual sensual awareness in women is due to thousands of years of sexual oppression and the absence of an opportunity to develop and express their own eroticism. Even today, a woman artist often explores visual sensuality only as an observer of herself or other women; as a result, female nudes produced by female artists differ from the ones produced by male artists. The female nude from a woman's perspective is presented as powerful rather than powerless, possessing human dignity and spirituality. I explore the female nude from the female point of view; however, I have also fixed my gaze on the opposite gender and investigated the complexities of beauty, sensuality, and earth-based spirituality of the male nude.

The appreciation of ritual and desire to incorporate it into contemporary life led me to experiment with ritual performance art. I believe that ritual art can enhance and inspire spirituality and creativity in human beings. It can bring the richness and enchantment of numerous ancient and non-Western cultures of past and present into our secular and impersonal contemporary society.

My philosophy of the purpose of art is inspired by people-oriented matristic cultures. I believe that a work of art must harmoniously interrelate with the environment and the flow of urban life. Art must be created as a vibrant and integral part of everyday life. Instead of being a part of an isolated esoteric realm, incomprehensible to the public and removed from the framework of everyday existence, art must take on a positive role in the lives of the people. Art should not be elitist. Art must reflect the culture that generates it and affect the public in an energizing, active, constructive, and educational manner. It should not be allowed to harm the environment or promote disruptive and negative activities, such as the obstruction of a view or traffic, when situated within urban context. Art must be an enhancement of the society that produced it. Visionary art often predicts a particular direction that a society will adopt in the future. My goal is for my artistic production to fulfill these requirements.

# 2

## *The Face of Mother God*

In order for humanity to succeed in transcending the patriarchal social structure and step into the portal of a gender-balanced society that is spiritual, peaceful, and respectful of Mother Earth, it is necessary to readjust and rethink our myths, archetypes, and spiritual beliefs. All organized religious systems that presently function within the dominant cultures visualize their gods almost exclusively in male form. My belief is that in order for a society to succeed in transforming itself into a new, egalitarian structure that is spiritually and ecologically conscious, it is imperative that both women and men should be able to visualize God in both female and male forms, with equal ease. Only when humanity is able to revive, re-accept, and re-absorb the image of the omnipotent and universal creator as female, can the gender-neutral or genderless concept of God be brought out for philosophical discussion and accepted by humanity on both conscious and unconscious levels. Since a single-gendered patriarchal culture has been dominant worldwide for nearly two millennia, it is impossible for the majority of human beings to visualize an all-powerful creator in the body of a woman. Even if the concept of God is dematerialized into a pure energy or spirit form, this spirit-energy is usually perceived by the human mind on a subconscious level as either all masculine or more masculine than feminine.

Every human being has a natural inclination to visualize her or his concepts and ideas, and the arts can and must continue to provide for this tendency. The images of God the Mother alongside the usual God the Father should be easily available. Only when both God the Mother and God the Father are equally venerated will the women and men of the world be able fully to embrace their rights to co-create the future of this planet. The contemporary philosopher Mary Daly explores this notion in her books, *Pure Lust* and *Beyond God the Father*, and her conclusion is that it is necessary to bring God the Mother back into the culture in order to achieve a balance among women and men in all other aspects of life. For two thousand years, artists have provided human beings with a multitude of images of the male god: as an old man—God the Father and as a young man—the Father's only Son. These images fill cathedrals, churches, temples, art museums, and books. Even when this male God is dematerialized into the Holy Spirit and is visually represented by the dove—a pre-Christian symbol of the divine feminine—it is still interpreted by organized religions as a purely male spirit, even though the dove was subsumed into Christianity from the old Mother God religions. Artists usually place the male God or the male divine Trinity in the heavenly realm, residing on a layer of clouds and surrounded by lower-ranking spiritual beings, most of whom are also male. Even the priesthood, considered by many organized religions to be spiritually superior to lay people and, therefore, closer to God, is still predominantly male. In spite of this, God the Mother was never totally excised from the genetic code and the subconscious minds of human beings. She appears in Christianity as the Virgin Mary, the Mother of God, and she is the occult Mother God in the psyches of most people who were raised as Christians. Even as you read this book, the role of the divine feminine is being re-evaluated within the Christian establishment, and some clergy and religious philosophers are ready to incorporate the original sacred feminine of early Christianity into contemporary organized religion, equating God the Mother with either the Holy Spirit or the Virgin Mary, or both. Some propose that she could be perceived as the mother of the divine son and the divine daughter. On the other end of the spectrum of Christianity is the complete public denial of the existence of God the Mother. Since the Reformation, many branches of Christianity have minimized or erased the role of the Mother of God, and the devotees of these religions are still deprived of the joy of celebrating the divine feminine principle in its veiled form. The need for this void to be filled is now emerging.

My Latin heritage has gifted me with the variety and richness of the images of a Great Mother, providing me with an easy transition between the time of discovery of ancient myths of the world, that include the divine feminine principle, and the realization that the sacred feminine must surface into the mainstream of our society. Discovery of the old myths and archetypes came early in my life. I had learned to read by the time I was five years old, and I was immediately attracted to the world's myths and religions that worshiped God in female as well as male form. The study of matriarchal religions and civilizations became my lifelong passion. Images of the divine feminine started to appear in my childhood sketches, and later in drawings and paintings created during my undergraduate studies at Arizona State University. Ultimately, they evolved into a series of art works on the theme of female spirituality during my graduate studies at Florida State University. During my doctoral studies years I acquired an interest in writing, and as a result have written articles and books on art, spirituality, and ritual in art.

## *Matriarchal Civilizations*

My investigation into the prehistoric and ancient cultures led me to the realization that the Great Mother was worshiped all over the globe[1] before male gods were invented by humankind. Although she had thousands of names, depending upon the geographical locations and languages in which she was worshiped, she was consistently believed to be the creator of all that exists. She was omnipotent, the giver and taker of life, the provider of abundance and fertility in nature. She ruled over the earth, the waters, and the sky. She was worshiped as the Great Creator of humans and animals. The earthly and heavenly realms were believed to be equally loved by the mother of all. The religion of the Mother permeated all aspects of human existence. The status of women in those matriarchal cultures was equal to the position of men. Female sexuality and spirituality were respected, and human beings shared a profound respect for their environment, a respect that bordered on reverence. The trees, plants, and creatures that inhabited planet Earth were presumed to have equal place with human beings in the world of the Great Mother. The matristic societies promoted and maintained periods of lasting peace and provided themselves with relative abundance from nature, with minimal consequences to the ecosystem. Traditionally, women were the gatherers, contributing to their society the majority, about 70 percent of the nourishment, while men were the hunters, killing animals for the balance of the food supply and for the hides. The number of animals killed was small, and a ritual was performed to pay respect to the slain creatures and to ask for their forgiveness. Later, women developed agriculture, the lunar calendar and the first script or written language, which they often used to decorate their clay vessels, as described by the archaeologist Marija Gimbutas in her recent books, *The Civilization of the Goddess* and *The Language of the Goddess*.

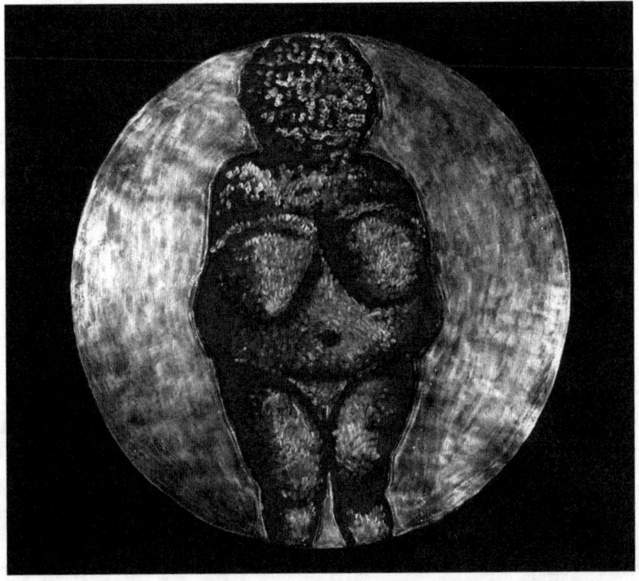

**2–1. Magic Circle Series: Mother God of Willendorf** © Kyra Belán, 1993
Acrylic on paper, module, 52" x 73"
Inspired by the Venus of Willendorf, prehistoric, c. 25,000 BCE

## *Transition from Matriarchal to Patriarchal Societies*

The years from approximately 3,000 BCE and 300 CE represent a period in history of humanity when weapons of bronze and metal were invented and herds of cattle were forced into captivity for human use and consumption. This was the accomplishment of the males, the traditional hunters of the tribes. Thus the men gained a high degree of social power, and the power imbalance between the genders was established. At this time, the worship of the first male god, as the son of Mother God, was initiated. He was a seasonal god, dying in the fall and resurrecting in the spring, and a prototype for many future gods of the first patriarchal religions. Mother God's functions were eventually divided among the numerous goddesses and gods, such as the ones worshiped by the Greeks or Romans. The polytheistic religions were well suited for the early models of male-oriented societies. These early models were replaced by stricter forms of andro-centric social order, which eventually dispossessed women of their lands, birthrights and human rights. At that point in history, Mother God either almost completely disappeared or was worshiped in secret. In our dominant Western cultures, the Goddess was transformed into a shadow of herself. She is now Mary, the mother of God, but officially not a god herself; she is the Virgin who gave birth and represents an anomaly that no living woman can duplicate or emulate. Yet she remains, within the male-dominated society, as the veiled Great Mother God archetype. Today her frequent apparitions, sacred sites, and miraculous events are frequently covered by the press world-wide. For many centuries, artworks have been created to celebrate her, and populate the museums, the private collections, and the cathedrals all over the planet. Many books on this art, including by this author, have been published to provide the viewer with many magical and beautiful images.

Mary's divine substance is even corroborated by Catholic dogma: she is interpreted to be, like her divine child Jesus, devoid of original sin. Like her son, she eventually ascended to heaven; she is revered as the Queen of Heaven and the loving Mother of the church and of humanity. The need for her existence in the spiritual realm of humanity is clearly expressed in contemporary society: throughout this century, numerous apparitions of the Mother have occurred all over the globe, and the attending worshippers receive messages from her, usually through a person to whom the Great Mother appeared or appears. This person is frequently a woman. Miracles, healings, and extraordinary phenomena also take place and are seen by the attending masses of people on the sites. One such phenomenon is the dancing of the sun in the heavens during the apparition time, another is the miraculous movement of the statue of Mary. The various phenomena are often viewed by thousands of people. They may be people's psychic experiences, hallucinations, or archetypal manifestations of the sacred feminine. Whatever the situation, in the minds of the people, the effect of Mary's presence constitutes a very powerful experience (see Color Plate 1).

To move from the general to the particular, let me cite an event from my own experience. In 1994 the miraculous apparitions of *Nuestra Señora*, Mother Mary, began to occur on every thirteenth day of the month in my own neighborhood in South Florida. After resisting the temptation to attend this local Lourdes event for several months, I ventured to the site and stood among the crowd of four thousand people (this figure is an estimate of local newscasters) to witness the reactions of the worshippers and to try to comprehend the mass spirituality taking place around me. The attending crowd, representing all ages, was about half Hispanic, and half Anglo. The praying and singing took place in both Spanish and English. The preliminary rituals and crowd-control activities were organized by various women volunteers of both Hispanic and Anglo heritage. They were providing a support system for the woman—whom I will call Nelida who, in a trance state, was believed to be receiving visions and communications from Mary. There were also women who facilitated direct contact with Nelida for those people who had the desire to be healed or to have a personal word with her. The crowd was extremely well behaved and passionately involved in their spiritual quest.

After about an hour of ritual prayer it was announced that the Virgin Mary had appeared to Nelida and was giving her a message of love and predictions of future world events. During the sacred visitation time, which lasted an hour, the public was frequently looking at the sky, waiting to see a sign or an apparition of Mother Mary, and taking photographs. I started snapping pictures of the overcast sky. The clouds were covering the sun most of the time on that rainy day, but occasional glimpses of the sun would appear. As I looked at one of the Polaroid pictures that I had just taken, I saw what appeared to be a face and a softly luminous human form in the clouds; the surrounding crowd also saw the same configurations in the photograph (as well as two other less defined faces and what looked like a galaxy). The crowd passed the picture around reverently, and finally, returned it. My other Polaroid images showed more "faces" and luminous blotches of light that looked like winged figures. At the end of the hour, Nelida appeared with the message of love from the Virgin Mary for the crowd, who held hands. This ended the apparition ceremony. The Polaroid picture was interpreted by the crowd as the manifestation of Mary and her son Jesus, while I saw in it what could be a figure of the sacred feminine, or a symbol of female spirituality. Photographs such as these are open to many interpretations, since the images are soft-edged and nebulous. Other incidents during the sighting or "presence" of Mary seem to point to the fact that a heightened state of spiritual awakening within a large crowd resulted in some physical effects. At one point I heard a scream of joy from a woman who was waving her rosary. According to her, it was changed from a brassy brown color to a shiny gold. Many saw the sun "dance" and the colors around change, yet what I saw was a normal, clouded sky, with the sun occasionally emerging. Then, at the very end of the "visitation," while taking my last Polaroid shot, I also saw, through the camera lens, the sun dance and the colors change from reds to oranges, and then to strong and luminous golds. Perhaps it was a mass hallucination in which I suddenly became a participant, perhaps the crowd's (and my) spirituality was heightened to the point that effected a change in a normal perception of reality, or perhaps the female aspect of the divine universal force was stronger than usual at that point in time and space. Unexpectedly, I became a part of an experience that was more unusual than I had anticipated, and since that event, my artistic productivity has increased. This statement is, of course, subject to interpretation. Yet, whatever was happening, it was about the presence of female spirituality affecting the minds of the people of our planet. The general effect on the crowd was energizing and unifying.

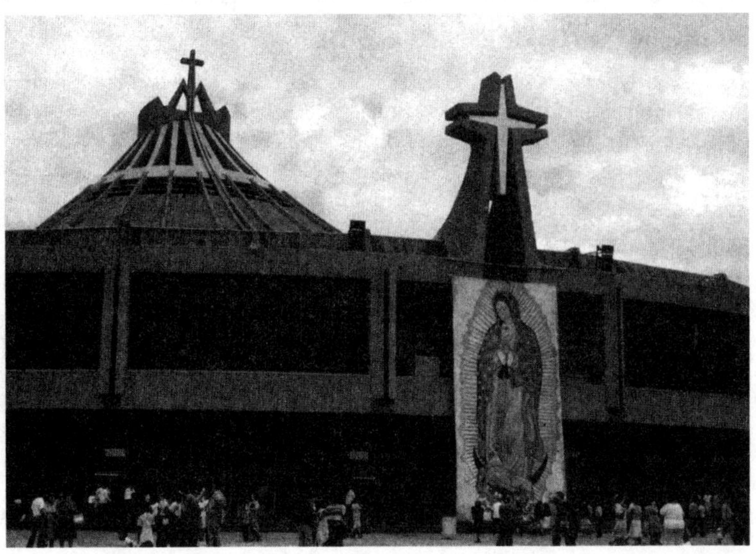

**2–2 The Temple of Our Lady of Guadalupe**, patron of Mexico and the Americas
Mexico City, Mexico

My decision to create new images of God in female form came out of a desire to restore the sacred feminine power to both women and men in our society. By creating female faces of God, I attempt to extend the divine essence into that half of humanity which is not yet visually entitled to it, and by extension, I recognize the divine nature in myself and all human beings. This realization gives me an incredible feeling of joy, and makes me a more complete being, on both physical and spiritual level. My self-respect has increased, as well as my respect for other women and their accomplishments. I also realize that preference for the male sex and the animosity for her own gender is so deeply ingrained in any woman raised under patriarchal order that she is usually unaware of it. Even those women who consciously believe that both genders are equally endowed with creative talent and intelligence somehow feel less compelled to attribute the term "genius" to a woman or to vote for one to become a president of an important institution, corporation, or nation. Volumes of art books are filled with the work of the great male artists, while the great female artists are either totally absent, or represented by a minute one to five percent of the pages. Their art, if reproduced at all, is often rendered in black and white. Most women are so used to this that they accept it as a norm; unconsciously, a woman's artwork is regarded as somehow less important or valuable than that of a man. The percentage has recently improved, and some college-level texts feature as many as twenty to twenty-five percent of great women artists. Yet the visual art establishment, like other patriarchal structures, does not treat women as equals. Creativity is still seen as primarily the realm of the male gender, since the creator is visualized as male.

The inclusion of the female aspect of God into contemporary imagery of the world will deeply affect both genders on all levels, in all professions and walks of life. Women and men will be able to express themselves beyond the boundaries of their stereotypical roles and explore their potential beyond those prescribed roles. Based on the enthusiastic response of male viewers who attend my exhibitions and lectures, I can conclude that most men are receptive to sharing the earthly and spiritual realms with women. The responsibilities of forming a better future for the children of this planet can and must be shared by both genders (see Color Plates 2 and 3).

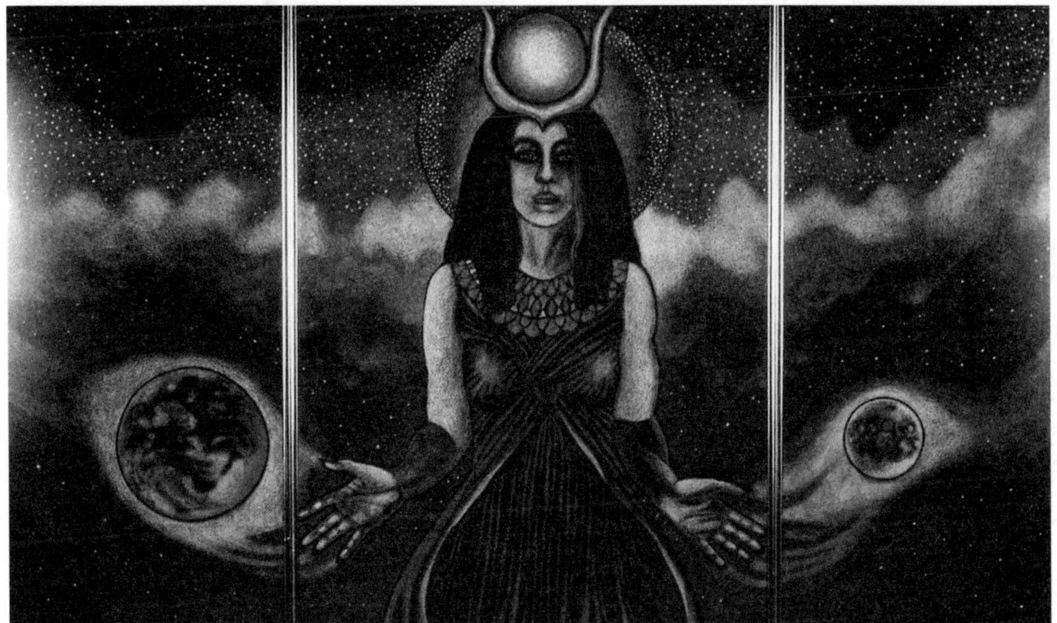

**2–3 Goddess Isis Creating the Earth and the Moon** © Kyra Belán, *1989*
Drawing, colored pencil, 29" x 38"

As a personal experience, changing the face of God has proved to be liberating; the subconscious biases against my own sex instilled in me by the patriarchal environment have vanished. I give myself permission to explore in my art any aspect of human emotions or messages that I consider important.

The process of creating Goddess images included studies of the divine feminine as represented in ancient religions of the world. Beyond the research into the materials available at the university libraries, I have visited an extensive number of archeological sites that offer an unlimited quantity of first-hand information on the subject. The history of the sacred feminine is available to all; it can be observed at numerous archeological sites and digs all over the planet. With some knowledge of the myths and symbols of the old matriarchal past and the non-mainstream matristic present, it is easy to discover the extensive female historical heritage that surrounds us.

This enormous pool of primary information, coupled with scholarly research, provides me with a foundation of symbols and images from the religions and civilizations of the Great Goddess. In this book I am not just bringing forward the past, but also creating and re-envisioning female spiritual archetypes, myths, and symbols that are in the process of becoming an integral part of a new gender-balanced society of the new millennium.

## *Goddess Isis Creating the Earth and the Moon*

This image, a triptych in colored pencils on black paper, depicts Goddess Isis in the center, wearing the sun disc on her head between the crescent/cow horns, traditional Egyptians symbols for this divinity. Rendered in a stylized realism, she is shown in the act of creating planet Earth and the Moon, its satellite. Using contemporary approach, Isis is portrayed in her traditional Egyptian role as the creation divinity. The background space suggests formation of the stars and the universe.

## *Goddess Isis, the Virgin Mary, and Mary Magdalene*

Goddess Isis was perceived by the Ancient world as the loving Earth Mother, the Creation divinity, the Great Healer and the Magician. Direct successor of the old omnipotent Goddess of prehistory, Isis is seen as the most ancient divinity of Egypt. Ultimately all the other goddesses and gods are aspects of the Great isis. In my book, Madonnas from Medieval to Modern, (Parkstone, 2001) Isis is featured as one of the divine predecessors of The Virgin Mary. In fact, the worship of Mary was introduced into early Christianity because the religion of Isis was more popular. When Mary's role in the new religion of Christianity was equated with that of Isis, the Virgin was accepted by the worshipers as the Mother Goddess, and syncretically merged with the Egyptian goddess.

Consequently, Christianity gained force; by sixth century the last temple of Isis was officially closed, and her religion became occult for many centuries that followed.

Goddess Isis and the Christian Mother of God were also merged in Europe into an image of the miraculous Black Madonna, worshiped at numerous Christian churches, particularly in France. These Madonnas are still extant today, and the belief in their ability to perform miracles and grant wishes is as popular as it was in the past. These Black Madonnas are also associated with Mary Magdalene, whose worship in early Christian Europe was extensive. The myth that The Magdalene represented the divine feminine in Christianity persisted, as she was seen as the companion/spouse of Jesus. This line of thinking was inherited from the numerous early patriarchal myths, when initially the Great Goddess became paired with a god as the divine couple. The worship of the divine couples and the concept of sacred marriage or *hieros gamos* also included Isis; according to the variation of the myth, she and god Osiris, together with their son Horus, formed a divine trinity.

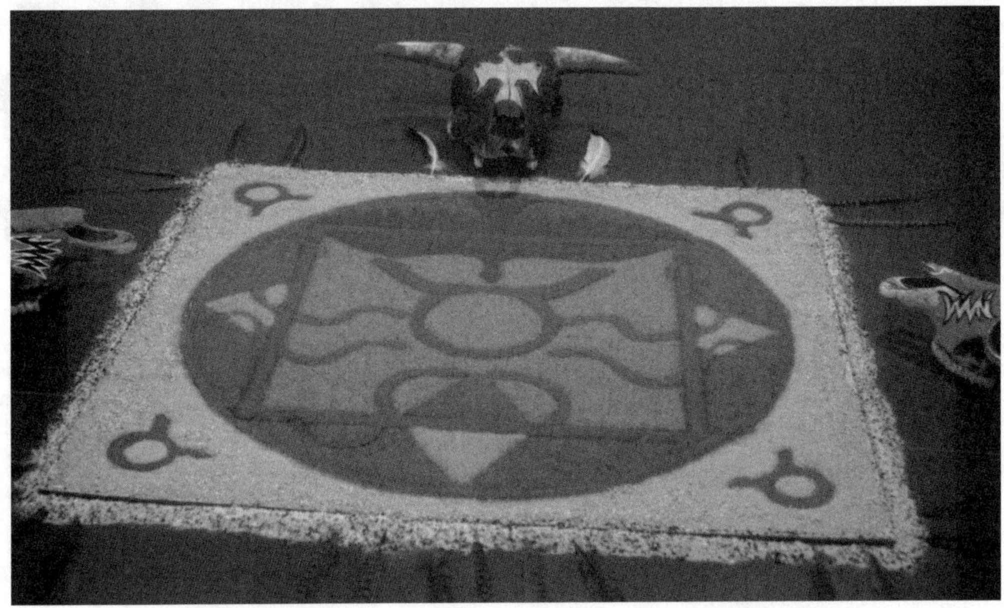

**2-4 Magic Circle II: Goddess Isis** © Kyra Belán, 1979
Deatil of Installation: sand painting, feathers, skulls
An Alternative Gallery, North Miami, Florida

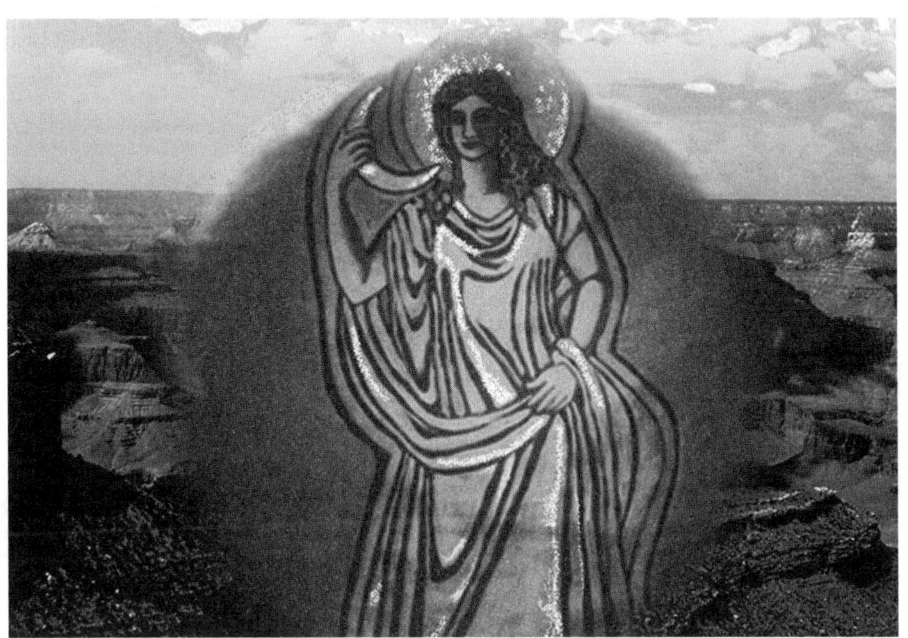

**2-5 Mother God Cybele** © Kyra Belán 2004
digital art
inspired by the Great Mother God of Rome imported from ancient Phrygia

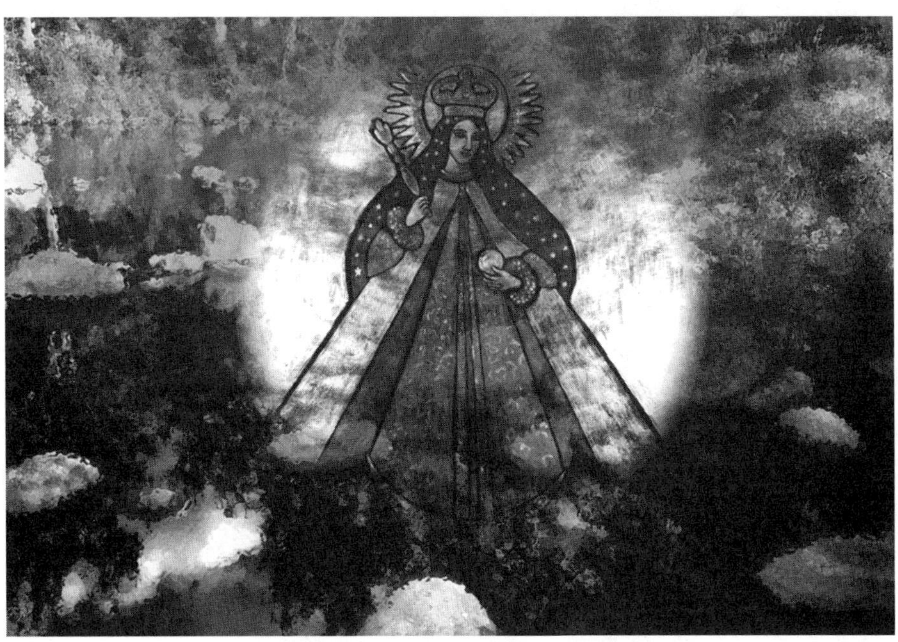

**2-6 Sedona Madonna** © Kyra Belán 2003
digital art
inspired by the Christian Mother of God, Goddess Pachamama of Peru
and the Native American Mother Earth as Sacred Life Giver

# 3

# *Mother God, Mother Earth*

In this book the icons of Mother God can be classified into several types or categories. The Goddess may be depicted as a woman, or a fusion of earth-based spirituality and female sexuality. The resulting image is a self-portrait or a portrait of another woman. The Goddess, in this case, is depicted as an incarnation of the sacred feminine on the planet. Mother God is re-created and re-envisioned in my artworks through my interpretations of earlier sources: the familiar images of the Great Mother that are found in prehistoric, ancient, Hindu, Native American, African, and Eastern cultures and in the traces of the divine feminine in Western patriarchal cultures. Finally, archetypes of Mother God that display attributes from diverse mythological and religious sources, originally a part of the past and present matristic cultures of the world are recombined into images of the Divine Mother that are a contemporary version of the visual manifestation of the sacred feminine. These Goddesses may also be self-portraits or portraits of women, or they may have features of an idealized woman, a personification of beauty.

I employ diverse media and techniques and often recombine them with new art technologies and approaches, such as mixed media, installations, process art, earth art, performance, video, and electronic or digital art. Visual content varies from pictorial to conceptual. The intent is to send into the world new ways of visualization and perception of God in female form.

During the seventies, I produced a series of paintings and drawings that included the myths of Mother God. The average size of a painting was 6 feet x 8 feet, and the drawings were usually 40 inches x 48 inches, rendered in a realistic style that included elements of the surreal and magic. The paintings were executed in oil or acrylic and the drawings in graphite, colored pencil or both. I explored themes from Egyptian, Greek, and Roman mythologies, combining them with contemporary motifs. Yet most people failed to understand the content of the works at that time, since both genders still perceived women as relatively powerless and lacking in historical heritage or importance. My images were often ridiculed and censored by those men or women who perceived them as vaguely threatening, since they contradicted accepted beliefs in the exclusivity of male spirituality.

One of the paintings produced during the early seventies while in graduate school, titled *Isis the Creator* (1974, oil on canvas 72 inches x 96 inches), features the Goddess in the center middle ground of the painting, wearing her solar headdress, a reference to her creative power and her status as the Sun Goddess. She is one of the female solar divinities that were abundant in ancient religions. Usually, the Sun Goddesses derived from the prehistoric, omnipotent Mother God, and Isis is one of them. The cow horns that surround the solar disc are symbols of the lunar or cyclical aspects of Isis. She is seen standing in front of a canvas that she is painting. In the foreground are five nude male figures, gods created by her through the act of painting. The animal world is represented by the owl, a symbol in many mythologies of the wisdom of the Goddess. The bats, according to Chinese symbolism, are seen as beneficial creatures of good fortune; they also populate the painting's illusionary space. One bat is shown drinking the life-giving red wine from a transparent vessel. The wine is symbolic of the sacred blood of the Great Mother.

## *The Myth of Isis*

According to Merlin Stone, Barbara Walker, and many other contemporary feminist theologians, the religion of Mother God Isis lasted for at least four thousand years, and her last temple was closed in Europe during the sixth century CE. Her place of origin is Egypt, but her religion spread throughout Africa, the Near East, and Europe, posing a serious threat to Christianity.

Mary, Mother of God, was inserted into Christianity to eliminate the worship of Isis, an act that greatly helped to establish Christianity as the dominant religion of the West. This was largely due to the fact that Mary was understood by the population as the divine feminine and as the female component of the Christian Trinity. Excellent examples of this Marian devotion are the Gothic cathedrals. They are usually built on top of the former Goddess temples and dedicated to Our Lady.

The Great Goddess Isis was regarded by the Egyptian population as an omnipotent universal creator, and all the other goddesses and gods were worshiped as her extensions or aspects. During the most patriarchal period of ancient Egypt, a parallel myth of Isis pictured her as the female component of a divine Trinity [2] that included her spouse and son, a diluted version of the original Trinity or triune aspects of all earlier Great Mother Gods. Her ancient temples constitute our precious artistic heritage, and are tourist attractions as much as sites of reverence among the seekers of the divine feminine in our past.Today she is worshiped secretly or openly by the neo-pagans of Europe and the United States. A temple dedicated to the worship of Goddess Isis that is located in England continues the tradition of this very old and lasting religion.[3]

Some of the important symbols of Isis include the Sun, as she is a Sun Goddess. Birds and serpents are also sacred symbols of the goddess, showing similarity with the omnipotent creator-goddess of the earlier times. She is particularly associated with other solar divinities, such as Sekhmet and the Cobra Goddess. Her sister Nephtys is seen as her own chthonic aspect. Goddess Hathor, the Great Cow Goddess is also perceived as Isis. Celestial bodies such as the Sun, the Moon, and the stars were associated with Isis and other goddesses and gods. The animals were highly respected and loved by the ancient Egyptian people, and therefore were often considered sacred and worthy to represent the divine. The Celestial Cow was considered the giver of life, and a metaphor for the Goddess Hathor, the creator of the Milky Way.

## *Athena/Demeter/Core*

Another metaphor for artistic activity as the act of creation is explored in an oil painting that was completed in 1974, 6 feet x 8 feet. This work, titled *Athena as the Goddess of Earth*, is inspired by the myths of the ancient Greeks. The Goddess is positioned within a golden section of the rectangle of the canvas. She is depicted as a woman wearing a long white garment, standing in front of her canvas with her back facing the viewer. She is holding a brush in her left hand, therefore she is ambidextrous. Her canvas is aligned with the horizon line where the ocean and sky converge, dissolving the distinction between the illusion and the real world. This effect of a painting that is contained within another painting is an ambiguity that fuses internal and external realities, and is a tribute to Surrealism. This illusion also symbolizes the act of creation by the Goddess. The spectator can see only her back and is forced to imagine her face. This allows each female spectator to see herself as the goddess and every male viewer to discover his anima. Athena/Demeter's creative effort results in the instant birth of her Daughter God Core, seated next to her, while three male figures also surround the Goddesses. They share their realm with a large reptile, an allusion to the theory of evolution. Several birds that populate the painting are symbols of the power of Mother God over the heavens.

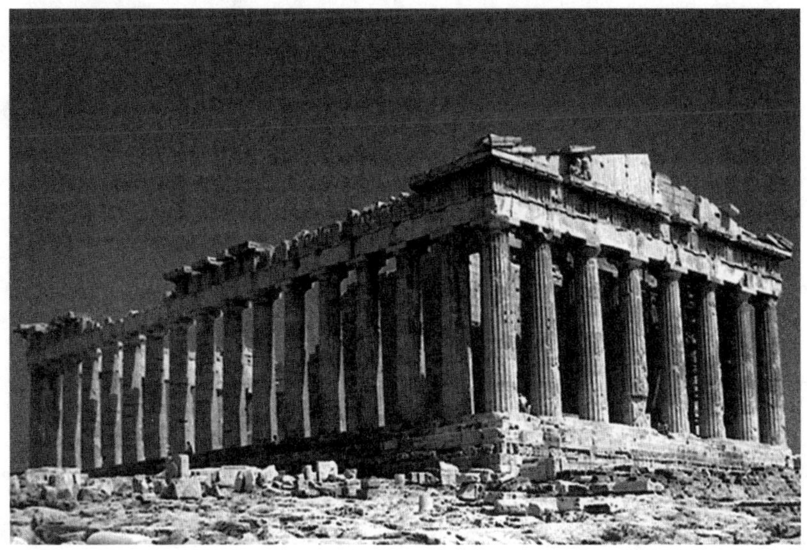

**3–1 Iktinos & Kallicrates**
Parthenon (447–438 BCE), temple of Goddess Athena. Athens, Greece

## *The Myths of Athena, Demeter, and Core/Persephone*

The archeological evidence indicates that in pre-patriarchal mythology Goddess Athena was an omnipotent Great Goddess; even in her less complete version of early patriarchy she still retained a powerful role as protector of her people, and was the goddess of wisdom and the arts. Athena retained her pre-patriarchal role as the protector of the Greeks, and as such was extensively worshiped during the classical/patriarchal times. Her temples were numerous and constitute our best classical heritage in architecture. The patriarchal Athena became the "motherless" child, as in the new myth she become the daughter of Zeus, in reality a much newer god. Zeus swallowed her mother Metis, so he can "birth" his child himself, therefore 'proving" that the function of the life-giving mother can be also a man's role. Athena is a virgin goddess, which made her more powerful and independent in the eyes of the ancients. She was often a mentor to men, their guide in battles (she always won), but she is on record as mentoring women, but the patriarchal men expected the goddess to favor them over the female gender, a view that is being re-envisioned today due to the new research that traces her matriarchal origins.

The religion of Mother God Demeter and Daughter God Core extended through the world of Antiquity for about four thousand years. Every Greek person belonged to this complex cult of the two Goddesses, and all were initiated into the various levels of the Eleusian Mysteries, or secret rituals, later to be joined by the conquering Romans. The complex and emotional rituals of the Mysteries greatly enhanced the lives of the ancient populations. Most likely, this was the oldest of the post-prehistoric Greek religions, and it did not interfere with the worship of other Greek divinities. Mother God Demeter functioned as the generous Earth Divinity. She provided an abundance of nature for her people. Daughter God Core, or Persephone, was the Goddess of Creation and Rebirth, emerging from the underworld every spring to activate the growth of vegetation and bring new forms of life into existence. The ruins of the temple dedicated to Demeter and Core at Eleusis, and the temple dedicated to Athena, the famous Parthenon in Athens are among many other temples that still serve as grand memorials to the celebrations of female spirituality.

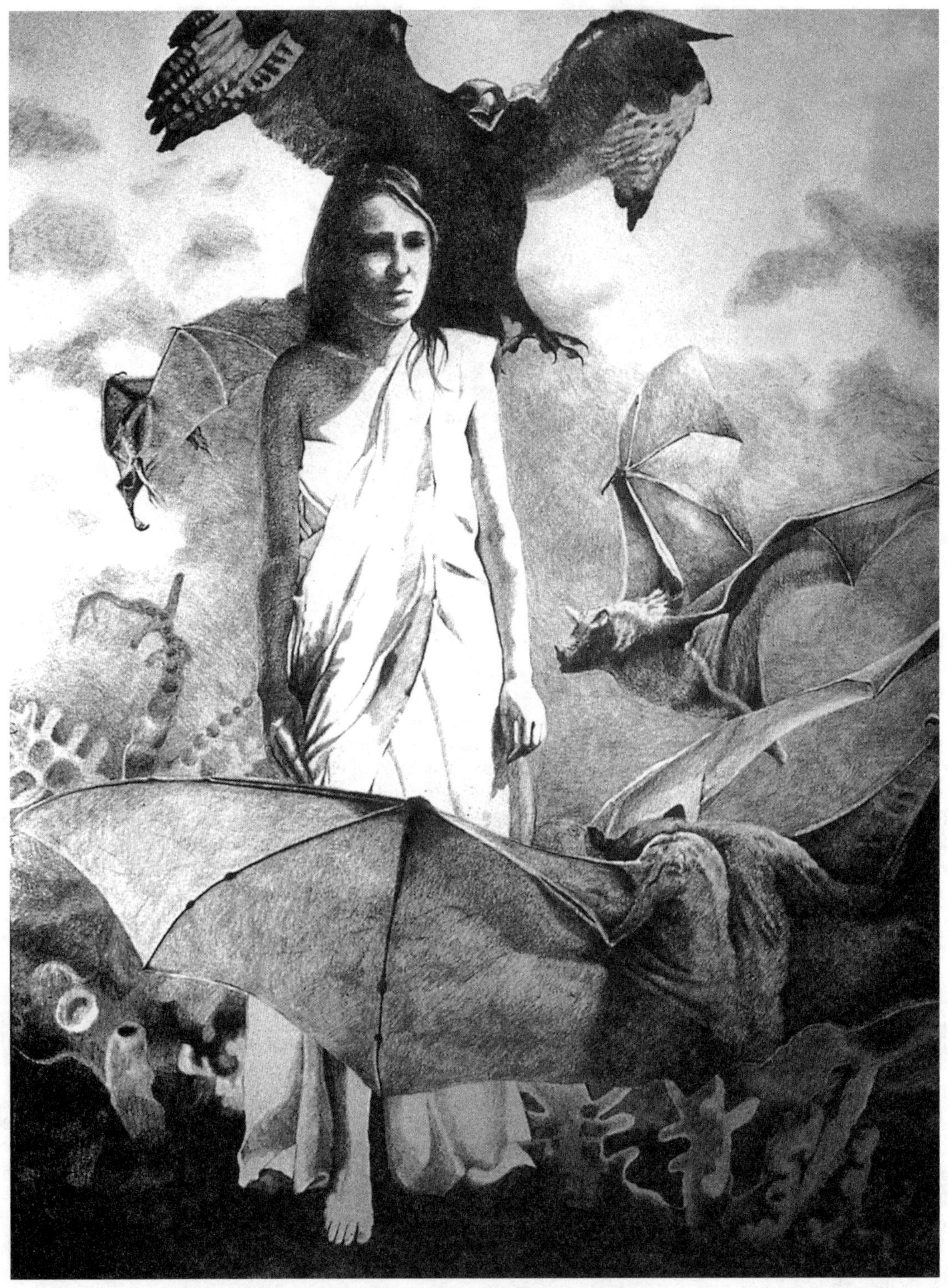

**3–2 The Return** © Kyra Belán, 1974
Drawing, graphite and colored pencil, 50" x 38"

Nature infused with the divine feminine is the theme of a drawing in graphite and colored pencil, *The Return* (1978). The self-portrait shows a standing female figure, wearing a white robe. She is surrounded by natural elements of sky, and a fusion between the earthly and underwater realm. A large eagle is perching on her shoulder, her wings spread. The eagle was a symbol of Great Goddesses in prehistory and antiquity, and it is also a symbol for female and male spirituality within Native American religions.

On each side of the figure are large bats, with the biggest bat positioned directly in front of the Goddess, with its wings spread. Their presence symbolizes the remembrance and unfoldment of forgotten matristic civilizations and cultures that reside in the cells which constitute the subconscious worlds of the people of postmodern society. However, according to the traditional belief of Western culture, the bats are symbols of darkness and evil. Euro-centric spectators, viewing this artwork through their value systems, usually presume that the image represents good versus evil, and the Goddess figure is often interpreted as the image of Christ. This last reaction is prompted by the absence of female spiritual role models, since the Reformation minimized the importance of Mary within new branches of Christianity.

A diptych drawing, 60 inches x 84 inches, in graphite and colored pencil, was also completed in 1974. The following year, I attached a feather collage to one of the birds. The diptych was titled *The Phoenix.* The title represents one obvious clue to the message of this work. It revisits ancient Egyptian and Oriental legends of a bird that in order to rebirth itself, descends into the flames of a fire and later rises anew out of the ashes. This process is repeated forever, and the bird is rendered immortal. The background is divided into three sections, symbolic of the prehistoric and ancient Mother God Trinity of the Virgin-Creator, Mother-Nurturer, and Crone-Transformer.[4] In the middle section, the sky can be observed, replete with white birds in flight. The two side sections seem to depict shallow space. A nude female figure stands in the center of the sky section, with her hands raised. She is holding a fabric, which alludes to her role as the weaver of destinies. Two male nude figures reclining at her feet personify the decline of patriarchal duality and of male supremacy. The female figure is a metaphor for the rising of the divine feminine and the re-emergence of female values within current social order. Two flying birds in the foreground are easily identifiable as an owl and an osprey, symbols of the wisdom of the Goddess. The third bird, sitting next to the rising Goddess figure, is covered by a collage of dark feathers that transforms it into a creature of imagination, the Phoenix.

One more myth of the ancient Greeks is remembered in a drawing that measures 50 feet x 38 feet. Completed in 1975 and titled *Artemis*, it is a work in graphite on paper. Goddess Artemis, semi-reclined over a woven fabric, is nude. She is an allusion to the universal archetypal symbolism of the Goddess as the weaver of destinies. Artemis is also the lady of nature and the animals. Flying birds in the background symbolize her creative power as the sky Goddess. The bird, since prehistory, has served as an archetype that represents the Sky Mother, the creator of the heavenly realm, and one of the aspects of the Mother God Trinity. At the feet of Artemis, two birds of prey, a hawk and a falcon, keep her company. Represented in her human incarnation, the Goddess is seen as both divine and human.

## *The Myth of Artemis*

According to the original matriarchal mythology, Goddess Artemis functioned as an omnipotent creator. Later, during early patriarchy, she became the Goddess of Nature and animals and the protector of children. A beloved divinity of ancient Greek civilization, she was worshiped in numerous temples. One of her temples in Greece is located at Delphi. It is also dedicated to her mother, Leto, and her younger brother Apollo. She helped her mother give birth to him, assuming the role of a sacred midwife. She is the Virgin Goddess, which means that she chose not to marry any god or mortal man. Temples dedicated to Artemis in Greece were populated by a priesthood that included children, usually girls, but sometimes also boys. In Rome, the Goddess was worshiped under the name of Diana. Her religion became occult after the persecution by Christianity, but still remains today as one of the no-longer-secret religions of Neo-Pagans.

One more work from the same period, a colored pencil drawing titled *Isis among Florida Anemones*, was completed in 1976. It shows a seated and draped female figure, a self-portrait as an incarnation of Goddess Isis. She is shown in a state of contemplation and is surrounded by a biomorphic environment that includes elements of the fantastic. Two owls in flight are above this woman-goddess, while a third owl is peering from behind her shoulder. The surrounding terrain is composed of numerous oceanic plants, creatures, and corals. There are anemones, reminiscent of vaginal forms, while other "plants" resemble phallic shapes. The presence of these sensual forms conveys the message of harmony between the sexes. Natural elements of this environment of fantasy create the feeling that planet Earth is a place of beauty and harmony.

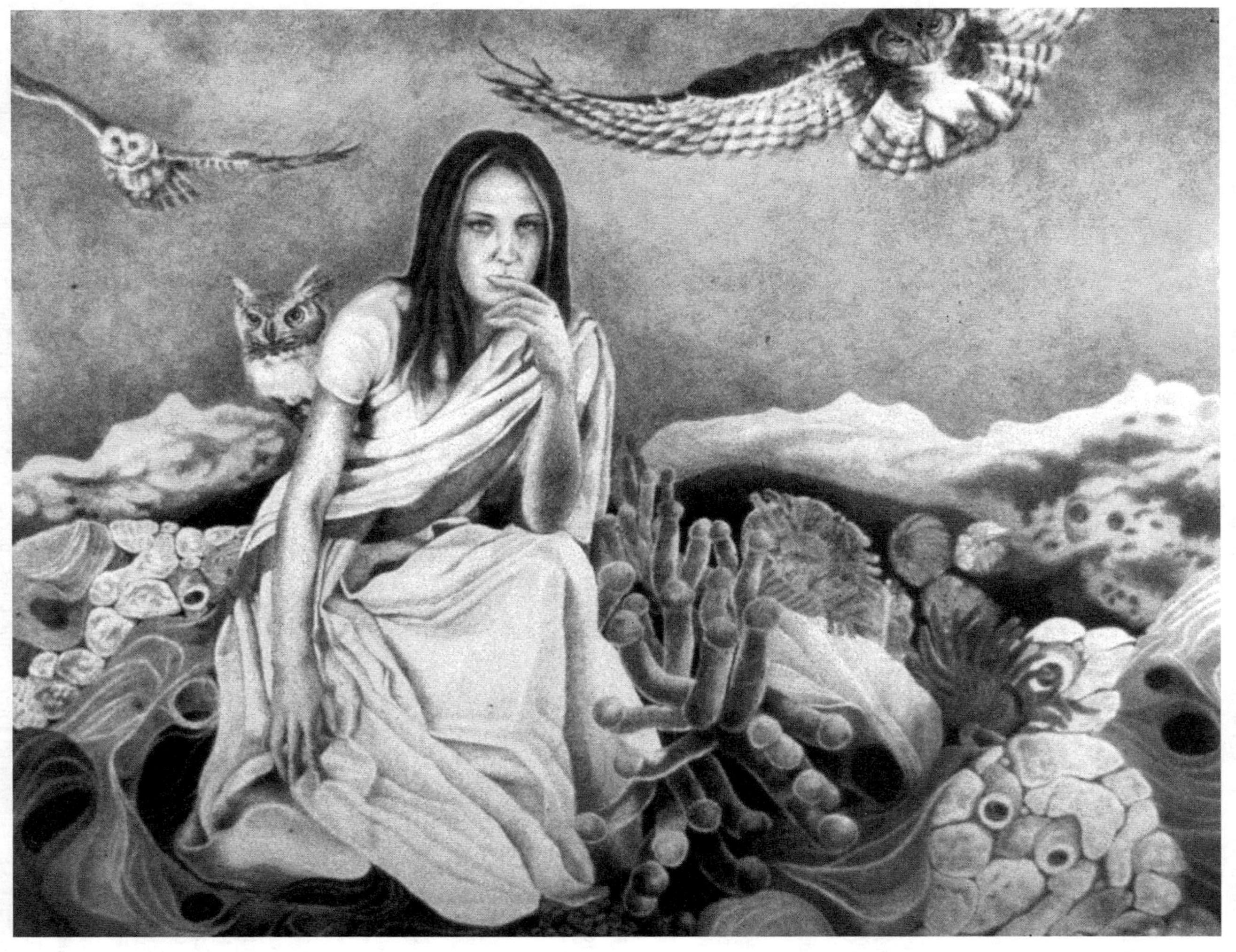

**3–3 Isis among Florida Anemones** © Kyra Belán, 1976
Drawing, colored pencil, 40" x 48"
Collection of Alessandra Comini

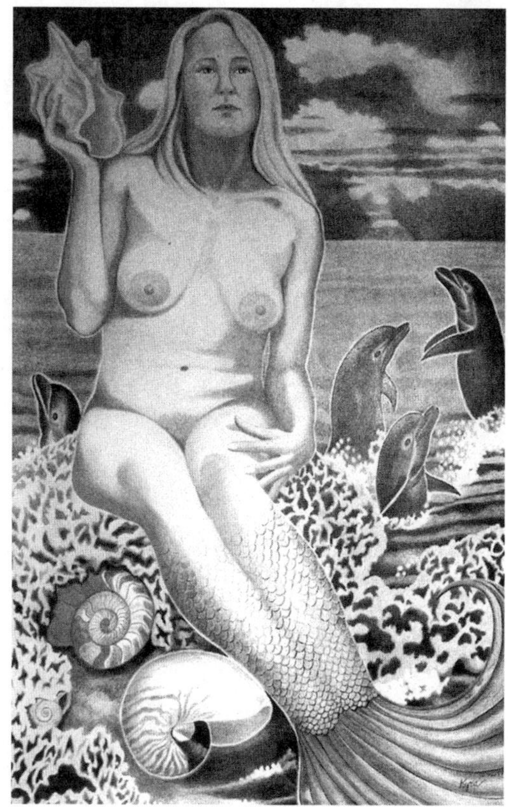

**3–4 Goddess Aphrodite** © Kyra Belán, 1992
Drawing, colored pencil, 40" x 34"
Collection of Vicki Hendricks

A drawing in colored pencil. that was completed in 1992, depicts a portrait of a woman as Goddess Aphrodite. The seated figure is surrounded by a sky with some scattered clouds and an ocean populated by several leaping dolphins. She is seated on what appears to be a grouping of sponges and corals. The shells are important symbols of Aphrodite, a Greek divinity closely connected with the oceans and waters. The nude figure holds a large shell. Below her knees, her legs become transformed into a colorful fish tail. This Aphrodite-mermaid is an allusion to the metamorphosis of the ancient myth: during Christianity, the Goddess was reinterpreted as a siren-mermaid, a fantastic inhabitant of the world of the seas who enchanted the sailors by her beauty.

When reinterpreting images of female divinities, I often include several layers of mythology, from the oldest to the most recent interpretations. The single images of the Goddesses represent a personal microcosm of archetypes, as distilled through my experience as a contemporary woman, and enhanced by the opportunities presented by recent research and advances in modern archeology. Perhaps the most valuable ingredient is my personal experience of visits to museums and archeological sites all over the world, where the reality of this important past crystallizes into a sharp focus.

## *Goddess Aphrodite*

This divinity was originally an omnipotent creator of prehistoric and ancient Europe. During classical antiquity, the Greeks worshiped Aphrodite as the creator of all the waters and as the goddess of love. The Romans called her Venus. Numerous monuments and temples were built to honor her. Her son, Cupid, is usually depicted as a little angel who holds a bow and arrows. Both mother and son divinities are still used as symbols of love in our contemporary society. Aphrodite, like many other ancient goddesses that followed the Great Goddess who was symbolized by a bird, inherited the bird, a dove, as her important symbol. The essence of the divine feminine, the dove was adopted as a symbol by early Christianity for the Holy Spirit. The Holy Ghost, originally interpreted by many Christians as female, was later changed into a male, but still retained the sacred feminine symbol, the dove, as its pictorial interpretation. Numerous works of art depict the dove hovering over the Virgin Mary, as the public tended to perceive the two as interrelated.

# 4

# *Mother of the World*

In the late seventies, a book by Merlin Stone, titled *When God was a Woman*, was released, accelerating the popularization of the knowledge of a female divine heritage through the history of civilization. This book had a serious impact on my art and writings. It reassured me that I was not alone in my search for female spirituality, and it legitimized my profound desire to create images of God as a woman. At that time, I was formulating ideas for a series of works on the theme of Mother God that would not only include paintings and drawings, but would also incorporate environmental or site specific installations, multimedia, earthworks, and ritual performance.

Environmental installations, earthworks, and performance art are usually temporary works, and have to be photographed or videotaped for documentation and future reference. The concept of a series that would utilize a variety of media, techniques, and stylistic versatility took form in my mind. I realized that each installation and performance had further potential to become an edited video artwork or video documentary. I decided to start a long term project.

I began *Magic Circle Series* in 1978, as an ongoing project and a traveling exhibition. The word "circle" was incorporated into the title because it is possibly the oldest abstract symbol for the prehistoric omnipotent Mother God. It is still used today as a symbol of female divinity, spirituality, and continuity of life in many non-Western civilizations, such as Tibet and the Native American nations that recognize and worship the divine feminine principle.

Each one of the individual components of the *Magic Circle Series* has a theme that explores one or more aspects of female spirituality. Since there is no dichotomy between the heavenly and earthly realms in all the Goddess religions or in my personal beliefs, the physical and spiritual cosmos is understood in my work as one diverse and extensive unit of a variety of forms of energy. The project is a celebration of Mother Earth, physical and spiritual, a macrocosm of diverse energy patterns. Female spirituality, earth-based and universal, is celebrated in order to manifest the images and concepts that promote peace,harmony and balance in our society.

The materials and techniques used for the series vary according to the particular locations. The interior spaces are used for installations and performance art. The outdoor earth art is also site-specific, and the materials, techniques, and performances are always adapted to the environment. As a result, some installations, earthworks, and performances of the series are complex and extensive, while others are compact and simple. The sites used are not necessarily traditional gallery or museum spaces, but can be public or natural locations.

## *Matriarchies and Art*

The matriarchies that originally worshiped Mother God were social structures of a generally non-hierarchical, Earth-loving, and peaceful nature. These societies lasted for many thousands of years; they are a proof that a possibility of peaceful co-existence on earth can be accomplished in the future if we re-adopt some of the characteristics typical of matriarchal paradigms. Exposing the public, through art, to the reality and the possibility that various types of societies can exist on this planet is crucial, and may help influence the transformation of the current social order into a peaceful society of the future.

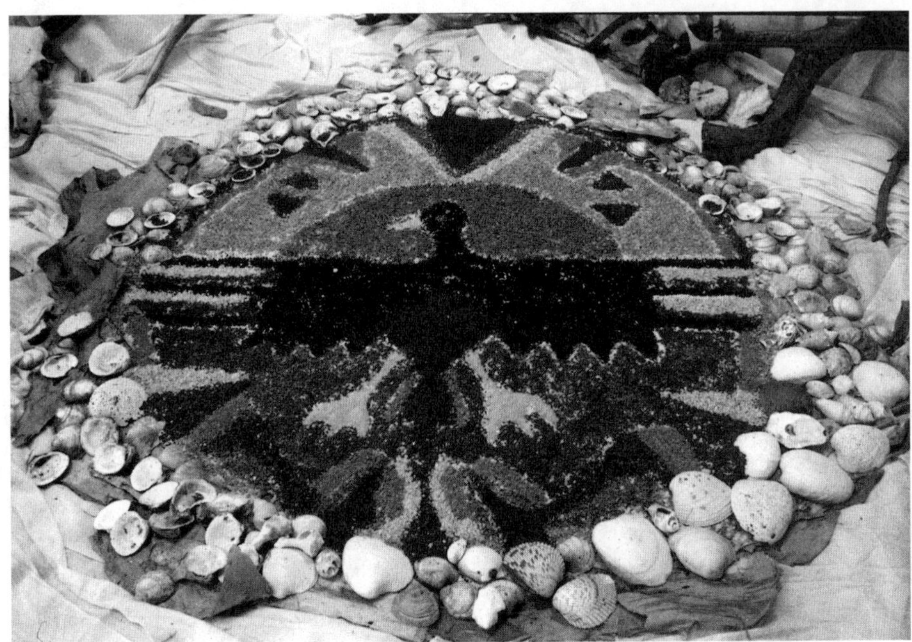

**4–1 The Magic Circle** © Kyra Belán, 1978
Detail of multimedia installation
The Grove House Gallery, Miami, Florida

The first work of the series, *The Magic Circle*, consisted of an installation at the Grove House Gallery in Miami, Florida, in 1978. The walls of the gallery displayed colored pencil drawings of goddesses and nude male gods. Colored pebbles and sands arranged in a six-foot-diameter circle were surrounded by shells and "feather trees" of dried wood and colorful dyed feathers. The first public ritual performance of this series consisted of the creation of a stylized bird within the circular floor sculpture. I accomplished this by letting colored sands sift through my fingers and fall into the appropriate locations within the design. The image was an abstraction of a thunderbird, the symbol of the Earth Goddess of the Native Americans. Thus, the first work of the series paid homage to the Native American female spirituality.

The *Magic Circle II* took place at An Alternative Gallery in North Miami, Florida, in 1979. The gallery walls were covered with colored pencil drawings of the goddesses and gods. During the ritual performance, I completed a sand painting within the center of the gallery space. The design of the circular sand painting included symbols of the Egyptian Goddess Isis, the prehistoric Mother God, and the Native American Mother God. It was surrounded by an arrangement of feathers. The performance was concluded by a ritual walk: I led several "worshipers," wearing a feathered mask and carrying peacock feathers, symbols for Goddess Hera. We also lit candles and carried them in a procession around the circle to honor the Great Mother, while the attending public watched.

The next location for the traveling project was the A.I.R. Gallery in New York City (1979). *The Magic Circle III* consisted of a circular floor installation about ten feet in diameter. The circular design was formed by arranging mirrors, feathers, and masks. During the ritual performance, I walked around the circle, picked up each mask, put it on my face, and did a short ritual dance. After completing each ritual movement, I took each mask off and returned it to its designated location. The meaning of this ritual is a metaphor for the changing roles of women in our society, and for the rediscovery of female spirituality as represented by the circle, symbolic of the life force and the eternal Mother of Nature.

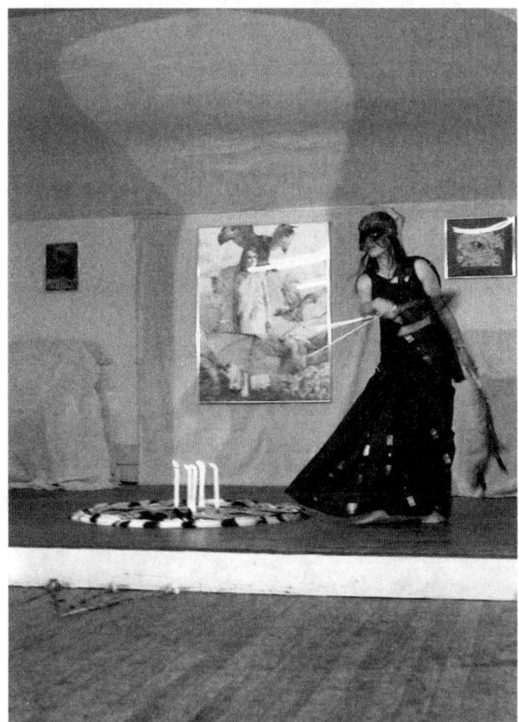

**4–2 Goddess Isis: Magic Circle IV** © Kyra Belán, 1980
Detail of installation and performance
Unitarian Church, Ft. Lauderdale, Florida. Photo: Karen Metcalf

An invitation in 1980 from the Unitarian Church in Fort Lauderdale, Florida, resulted in an artwork titled *Goddess Isis: Magic Circle IV*. The church membership felt the need to be in touch with their divine feminine energy, and I was encouraged to use the altar and the surrounding area of the church for an installation and a ritual performance. This was videotaped and later edited into a video artwork. The altar was draped with white cloth, and the images and symbols of the Goddess, all pencil or colored pencil drawings, were hung on the walls. On the floor I assembled a circular sculpture, of approximately seven feet in diameter, allowing enough space for a ritual walk and a dance. The materials used for the design of this environmental sculpture consisted of mirrors, colored sands, feathers, and candles. The performance started with an audio-visual presentation of projected Goddess images and a recording of my voice. It provided the public with an overview of the history of matriarchies and their Mother God centered religions. The historical overview was followed by the chanting of the poem celebrating the return of the Great Mother. Next, three other "priestesses" and I performed a ritual of candles and dances. The event was concluded by an offer of flowers to the viewing audience. The flowers were symbols for the celebration of the return of the feminine principle that values peace, equality, and concern for the well being of the planet. The activity of handing them to the audience created a participatory connection between the artist, the artwork, and the viewers.

The Fine Arts Gallery at Broward Community College in Davie, Florida housed another work of the series, titled *Isis: Magic Circle VI*, in 1982. A large video projection screen was placed in the center of the gallery space, against the wall. The circular floor installation was located in front of the screen. I covered all the walls with reflective black plastic, cut in sections and layered, to produce a "black vegetation" effect. The focal point of the circular installation, located in front of the screen and in the center of the gallery floor, consisted of a cow skull surrounded by corals, rocks, and feathers. The exhibition included a projection of a pre-recorded ritual performance: I performed ritual dance movements around the circular installation in a costume that was based on the traditional garments of Goddess Isis. The video was projected onto a large video screen, while the live version of the ritual dance was actually taking place. The blurring of the barriers between the real performance and installation, and the illusion of the pre-recorded ritual and sculpture was meant to challenge the spectator to see both as valid reality constructs.

The presence of repetitive images, motion, and sounds was conducive to a meditative or entranced state in the spectators, or a mood of spirituality. The visual message emphasized the importance of peace and spiritual balance in our lives.

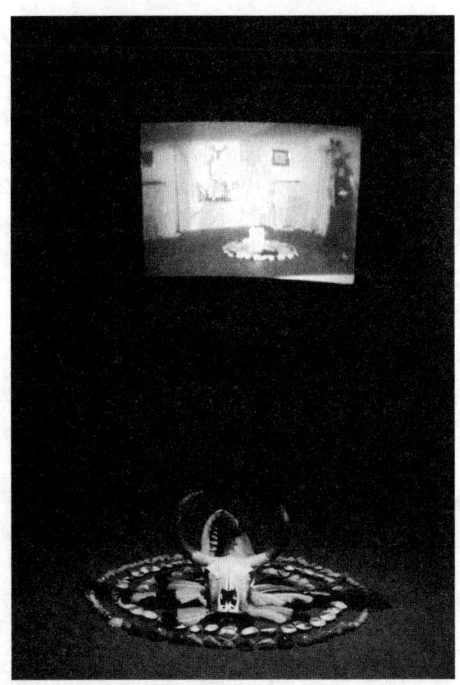

**4–3 Isis: Magic Circle VI** © Kyra Belán, 1982
Detail of the installation, video projection
Fine Arts Gallery, Broward Community College, Davie, Florida. Photo: GL Sullivan

The concept behind the fifth and sixth *Magic Circle Series* installations was similar to the previous one, while the *Magic Circle VII*, for the first time, was presented in an outdoor setting at the New World Campus of Miami-Dade College in 1984. The floor sculpture was assembled inside a patio, almost totally enclosed by a building of several stories. The building's high glass roof allowed the filtering of natural illumination. All the small trees within the tiled patio were adorned with red and white streamers. Throughout the duration of the installation and ritual performance they gently moved in the breeze that came in through the two open entrances. The circular installation was located on a raised multi-leveled platform, and the design was formed with materials that included colored sands, shells, feathers and mirrors. Numerous candles were added to the floor sculpture. The ritual performance began during daylight, but continued into the evening. Attired in the costume of a priestess, I led the "worshipers," as we formed a ritual procession that later evolved into a dance. An edited video artwork was later produced.

Up to this time, the *Magic Circle Series* often celebrated numerous female divinities, while primarily honoring Mother God Isis, whose religion lasted for several millennia and expanded over many territories beyond ancient Egypt. She was one Mother God who remained omnipotent even within the emerging andro-centric societies whose new religions generated many powerful male divinities. The next work, *Great American Goddess Coatlique: Magic Circle VIII* (1984), was focused instead upon the most powerful deity of the New World, the Mother of all the goddesses and gods of the Aztecs. This omnipotent Mother God was their principal divinity. Like the followers of the religion of Great Goddess Isis, the Aztec civilization believed that every divinity and all of nature existed as her manifestation. The similarities between the iconography of her religion and that of Isis are striking: both Goddesses possess solar powers, and birds and serpents are among their symbols.

This work of art occupied both the wall and floor space of the Fine Art Gallery at Broward Community College's Davie Campus. Colored pencil drawings of Goddess images and symbols were arranged on the walls. A large triptych depicted my interpretation of Mother God Coatlicue (or Coatlique); the five feet by twelve feet colored pencil drawing on paper was installed in the center of the wall that faced the floor sculpture. The sculpture consisted of a circle seven feet in diameter, surrounded by an 80 foot long spiral serpent (see Color Plates 4 and 5). The circle and the serpent were formed out of white quartz sands, colored sands, rocks, feathers, and other materials. The ritual performance included sound, light effects, a procession, and a dance. During the performance, one wall was removed to accommodate the public. The performance was recorded on video and later edited.

## *In Quest of Coatlicue*

During 1985, this artwork was followed by another environmental installation, again a tribute to Goddess Coatlicue. Part of the previous work, the large triptych of Coatlicue, was included in the new work, titled *In Quest of the American Goddess Coatlicue: Magic Circle IX.* Often, after de-installation, a substantial part of the work of art has to be destroyed, but it is important to me that some parts or materials from previous works are incorporated into the next production of the series. Because of the site-specific nature of the series, the same configuration of the remaining works never happens again, yet some portion of the previous work is often present in the subsequent one. Much of the floor space was used for the creation of a 55 foot long double-headed plumed serpent, a symbol for the Mother God's earthly and celestial realms. The serpent was formed out of white sands, clay, colored sands, rocks and feathers. It surrounded a circular floor sculpture that was also made out of white and colored sands, feathers, and hand painted latex serpents (see Color Plates 6 and 7). A ritual performance took place within the plumed serpent and around it (see Color Plate 8). The ceremony, inspired by the ancient Aztec rituals dedicated to Goddess Coatlicue, included a procession, sound-making, dances, and candle-lighting rituals. As usual, the process was videotaped and later edited into a 15-minute video art.

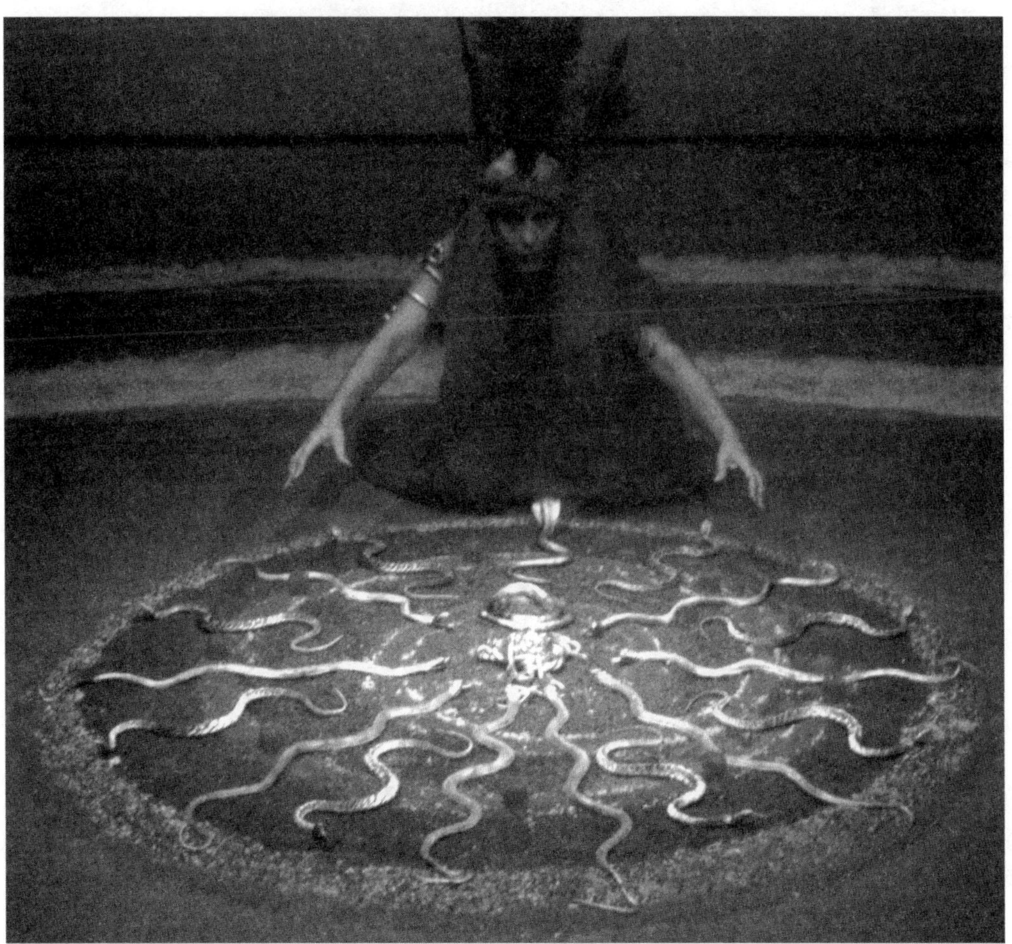

**4–4 Great American Goddess Coatlique** © Kyra Belán, 1984
Detail of installation, artist performing

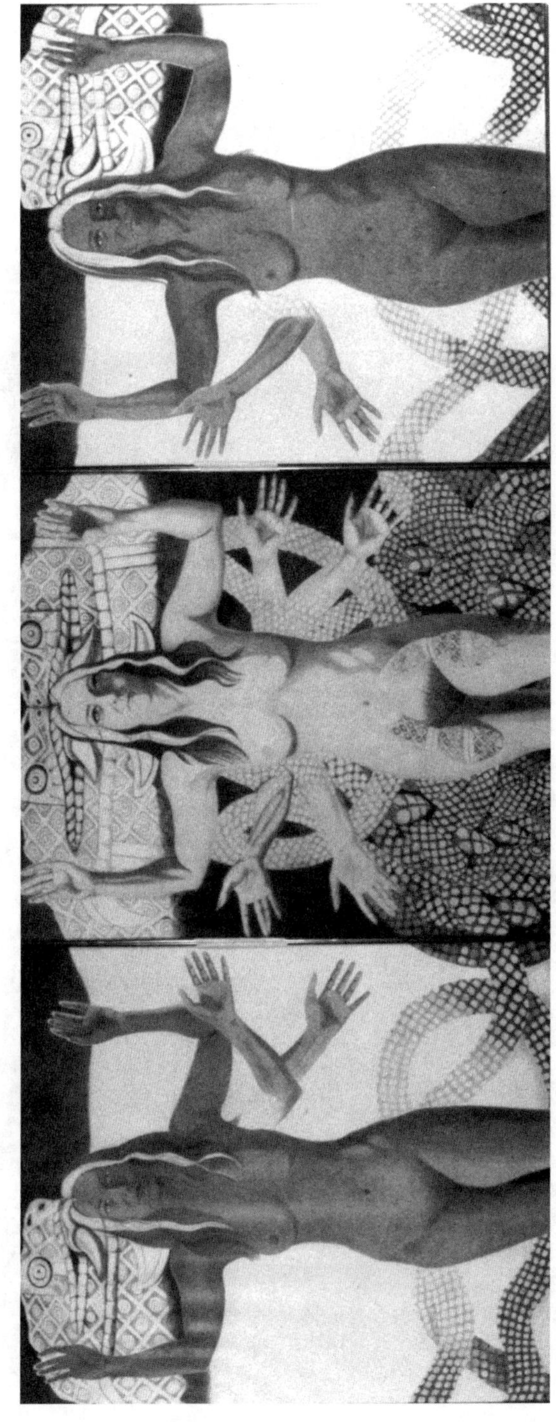

**4–5 Goddess Coatlicue Creating a Woman** © Kyra Belán, 1984
Drawing, colored pencil, triptych, 50'' x 126''

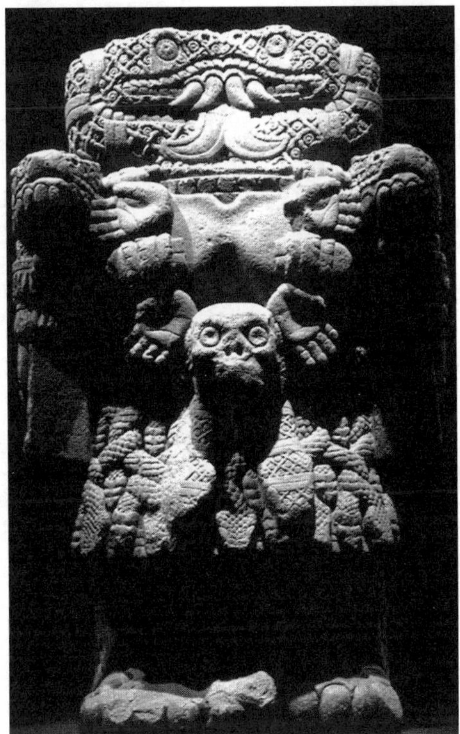

**4-6 Goddess Coatlicue**
Aztec, Museo Antropologico, Mexico City

## *Goddess Coatlique or Coatlicue*

This Great Mother God of the Aztecs was an omnipotent divinity. She was the creator of all other goddesses and gods, the sun, the moon, and the stars, and all that is. Coatlicue, as the creator, also received her people in her special paradisiac realm after their deaths. Her symbols include the serpents that stand for immortality, the eagle that represents her sky powers, and the human sculls and hands, symbolic of her chthonic and regenerative powers. Today she, like Tonantzin, the Earth Mother, is still worshiped in Mexico as syncretic *Nuestra Señora de Guadalupe* (Our Lady of Guadalupe), official protector of Mexico. Ritual dances, performed by women and men, attired in Native American Aztec costumes, take place in front of the cathedral that is dedicated to Nuestra Señora de Guadalupe several times during the year. The dancers also vocalize their praises and devotion to Nuestra Señora.

The most popular symbols of the Creator Goddess Coatlicue include the serpent, the eagle, human hands, and sculls. Coatlicue is believed to offer an after death realm for her followers; she is a transformative divinity, like Kali of India. A life giver, she also transforms nature and people in death, sending them into another dimension. Therefore, the cyclical nature of the cosmos is maintained and reinforced.

## *The Great Goddess*

One more outdoor installation, titled *Great Goddess: Magic Circle X*, was temporarily installed in 1985 on the open coral rock platform, over the series of steps leading to the front of the east entrance to the Metropolitan Museum and Art Center of Coral Gables, Florida. Quartz rocks, coral rock, and shells were painted in yellow, red, blue, gold, and silver and transported to the location. There I assembled them into a circular sculpture ten feet in diameter, reminiscent of a Sun disc; it was flanked by two crescent shapes on each side.

The symbolic Sun shape was arranged with red, yellow, and gold rocks, and I constructed the crescent Moon shapes with blue and silver rocks and shells. Over a dozen female participants were dressed in either white or black, representing the passage of time, and the polarity of day and night. I was wearing a long red garment, the sacred color of the Goddess in her role as a life-giver. The ritual walk and dance were dedicated to the Mother Creator of prehistoric times, perhaps best known as the Goddess of Willendorf.

# *Goddess or Venus of Willendorf*

The image of this Mother God is often believed to be the oldest known art object in existence. A small sculpture in the round, this figure dates between 25,000 BCE and 75,000 BCE. She is one of many thousands of prehistoric sculptures of Mother God found all over the globe, confirming the fact that the original divinity was perceived by human beings as feminine for many thousands of years. Mother God of Willendorf personified the omnipotent powers of the prehistoric female gods; she was the Goddess of Earth, the giver of life, which included the skies, waters, and all living beings. She was also the transformer, or the giver of death, completing the cycles of birth, life, death, and rebirth of nature and all that exists. First traces of the appearance of a male god, as her son, are dated at approximately 5,000 BCE in some regions of the globe. Initially, he was a dying and resurrecting nature divinity, later evolving into a more permanent son and consort of the Goddess (See image 2–1).

# *Sun Goddess*

The Sun Goddesses have a prominent place in world mythologies. Numerous female solar divinities seem to be the direct descendants of the old omnipotent creator, the prehistoric Mother God. In Egypt, possibly the most ancient of the Sun Goddesses is the lioness-headed Goddess Sekhmet. Even the ancient Egyptians were unable to trace her origins to a specific date, calling this divinity the Oldest of the Old. Hathor and Isis, also interpreted as aspects of Sekhmet, and the Cobra Goddess are other Egyptian divinities that possess solar powers. Goddess Amaterasu of Japan, worshiped to this day, is also a Sun Goddess.

One of my site specific installations, *Sun Goddess, Emergence of the Myth: Magic Circle XI* (see Color Plate 9), completed in 1986, was dedicated to the celebration of female solar divinities. The central part of the interior environment was occupied by a sun-shaped floor sculpture 14 feet in diameter. The materials used included painted wood, painted quartz rocks, and painted shells. Ceremonial performance of sound, walk, and dance took place around the sun-shaped sculpture; colored pencil drawings of proposals for monuments and earth sculptures, dedicated to various Mother Gods, and documentary drawings of previous installations were displayed on the walls.

An Egyptian Sun Goddess that was evoked in the previous work, Sekhmet, was celebrated in her role as Mother Nature in an earthwork titled *Nature Goddess Sekhmet: Magic Circle XII* (see Color Plates 10 and 11). This work was commissioned by the Metro-Dade Art in Public Places for Miami Site in 1987, an art park for temporary earthworks and site-specific works. The installation of this earth art, that marked the opening of the park, took three weeks. It remained on site for several months and then was de-installed, or literally destroyed. On my request, the opening and performance date was set to coincide with the Spring Equinox. When possible, I prefer to have exhibitions during solstices and equinoxes, which are the four major holidays of the prehistoric, ancient, pre-Columbian, early Western, and non-Western cultures of the world that celebrate the divine feminine. Other favored dates include festivities that celebrate Goddess religions of antiquity or contemporary cultures.

By the entrance to the park on Key Biscayne, I displayed red banners with painted images of Goddess Sekhmet. As the spectators entered the park, they were faced with a cluster of royal palm trees, green grass, and a lake. The earthwork consisted of a low circular mound of 12 feet in diameter, tapering from 2 feet high at the center to the level of the grass. It was assembled with a layer of white crushed coral rock, topped by a layer of white quartz rock, which was hand painted in bright red, yellow, and gold hues. Two large serpent-shaped mounds were located on each side of the sun circle. The two serpent heads were about three feet high, and the bodies of the snake mounds were about two and a half feet wide, tapering down to 12 inches at the very end of the tails. One serpent was 150 feet long, while the other extended to just over 135 feet. The snake-shaped mounds meandered through the palms, and their tails embraced both sides of the lake. The last layer placed over the crushed white coral consisted of hand painted white quartz rock. It matched the top layer of rocks of the circular mound. The red, yellow and blue colors created a pattern on these larger-than-life serpents. The symbolism of the shapes is clear: the circle represents the life giving warmth of the sun created by the Goddess, and the permanency of the cycles of nature. The serpents are the archetypal icons of the Goddess in her role as the Mother of Earth.

The ritual performance was inspired by Native American ceremonies and consisted of a celebratory procession and dance around the circle and the serpents. In the role of a "priestess" and "shaman," I wore a long white dress, the ten "priestesses" wore long red dresses, and the "worshipers" of both sexes and diverse ages, including children, wore red shirts. The earthwork presented many viewing possibilities, changing considerably when observed from different vantage points. A reflection of the earthwork danced in the waters of the lake. This reflection was further enhanced by the activities of the ritual performance. At a later date, I performed a ritual alone, and it was videotaped. The video of the public performance on the day of Solstice and the video of the private ritual were later recombined and edited into an artwork.

## *Celebration of Goddess Medusa*

During the same year I celebrated Goddess Medusa by creating a 4-foot-high and 12-foot-wide mound of painted quartz rock, which occupied the interior space of the Fine Arts Gallery at Broward Community College in Davie, Florida (see Color Plate 12). Several serpentine forms, assembled of painted quartz rock, converged from two opposite corners of the gallery toward the painted rock mound, located in the center. The painted quartz rocks were recycled from the earthwork at Key Biscayne. In the center of the wall, opposite the mound and the serpentine forms, was a colored pencil drawing, titled *Goddess Medusa Creating the Cosmos*. Red candles were placed directly in front of the artwork on a pedestal covered with red cloth, resembling an altarpiece.

The mound dominated the site-specific installation. In its center was a hollow space that housed a translucent container of water, like a crater of a minor volcano. It was populated with several life-like painted latex serpents. Other painted serpents seemed to be crawling out, and over the surface of the mound, apparently in a process of descent. The presence of the serpents suggested the earthly powers of Goddess Medusa, and also recalled her mythological function as the protectress divinity of the Greeks of ancient days. The ritual performance consisted of a dance around the circle, the rhythm of percussion, and a candle-lighting ceremony. The participating "priestesses" were wearing long red robes, while I wore a long gold cape over a long white garment.

## *The Myths of Goddess Medusa*

An old matriarchal myth of the Goddess interprets Medusa as the protector of the Greeks and an aspect of Goddess Athena. Both Goddesses are the descendants of the Great Omnipotent Mother God of prehistory. During early ancient times, Medusa was celebrated alone as the protector and defender of her people, and her religion extended beyond Greece, as far as North Africa. Medusa was also celebrated as an aspect of then omnipotent Goddess Athena, later reduced by patriarchy to the role of the protector of the Greecs, and the Goddess of Wisdom and the arts.Within the more recent patriarchal Greek mythology Athena and Medusa become rivals; the myth tells us about the transformation of Medusa by Athena, the more powerful of the two divinities, into a snake-haired monster. This monster is often seen in male-dominated Hollywood movie productions. Yet even after the change in the myth, Athena and Medusa remained interrelated until the end of Athena's worship in Greece during the sixth century CE: the image of the snake-haired head of Medusa usually appears on the aegis and on the shield of Goddess Athena.

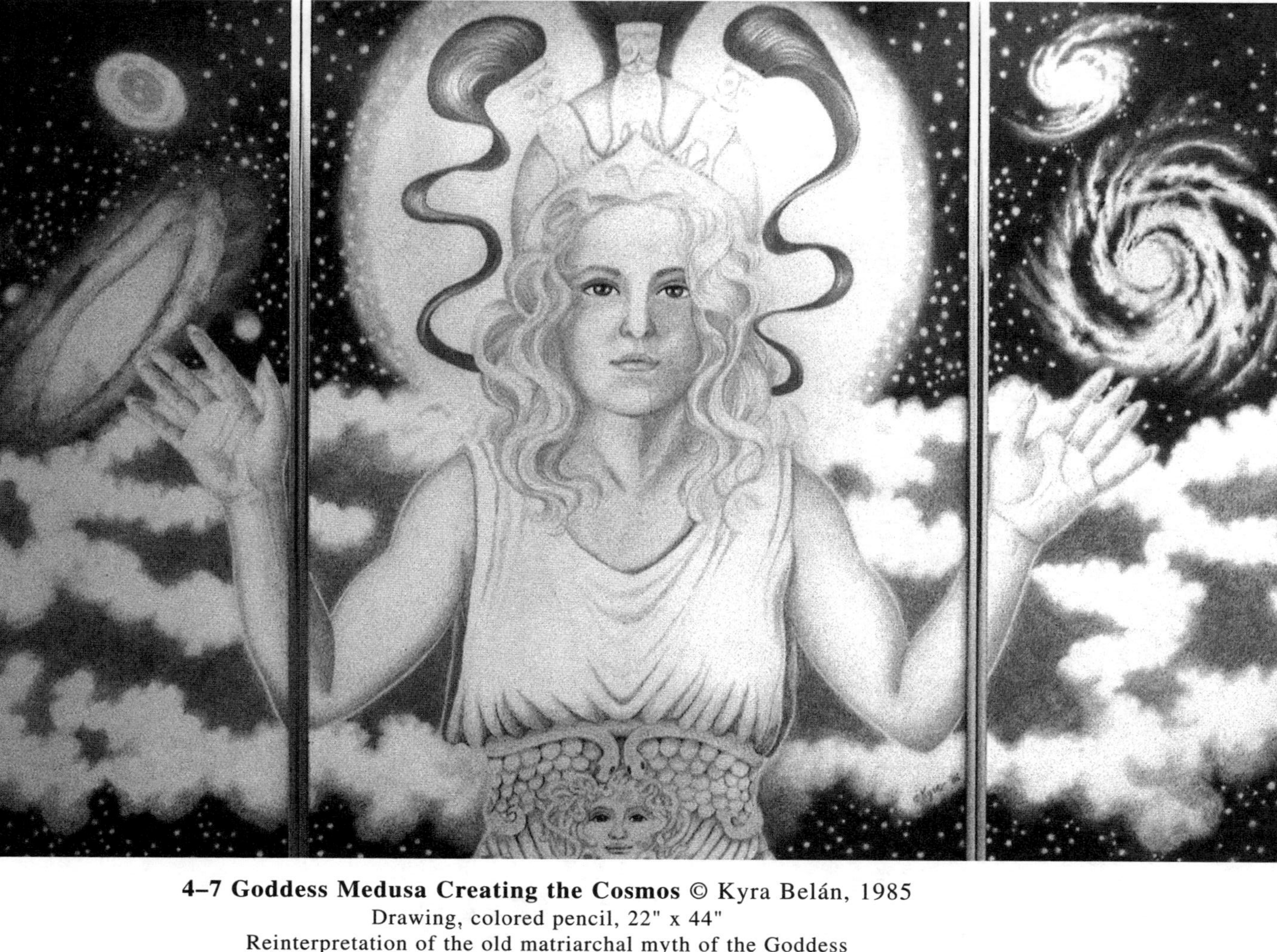

**4–7 Goddess Medusa Creating the Cosmos** © Kyra Belán, 1985
Drawing, colored pencil, 22" x 44"
Reinterpretation of the old matriarchal myth of the Goddess

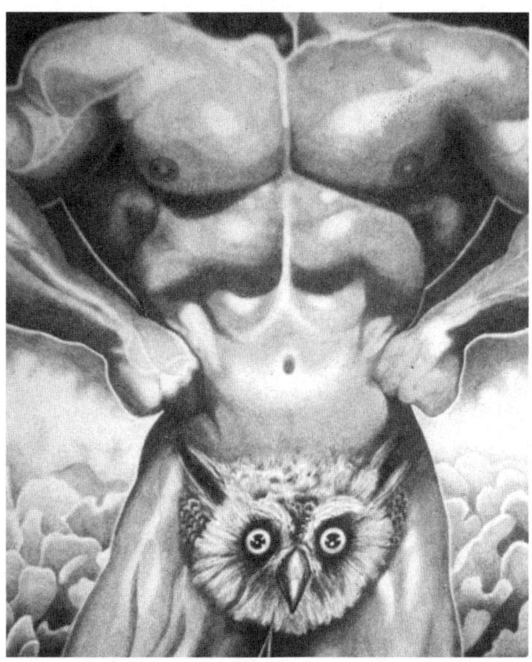

**4–8 The Adonis Series: Perseus** © Kyra Belán 1982
Drawing, graphite 30" x 22"
Matriarchal interpretation of the ancient Greek myth

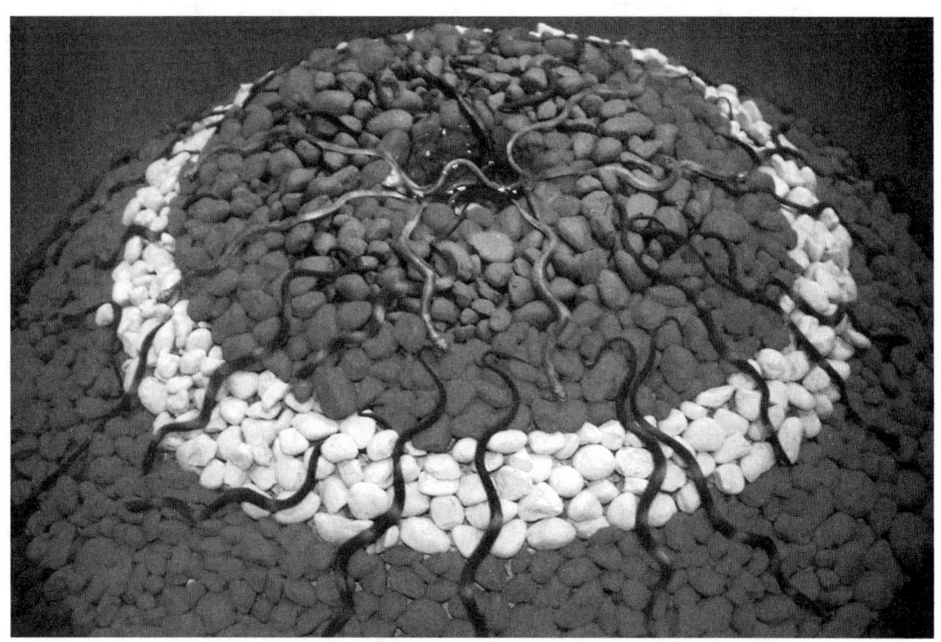

**4–9 Goddess Medusa: Magic Circle XIII** © Kyra Belán, 1987
Detail of environmental installation showing 14' diameter mound,
painted quartz rock and latex, serpents, plexiglass, water
Fine Arts Gallery, Broward Community College, Davie, Florida

# *Goddess Chicomecoatl*

To the Aztec civilization of Central America, Goddess Chicomecoatl represented Mother Earth and the earthly powers of a female divinity. Several artworks of the series are dedicated to her, including the interior space installations and performances at The Art and Culture Center of Hollywood, Florida, The Dupont Gallery at Washington and Lee University, Lexington, Virginia (1988) and the earthwork at The Rim Institute, north of Payson, Arizona (1988). Another earth art was created during the following year at The Rim (1989) to celebrate the Goddess of the Waters, Chalchiutlicue, also Aztec.

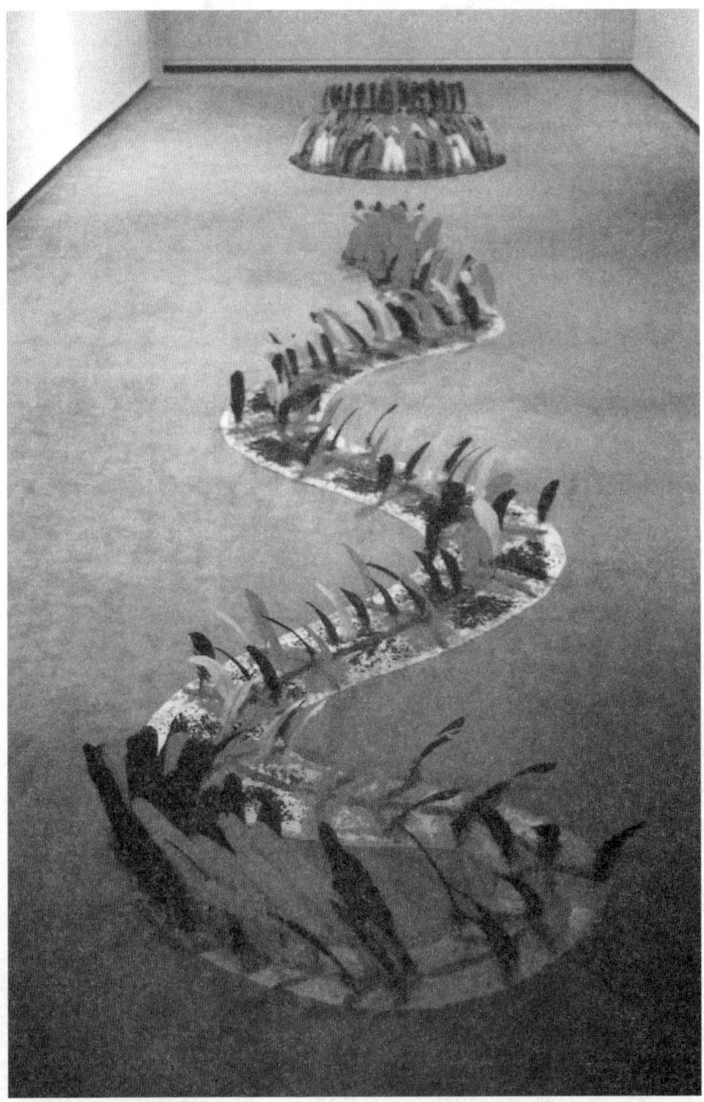

**4–10 Cosmic Goddess Chicomecoatl/Demeter:**
**Magic Circle XV** © Kyra Belán, 1988
Detail of environmental installation
Du Pont Gallery, Washington and Lee University, Lexington, Virginia

# *Nuestra Señora de Florida: Site Specific Installation*

The central theme of the site-specific installation designed for The Art Gallery, Broward Community College in Pembroke Pines, Florida (1991) was the image of *Nuestra Señora de Guadalupe*, successor of the Great Goddess Coatlicue, Earth Goddess Tonantzin, and the official protectress of the people of Mexico and the Americas. This time the archetypal image of Virgin Mary became the symbol for the divine feminine in Florida. A colored pencil triptych of *Nuestra Señora* served as a point of departure. She is shown wearing a red garment (red is symbolic of the life-giving power of the Goddess in many civilizations) and a star-covered blue cape, evoking her status as the Queen of Heaven of Christianity. Sun rays emanate from her body, an allusion to the female solar divinities and the traditional representations of the Virgin of Guadalupe. In the background is a scene of typical Floridian environment: convergence of the ocean and the sky, with several dolphins leaping out of the water, as if joyfully celebrating the presence of Our Lady. The concept behind this work celebrates female spirituality as global and multi-cultural (see Color Plate 1). The wall installation included various colored pencil drawings, all triptychs, of Goddesses. Numerous circular shapes, gleaming with gold, with colorful feathers attached and trailing down toward the floor, were incorporated into the wall installation. They were inspired by the Native American shields that the shamans and people of these cultures design for themselves. These include personal clan totems and symbols that are understood only by the owners of these ritual shields. I created large "shields," and painted universal Mother God symbols on their gold surfaces: triangles, circles, spirals, the Sun, the Moon, and human hands.

The vertical space of the gallery was transformed by the presence of multiple units of mobiles, made out of trimmed and painted tree branches. I attached multicolored feathers to the branches with clear threads to create an illusion of weightless floating in space. The floor area's principal installation consisted of a circular sculpture eight feet in diameter. It was constructed with painted rocks, shells, serpents, and trimmed and re-shaped tree branches. The branches were painted with red acrylic paint and stacked to a height of approximately four feet. Three other floor configurations, made of the same materials, either semi-circles or quarter-circles, were installed in other areas of the gallery floor, against the three walls. Colorful feathers were attached to some of the floor branches. A motif of the rebirth of nature, a constant component in the rituals of numerous Goddess religions, was explored in this work. The top layer of branches was painted while still fresh, and about a week after the exhibition opened to the public, small leaves appeared on these branches, growing right through the red acrylic paint.

The ritual performance consisted of percussion sounds, ritual processions, and dances. Over twenty participants, dressed in black, white and red, carried rattles and feathers. I wore a long red dress, a sheer blue cape and a blue headdress. The performance prompted a reporter from a small local newspaper to write a caption under the photo that explained the event as a group of Indians doing a war dance! In reality, the dance was a symbolic peace ceremony, but the power-oriented mentality prompted the reporter to understand this activity as a glorification of war rather than a tribute to peace.

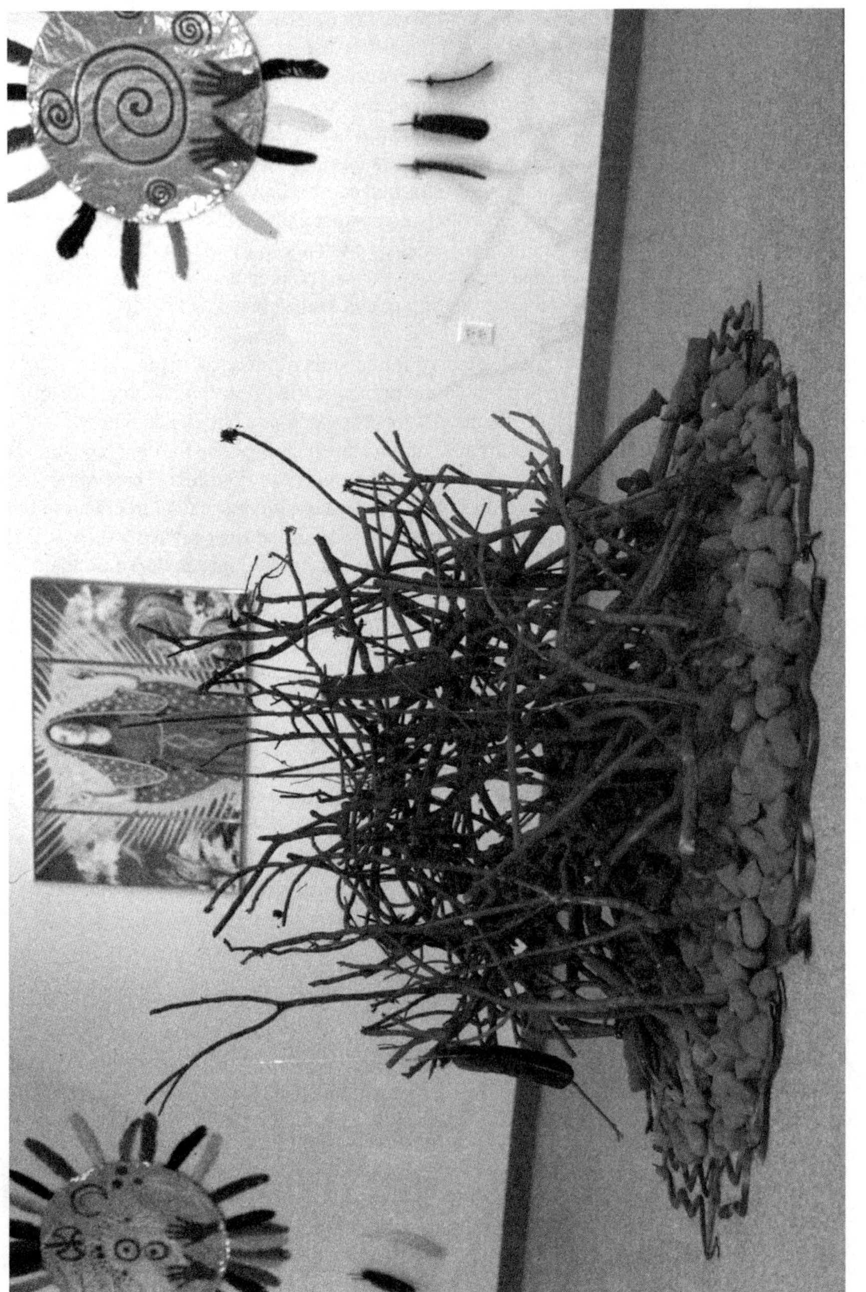

**4–11 Nuestra Señora de Florida: Magic Circle XX** © Kyra Belán, 1991
Detail of environmental installation
The Art Gallery, Broward Community College, Pembroke Pines, Florida

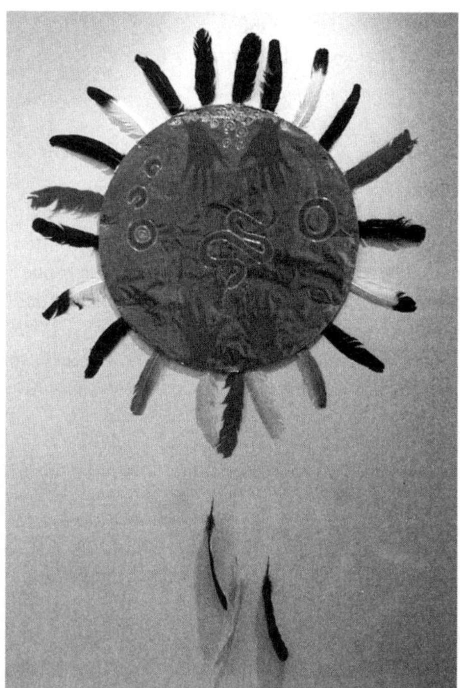

**4–12 Nuestra Señora de Florida: Magic Circle XX** © Kyra Belán, 1991
Detail of environmental installation showing one of the "shields"
The Art Gallery, Broward Community College, Pembroke Pines, Florida

## *Celebrating Juno*

An earthwork dedicated to Goddess Juno, the universal creator of ancient Rome, took shape in part from the recycling of the painted rock, the gold feathered shields, and some painted red branches used in several previous installations or earth art. This earthwork, an outdoor installation and a performance, was designed to be a temporary site-specific earth art at the Sri Naranda Yoga Center in Hallandale, Florida in 1993. The installation and the performance lasted one day, while the circular mound remained on the site for many months. The 14-foot-diameter circular form was inspired by a sunburst. It was assembled with yellow, red, and gold painted rocks, interrupted by some blue rocks over a layer of crushed white coral (see Color Plate 13). The low mound tapered down to the level of the grass. Three clusters of painted tree branches, to which several colored feathers were attached, formed a triangular enclosure for the stone circle. The gold feathered "shields" were attached to the trees and the framework of a stage, which was used during the performance.

The ritual performance was one of the longest, with over 40 participants assuming either performing or support roles. The performance took place on February 14, the traditional Roman and European day dedicated to the celebration of Goddess Juno, later to be transformed by Christianity into St. Valentine's Day. The traditional February celebration of the Goddess emphasized her aspect as the protectress of lovers, and her worshipers hoped either to enjoy and improve their relationships with the opposite sex or to find their mates on that day. In order to dissolve the artificial barriers between art and life itself, the second part of the ceremony consisted of a nuptial ceremony, my marriage to Charles Martin. The wedding ceremony was performed by an 82 year old Swami, Sri Naranda. Swami Naranda originated the non-profit Yoga Center and she has been a practitioner of yoga philosophy for over 40 years.

The ritual performance occurred in several stages. The participants of both sexes, as "priests" and "priestesses," wore white. In the role of the priestess and shaman, I wore red and gold during the first part of the ceremony and white during the second part, which included the wedding ceremony. The ritual sounds consisted of drumming, percussion and instrumental music that was composed for the performance. Charles Martin played his compositions during the first part of the performance on two keyboards.

During the first part of the performance, the participants walked through the garden and a canopy of oak and palm trees toward the earth sculpture, located in the middle of a grassy flat area. Then, producing drum beat and percussion sounds, the group danced around the circle. The nuptial ceremony took place on an outdoor stage, with a backdrop of gold feathered shields. It was followed by the procession and dance at twilight hour. Numerous candles that had been lit during the earlier part of the ceremony formed a luminous ring around the circular earth art after sunset, concluding the event.

## *The Myth of Goddess Juno*

Goddess Juno, also known as Juno Lucina, a solar divinity, is an ancient Roman Mother God and a direct descendant of the sole and omnipotent prehistoric Great Mother. She was also celebrated as the Goddess of agriculture, protectress of women and family, and a special divinity of lovers and those looking for a partner or a soul mate. One of her numerous festivities took place on February 14, and was primarily dedicated to those women and men who were trying to find each other to become partners in life. During early Christianity, this festival was abolished, but people continued to celebrate it. To eradicate Juno's memory from human consciousness, Christian fathers invented St. Valentine and allowed the festivity to continue to exist, while effectively erasing the memory of the divine feminine.

## *Mother Earth, Mother God: Site Specific Installation*

The theme of the celebration of the feminine continued in the site specific installation created for The 621 Gallery in Tallahassee, Florida, in the fall of 1993, and partially sponsored by the Florida Arts Council. The exhibition, titled *Mother Earth, Mother God: Magic Circle XXIII*, occupied a space that was 80' feet long, divided in the center by a tall partition-wall, with two walk-through spaces on each side. The tall dividing wall, and the high ceiling of this interior served as an inspiration to create a vertically oriented installation. New acrylic paintings on thick black paper were created to fill this space. Since the Earth Goddess was emphasized, the plumed serpent, associated with the Earth Goddess' powers, became the dominant image of the installation. I painted three vertical art works depicting the serpents, each 53 inches wide and 36 feet long. Two of the works, mirror images of undulating serpents, were placed on the partitioning wall (see Color Plate 16). They seemed to crawl up to the top of the wall. One image of a double-headed serpent of the same dimensions was placed on the opposite side of the wall, facing the back wall. All three plumed serpents, because of their size, were also gliding onto the floor. The rest of the walls displayed large paintings of Mother Gods of past and present religions. Many were inspired by familiar ancient sculptures, beginning with that of the Goddess of Willendorf. The colors were often iridescent or metallic, with a predominance of varying gold hues. As the spectators entered the gallery, they were met by the floor installation that preceded the two serpents which descended to the floor. It was a large circle, with an image of a double-headed serpent, coiled into a spiral and painted with acrylics. Rocks and feathers, some of which were recycled from previous installations, surrounded the circle and the sections of the giant serpent paintings that extended onto the floor surface. The ritual performance started with a ritual walk, drumming, and percussion, which I initiated. Then, the volunteer "priestesses" participated with me in the dance around the circle.

The next installation, titled *Mother Earth, Changing Woman: Magic Circle XXIV*, opened with a performance on Earth Day, April 22, 1994, at The Art Gallery of Broward Community College at Pembroke Pines. The square gallery space presents a challenge of multilevel ceiling heights. Two of the four wall levels ar 24 feet and 20 feet tall, allowing for a vertical expansion of the site-specific installation. The theme was closely related to that of the previous exhibition. The painted rocks from previous installations were again recycled within this space. The three artworks with giant plumed serpents were displayed on the tall walls, and as they descended onto the floor, several folds were formed. The surface of the south wall was covered by a modular mural of Goddess images (see Color Plate 17). A continuous mural of icons of Mother God, 53 feet high, was visible on the north and west walls of the gallery. In the central area, the circular floor installation was surrounded by painted rocks, while white quartz rocks with painted Goddess symbols formed a "medicine wheel" pattern within the circle. A number of painted latex serpents were also incorporated into the floor installation. The performance was initiated outdoors. A procession of over 25 participants, dressed in black, marched around the campus grounds. As their "shaman" leader, I was wearing a long black dress covered by a gold cape. Drumming and other percussive sound were created with a tambourine and a variety of shakers and maracas. This activity was followed by the procession into the gallery. Several ritual dances were performed inside the gallery space.

The indoor music consisted of drum, percussion sounds and electronic music composed for this work by Charles Martin. The image of Changing Woman, the ever-changing Earth Goddess of the cycles of life of Navajo people, was represented through the ritual aspect of the performance and through the symbols found within the installation.

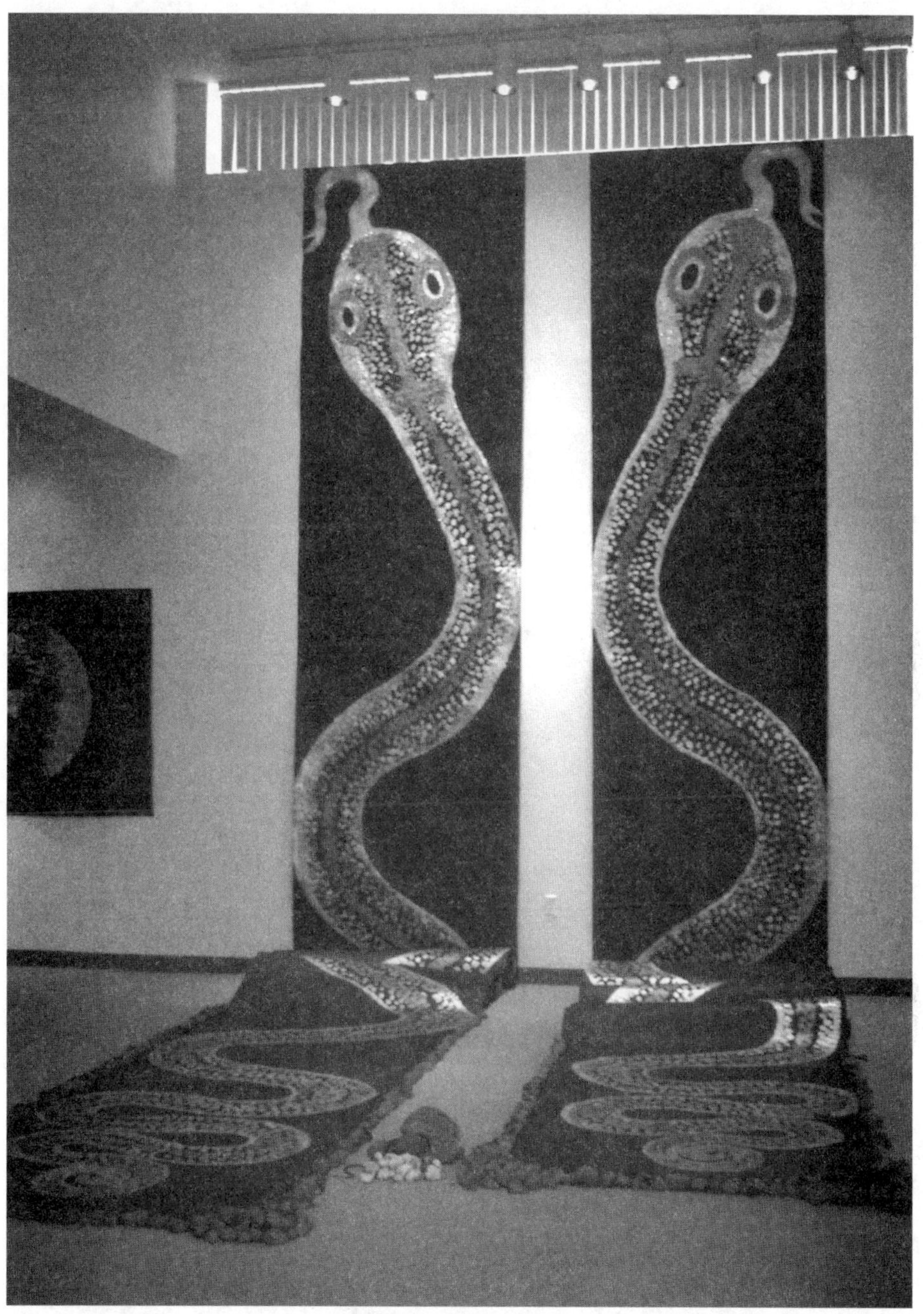

**4–13 Mother Earth, Changing Woman:**
**Magic Circle XXIV** © Kyra Belán, 1994
Detail of site specific installation, showing two Plumed Serpents
The Art Gallery, Broward Community College, Pembroke Pines, Florida

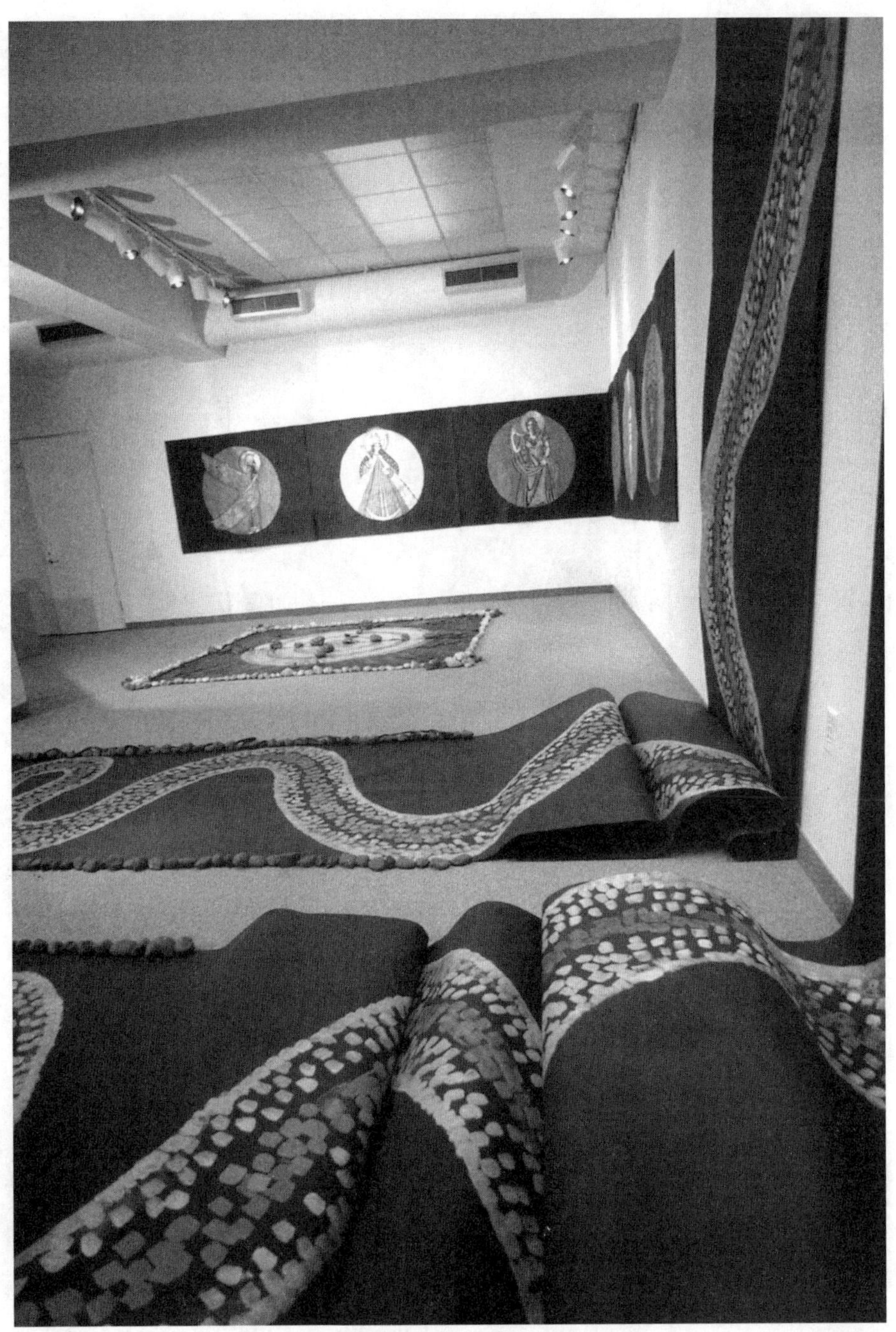

**4–14 Mother Earth, Changing Woman:**

**Magic Circle XXIV** © Kyra Belán, 1994

Detail of site specific installation.

The Art Gallery, Broward Community College, Pembroke Pines, Florida

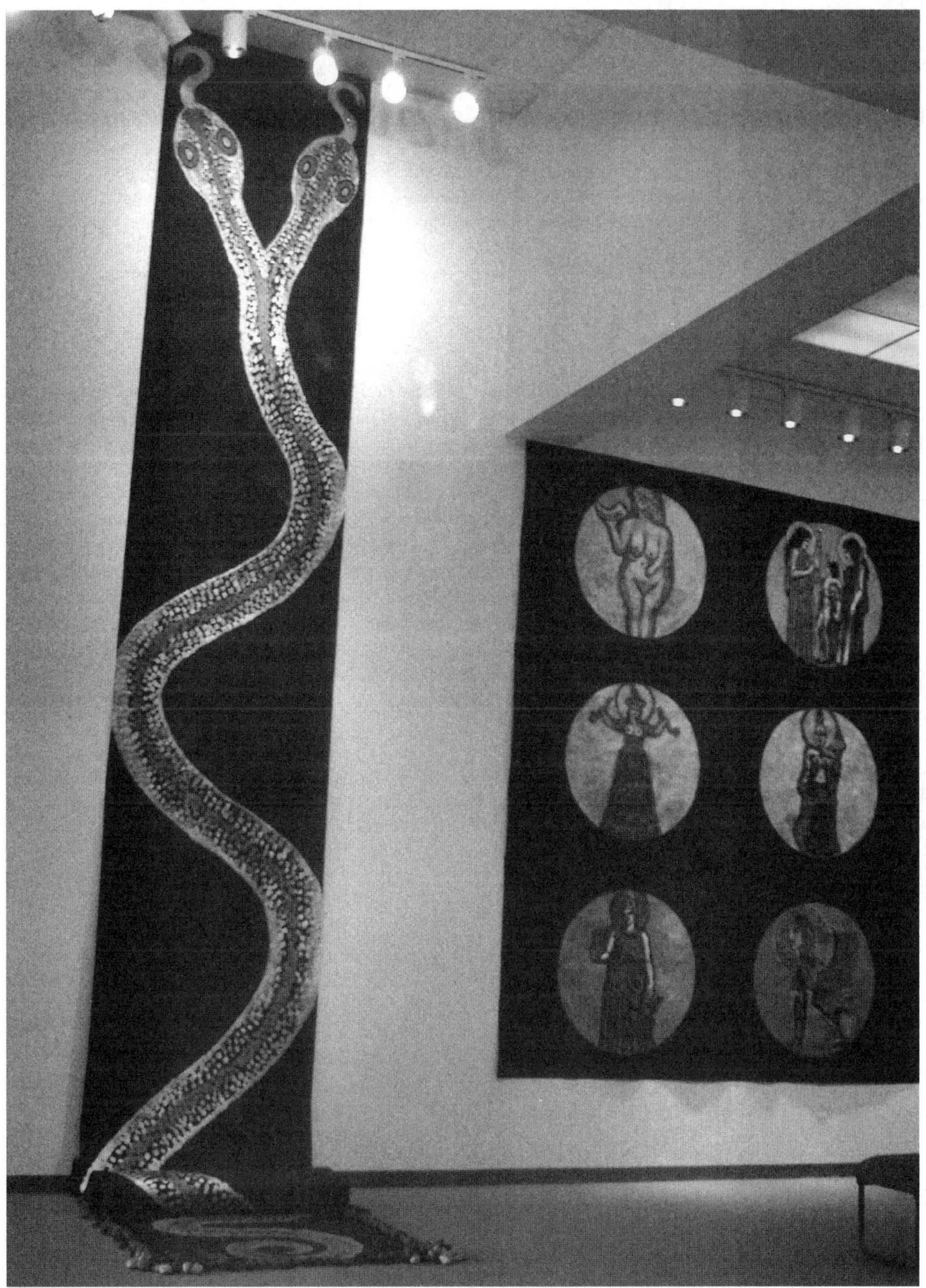

**4–15 Mother Earth, Changing Woman:**
**Magic Circle XXIV** © Kyra Belán, 1994
Detail of site specific installation with a partial view of the south wall
The Art Gallery, Broward Community College, Pembroke Pines, Florida

This exhibition was followed by an artwork that was a celebration of Summer Solstice. The ritual performance and site specific installation took form at the Yoga Vedanta Science and Arts Center in Ft. Lauderdale, Florida, in 1994. The exhibition was titled *Goddess Lakshmi: Magic Circle XXV*. Three walls of the exhibition space were used for the display of several groups of Goddess images, and the floor had the circular installation, around which the performance occurred. Painted latex serpents, painted rocks, and glitter dust were arranged within and around the floor sculpture. An image of Mother God Lakshmi was centrally placed on the wall that faced the circular floor artwork. A ritual walk and dancing, accompanied by percussion and electronic keyboard music composed by Charles Martin, took place on the eve of Summer Solstice. White was the main color worn by the participants, while I wore a white feathered headdress, a long white dress, and a gold cape for this ritual performance. Since prehistory, solstice celebrations have been traditional Goddess and Earth Mother festivities throughout the world, and are practiced today by numerous non-mainstream cultures. This artwork emphasized the importance of celebrating the cyclical nature of planet Earth.

## *Goddess Lakshmi*

The Great Mother Lakshmi, like other female divinities of Hindu religions, is perceived as triple, multiple, and one. She represents the active divine force from which the male gods must draw for their existence. According to traditional and ancient Hinduism, female divine essence is recognized as active, while the male divinities have a passive nature. They coexist with the primal female divinities by being imbued with their active divine energy, Shakti. On another level, Lakshmi is worshiped as the giver of abundance in nature. She bestows prosperity upon her followers. She is presently worshiped in India, other non-Western countries, England, and in America by immigrants from India and their descendants.

## *Magic Circle Series*

The *Magic Circle Series* is an ongoing lifetime project of site-specific installations, earthworks, and performances. It is an ever-changing and continuing work of art that undergoes numerous transformations and destructions. It is also being shown, in various configurations, as a traveling exhibition. The driving force within the artwork is re-introducing the divine feminine into the mainstream culture dominated by several one-gendered religious philosophies. The series helps to create visual language for a more spiritual, compassionate, peaceful, and interconnected world culture.

My images of the Goddesses were executed on paper, canvas or with mixed media. They can be exhibited separately or together. Besides my aesthetic concerns, the purpose for their existence is to reinforce the message of female spirituality within the public consciousness. By reintroducing the many faces of God the Mother into our society, I hope to help effect a change that will result in a balance between female and male spirituality. My goal is to offer the public an opportunity to visualize God in female form with the same ease that enables them to visualize the Omnipotent Creator in male form. The images of God the Mother, archetypal within human minds, expand the possibility of a harmonious, peaceful, and multi-cultural future for our planet.

# 5

# *The Female Gaze and the Male Nude*

My interest in the male nude developed early in college, while I was attending Arizona State University in the seventies. It was a time of significant social change that included the slow process of liberation of women from patriarchal oppression. As an undergraduate college student, I was passionately involved in my quest for acquisition of knowledge and artistic development. I was totally oblivious of the fact that beyond the college environment, women artists were pressured by society not to use male nudes as subject matter for their art productions.[5] I continued to develop my technical skills and to pursue my aesthetic interest in male figure drawing and painting throughout my graduate studies at Florida State University in Tallahassee, where I produced numerous artworks with the male nude form as my main subject matter. Although the university never placed any restrictions on my ideas, as I began to enter professional juried exhibitions and make arrangements for solo exhibitions, I was confronted with my first encounter of what would become a career-long problem: the censorship of frontal male nude figures and the unwillingness on the part of art galleries or museums to exhibit male nude forms.

A strong believer and supporter of artistic freedom, I first went through a phase of disbelief and denial. Subsequently, I tried to comprehend why this type of injustice was perpetrated on women artists. I began to research art history in a context of socio-cultural environment for historical precedents that denied me the freedom to get my images out to the public. The issue of my gender surfaced as the main obstacle. However, I assumed that this obstacle would dissolve within a few years, as society continued to change its view on the status of women. As my efforts to exhibit male nudes continued, the label of feminist was now attached to my name. This fact confirmed my suspicion that, by allowing myself to expand into the area of erotic art from the female point of view, I had antagonized the current social establishment. Yet it was hard for me to understand why an artist would be perceived as a political activist only because she does what she likes to explore. Later I realized that under the rules of patriarchy, all art was assumed to be created for the male gaze, whether by males or females. The accepted premise was that all art must be produced and preserved for the aesthetic consumption of male spectators and art appreciators. Contemporary society usually does not provide visual stimulation for the female gender in the realm of sensuous or erotic art. As a result, current research seems to indicate that women are less visually stimulated by the images of male forms than men are by the images of female forms. I concluded that this fact is a result of the lack of opportunity for the female gender to be as visually literate as the male gender. Images of the female nude, created mostly by male artists, exist in abundance in our culture. They range from romantic glorification of the female body to the most derogatory and degrading depictions of the female form. Nearly all the nuances of female sexual oppression have already been expressed through the visual arts. The female nude, in all the possible permutations of sensuality or oppression, from passive reclining beauties to scenes of torture, dismemberment, violence, and rape populate numerous museums and galleries of the world. They are seen on public display, available to both young and adult populations, providing visual standards and visual literacy for adolescents and adults.[6]

I wondered what had happened to the images of male nudes that had been created by women artists throughout the history of art. They are not a part of the establishment's gallery or museum displays. Not many of those works produced in the past exist today, because women artists had to create this kind of work in secret, and it has been destroyed. If this type of artwork exists today, it is not exhibited in mainstream museums and galleries. My artistic journey led me to cross over into the rarely explored, underdeveloped and forbidden territory: the journey into the realm of the female sensual gaze.

My status as a pioneer in this area has become clear to me; I also became acutely aware that this aspect of my art may largely remain a secret during my life time. This premonition has proved to be correct so far throughout the following decades. I kept submitting my male nudes to the juried shows, galleries and museums and received literally hundreds of rejections. I even traveled to New York, and managed to get my male nudes accepted into a cooperative gallery called Womanart, where artists had to pay a fee to exhibit their work. Yet the presumably progressive newspaper, *The Village Voice*, refused to publish a show announcement ad with an image of a male nude. Instead, the gallery director was asked to provide the paper with a female figure for the announcement. One more New York gallery, *Alain Bilhaud*, accepted the request to represent my art on the subject of the male nude, but suddenly closed down, and the owner left for France. Myart works, placed at the gallery on consignment, disappeared without a trace.

In the late 1970's, a small number of institutions included my colored pencil drawings of male nudes in their group shows, such as The Lowe Museum of Art in Coral Gables. Miami-Dade College's Wm. Pauley Art Center agreed to a solo exhibition of my artwork, sans censorship, and the resulting installation included numerous male nudes. The Fine Arts Gallery at Broward Community College in Davie (solo exhibition with an installation and performance) and Hanson Gallery in New Orleans (one work entered in a juried exhibition judged by artist Dorothy Gillespie) also were among those institutions that did not censor my art. However, in the 1980's, not a single institution or gallery accepted my male nudes, fearing that the backlash against women would bring some complaints from the public. In the nineties, one male nude was reproduced in a Ft. Lauderdale news magazine, XS (the magazine staff chose a conservative side view). Currently, the censorship of the male nude continues, as usual.

Censorship of male nudes created by female artists has effectively slowed down the development of the female gaze in our society. It is a true challenge for me to continue to produce art works that feature male nudes, since they cannot be seen by the public; yet the series continue. I enjoy expressing the liberating power of the female gaze through my art, and I am not alone. Contemporary women have been slowly discovering within themselves the ability to enjoy the visual aesthetics of the male nude forms. Re-enchantment with the world, including all its sensual aspects, is now the domain of both women and men. Since the right to gaze at the male is the prerogative of a modern female, this right must be translated into an artistic expression, and it must be incorporated into contemporary culture, just as the male sensual/visual experience has been for many centuries. Even though the products of the female sensual gaze may not yet be frequently seen, they can constitute a legacy for future generations of women, and will enable them to proceed on their own personal journeys into female sensual aesthetics.

I do not presume to be the first in the history of patriarchy to exercise the female sensual gaze, but the fact remains that most efforts of my predecessors, such as the work of eighteenth century Italian artist's Giulia Lama, have been destroyed. Italian Baroque artist Artemisia Gentileschi has emerged as an important figure of her time after the seminal book on her was published by art historian Mary Garrard. Her work includes numerous innovations in the treatment of subject matter: It is a known fact that she drew male nudes in secret, but none of them have survived the passage of time. My more recent role models include artist Malvina Hoffman. She sculpted the male nude in marble or cast it in bronze, but her art is still minimally accessible to women artists or the general public. Before the seventies, women artists were excluded from college and school art history texts, and very few articles or books on their art were published. Contemporary New York artist Sylvia Sleigh and several other female artists occasionally explored the male nude form during the seventies and have been included in a few textbooks on women artists. The last three decades demonstrate that due to constant censorship and even harassment, women artists are often not willing to dedicate their time and psychic energy to the creation of a large body of work that may never be exhibited or published. I have made an effort to maintain the creation of work that is never publicly displayed. However, my production would have been more extensive if the possibility of showing these artworks to the public had been more realistic.

Male artists were allowed to explore the male form for thousands of years, in many cultures. Since art history as a discipline began to develop in the Renaissance, male artists from Michelangelo to Mapplethorpe have been able to receive support from the establishment to show their work. My belief is that artistic experience is enriched by the participation of all races, genders, and sexual orientations. Finally, it is time for humanity to recognize the existence of the female sensual gaze. The world will be richer when one more artistic expression, stemming from a woman's perception, *the female sensual gaze*, is added to the heritage of the world as one more aspect of artistic experience. If my work represents a good start in this direction, my hope is that many other women artists will join in to explore this still largely uncharted territory.

# *Male Nude and the Divine Masculine: The Adonis Series*

My journey into the female sensual gaze began with my involvement with world mythologies, which serve as a source of my inspiration. These old religions, which include Egyptian, Hindu, Greek, and Roman male archetypes, allowed artists to create idealized male forms of the numerous male divinities. The gods of the old religions were closely connected to the Goddess, to nature, and to our planet Earth. In my art, the males possess the characteristics of ancient divinities and of contemporary men; they are connected with earth-based spirituality. They are men, heroes, gods, and archetypes. They bond with nature and the animals. Inspired by Native American and pre-Columbian religions, I also transform them into a form that is a combination of human and animal, such as a fusion of a man and an eagle, thus emphasizing their profound unity with nature. They are in tune with Mother Earth and feel kinship with the animals.

My preferred medium for the male nude series, titled *The Adonis Series*, is graphite or colored pencil on paper. The technique is elaborate and realistic, with a touch of the surreal. This method allows me to get intensely involved in the sensuality of the muscular curves of male bodies and surround them with colorful and often fantastic natural forms, derived from both vegetal and underwater realms. These rich environments envelop the nude masculine bodies with the tenderness and beauty of Mother Nature. Animals of different types may also be incorporated into the compositions. Several thematic approaches are explored: the male nude figure only; male and female figures together, with the latter either draped or also nude; the fusion of human and animal form into one fantastic creature; and the phallic form itself, as a symbol of male sexuality, fertility, and earthy spirituality.

One of the works that fits into the first category, the male nude form, is a graphite pencil drawing, 50 inches x 38 inches, titled *The Source*, completed in 1974. It depicts a standing nude figure, with his arms raised and his head tilted skyward. Behind him is an osprey, shown larger than life and in a protective stance. Her wings are open, as if shielding her human offspring. The role of the osprey as an archetypal symbol of the divine feminine is apparent in this work. Since prehistoric times, Mother God is often depicted in a form of a bird. The message of the image is that of a cosmic mother protecting her creation, a man who is in harmony with nature. Completed during the same year, a graphite and colored pencil drawing, 50 inches x 38 inches, titled *The Visit*, also shows a single male nude. He is reclining in the foreground, surrounded by organic forms inspired by the sea barnacles and anemones that suggest the shapes of a lingam and a yoni. The upper level of the drawing exhibits two fruit bats with their wings spread, in the activity of extracting nectar from the flower-shaped anemones. Also seen in the background is a draped female figure, holding a small feather in her hand. This bird feather, which presents a connection to the divine feminine, identifies the figure as either a female guardian angel or protective Goddess figure or the anima of the male figure. The nude is portrayed as relaxed, content, and attuned to his environment.

*Black Orpheus*, a colored pencil drawing, 48 inches x 38 inches, was completed in 1975. This artwork is a double portrait. The dominant male nude figure in the foreground is facing the spectator. The second nude male form is in profile, while in between them is a low-flying owl, an archetype for the creative female principle. The ground surface is covered with colorful and luxurious sea forms: plants and animals, often reminiscent of vaginal and phallic shapes. The space is shallow, due to the presence of a wall. There is a large rectangular window, through which one can observe several colorful clusters of crystals. The crystal has been admired and revered by the Native American and pre-Columbian Goddess worshiping civilizations, as well as by ancient Europe and Africa. The crystal was first connected with female divinity, but later its powers and symbolism were expanded to represent both the male and female gods and earth-based spirituality in general. Some people believe that crystalline structure contains and manifests a beneficial and powerful energy. The graceful male nudes appear at peace with themselves and the surrounding universe, yet they possess unmistakable sensual beauty. In this work, the Greek myth of the divine Orpheus, God of music, winds, and love, has been expanded to include images of the African-American male, dissolving the Euro-centric barrier.

The archetypal symbolism of the next two works, also completed in 1975, was again inspired by Greek myths. The first, a graphite drawing, 38 inches x 48 inches, *Athena and Paris*, shows nude Paris in the foreground, while nude Athena is centrally located in the background. The surrounding environment appears to be calm; only the soft terrain and the cloudy sky are visible. Two large birds of prey, an owl and a hawk, accompany the two nude figures. The sensuous body of Paris is emphasized by the fact that part of his face is cropped, forcing the spectator to concentrate her or his gaze on the torso and phallus. This work glorifies harmony between human beings and nature and the aesthetic beauty of the male nude. The female can be interpreted as a guardian angel or an anima. The subsequent work, a colored pencil drawing, 40 inches x 48 inches, *Athena and Mars*, has a dynamic composition. Two reclining figures, male in the foreground and female above and behind him, are accompanied by a large owl. Both Athena and Mars seem to observe a bird in flight, seemingly ready to perch between the two.

The owl is a well-known symbol of wisdom of the Goddess. Both divinities of the Greeks have a warrior aspect. In this work, the warriors are transmuted into seekers of peace and enlightenment and are in harmony with nature. The calm sensuality and beauty of Mars is the symbol for the emergence of the new male who integrates within himself both the masculine and the feminine values of peace and earthy spirituality.

Goddess Athena, as the anima of man, appears in the next colored pencil drawing, 40 inches x 48 inches, completed in 1976. The drawing, titled *Dionysus in the Land of Eleusis*, depicts a reclining nude male in the foreground. The figure is frontally positioned; his legs are spread, allowing a full view of his genital area. He is surrounded by a "vegetation" of anemones, sponges, and coral formations, many of which resemble the shape of a lingam. The ambiguous background contains two floating "windows," in which the image of Dionysus is represented embracing Athena, a nude female figure. They are both human and divine and represent the union of feminine and masculine spirituality and sensuality. The importance of a loving emotional involvement, and a sense of harmony are evoked in this drawing. It is my belief that the emotional state of happiness provides an important and exciting subject for a work of art. The figure of Athena, as the active creative force, is represented in the upper half of the colored pencil drawing, 40 inches x 48 inches, *Athena and Dionysus*. The spectator is confronted by a reclining nude male figure in the foreground. The relaxed and serene Dionysus is surrounded by sea anemones that are suggestive of vaginal forms, as well as various underwater phallic shapes. Corals are seen immediately behind the figure. The sensuous figure has dual significance: as a rendering of a contemporary flesh and blood male, and of the myth of Dionysus, consort of the ancient Great Goddess, the foremother of Athena. Dionysus was worshiped as the God of rebirth of nature and of the coming of spring, the motivating force of the re-awakening of nature. According to some myths, he was a divinity who re-enacted the yearly cycle of death and resurrection, emulating the circular progression in nature. Indeed, Dionysus is seen as deeply attuned to nature. The upper level of the drawing appears to have a shallow flat wall, with an arched semicircular window, through which the viewer can observe a deep space containing an arid mountainous landscape and a reclining nude female figure in its foreground. The woman-goddess Athena holds an owl feather. Two owls protectively extend their open wings over her head. The hand with the feather reaches out of the semi-circle, and into the lower space where the man-god Dionysus is located. The gesture can be interpreted as either the act of creation of the man-god by the Goddess, or her interconnection with him. This is a world of peace, love, and paradise: a fantasy of a probable idyllic past, present, or future.

*Quetzalcoatl* is a colored pencil drawing of a single male nude, which was completed in 1990. The figure is that of an idealized male nude inspired by an Aztec myth. He is the son of the Aztec Goddess Coatlicue, the Great Mother of all goddesses and gods. The pyramids in the background are similar to the pyramids of the Sun and Moon that can be found at Teotihuacan, a major site of pre-Columbian Goddess worship. He is wearing a ritual headdress in the shape of an eagle's head, adorned with the plumes of the sacred bird quetzal. A jaguar and a serpent at his knees are symbols of the powers of Pre-Columbian divinities. Strong and serene, he is at peace with nature. He is also an expression of female sexual fantasy. His lean and muscular body is well proportioned and beautiful (see image 5-1).

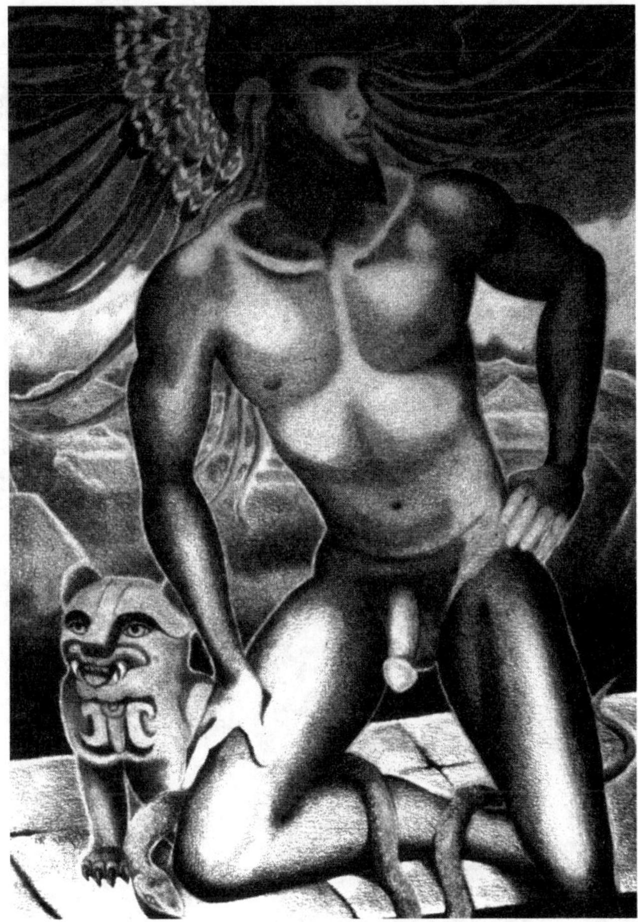

**5-1.The Adonis Series: Qietzalcoatl** © Kyra Belán 1990
Drawing, colored pencils, 30" x 22"

The male nude form is often represented in my art as inseparable from nature and its animals. Often the male figure and the animal form are metamorphosed into one. This is a statement about an atunement and harmony between human and animal realms, and evokes Native American, Australian Aborigine and other belief systems that promote the idea of equality between humans and animals. There is also a shamanic message about a human who has the ability to merge with his personal animal guide, to become one with this creature. One example of this motif is a graphite drawing, 30 inches x 22 inches, titled *Perseus* and completed in 1982 (see image 4-7). This character, inspired by the Greek legend about this hero or demi-god, is shown as a male torso with its head cropped out of the picture, displaying pronounced muscularity. From his groin area emerges a head of an owl. This bird is an ancient symbol of wisdom of the Goddess, but in more literal mythological interpretations, Athena's magical owl assisted her favorite semi-divinity in his heroic accomplishments. In this artwork, the nude body becomes one with the head of an owl; the image can be interpreted as the ritual covering of the phallus, or as replacement of the phallus by the owl's head. Another example of this union between animal and male forms can be observed in *Hercules*, a 30 inches x 22 inches graphite drawing completed in 1983. Hercules, another hero or demi-god of the myths of the ancient Greeks, was originally one of the "sons of Hera," the ancient meaning, according to Barbarra G.Walker, of the term "hero." Hercules is a muscular creature. This muscularity, however, is beyond the standards of Ancient Greeks and is more appropriate for an image of a contemporary body-builder. He is not totally human; his head is that of an eagle. His pubic area, besides his prominent phallus, displays feathers in place of pubic hair. He has merged with his familial animal, becoming an archetypal shamanic vision.

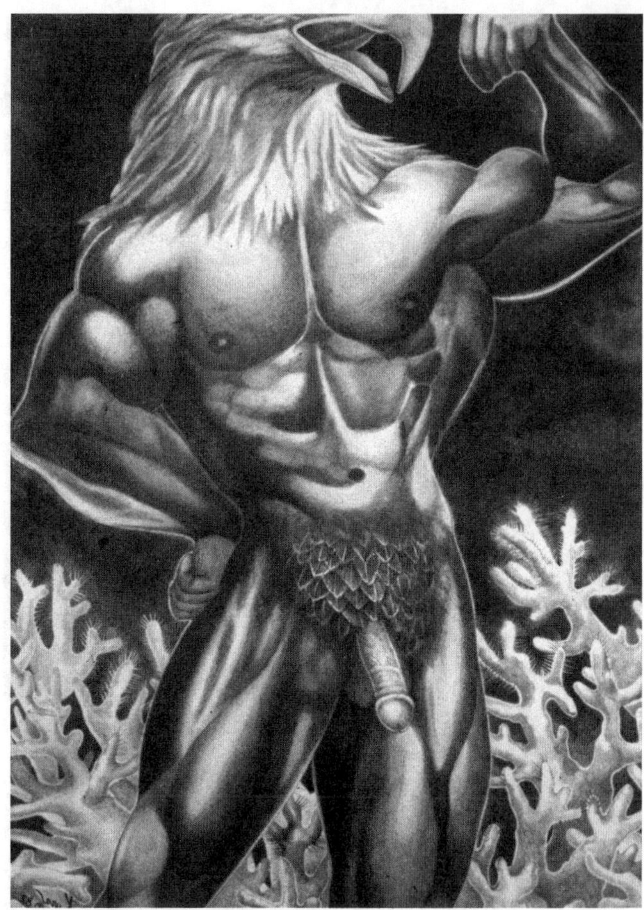

**5-2. The Adonis Series: Hercules** © Kyra Belán
Drawing, graphite, 30 inches x 22 inches, 1983

Some artworks present a double phenomena: the mutation of a human male nude into a human/animal form, and a polyphallic condition. The multiple phallus, usually detached from the body, appeared in the arts and artifacts of ancient Rome as a symbol for male fertility. An important attribute of fertility god Herm, the phallus was considered to be an image of good luck. Erotic Roman art is one of the sources of my inspiration and is combined with my erotic visions of sensual masculine forms. The drawing is a fantasy about a super-sensual male, capable of pleasing any multi-orgasmic female. *Medusa's Warrior* (1982),a graphite drawing, 30 inches x 22 inches, focuses upon this polyphallic vision. The frontal male torso, with well-defined contemporary muscularity, is partially a form of a bird: a winged creature, perhaps with a head of a bird (we are not certain, since the head is cropped off), and feathers instead of pubic hairs. Seven penises, in various stages of erection, sprout from his groin area. This is a superman of female sexual fantasy, an image of dreams and of the subconscious. A colored pencil drawing, 40 inches x 48 inches, titled *Minerva's Warriors* and completed in 1985, explores the same motif. The five bird-headed and partially feathered male nudes are seen walking through a fantasy world of clear skies and a landscape covered by colorful anemones, corals, and other fantastic vegetation. The nudes are very muscular, beautiful, and well proportioned. Triple phalluses can be observed on three out of five figures in the foreground. These mutant male nude figures may be interpreted as the familials of the goddess/woman/shaman who can subject them to her sensual powers.

The phallus as a symbol of male sexuality and female sensual pleasure is presented as the main subject matter for several compositions; it does not need to be attached to a figure. A drawing created with colored pencil, *Astarte's Paradise*, 40 inches x 48 inches, (1978), alludes to an old pre-patriarchal myth of creation. The composition depicts a clouded sky that dissolves into an environment of corals; floating within the ambiguous space are three circular windows. Each circle is occupied by a close-up of a larger-than-life pink hibiscus flower. The hibiscus in the middle circle is shown in the various stages of transformation that its several stamens are undergoing. A female hand, emerging from the cloud above, is depicted entering the circular space, and causing a metamorphosis to take place: The stamens of the flower are transforming into phalluses.

A companion artwork, of the same medium and size, *Astarte's Ascidians* (1979), has a similar composition: the blending of heavenly and underwater realms. The three circles slightly overlap and are populated by an assortment of phallic shapes, intermixed with various creatures of the ocean. The two silver shadows of the hands of the Goddess are located at the bottom of the pictorial space, as if in a process of entering the three circles. In this artwork, the creation myth is intertwined with scientific theory, which presumes that all life originally sprang from the underwater realm, and surfaced onto solid ground after a period of evolution.

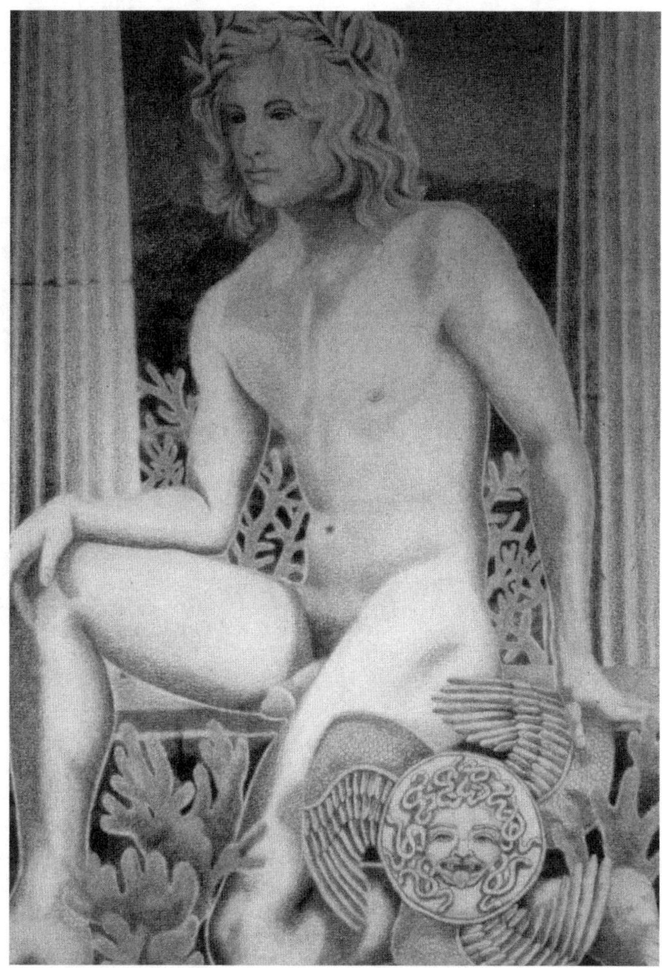

**5-3 The Adonis Series: Medusa's Worshiper** © Kyra Belán
Drawing, colored pencils, 1990

In my work, a male nude form is a balanced blending of sensuality and spirituality. This is apparent in a colored pencil drawing, completed in 1995, *The Earth Angel.* The nude alludes to the angelic qualities present in human beings. This drawing shows a reclining winged male nude surrounded by a natural environment of harmonious beauty. A summer sky occupies the upper portion of the background, where it converges with the ocean at the horizon line. The sensual beauty and spirituality of the nude, who is in a state of attunement with nature, is the essence of this work.

My exploration of the male nude form resulted in the creation of numerous drawings and paintings of the nude that place emphasis on the natural beauty, the muscularity, and the sensuality of a youthful male form. He is also a myth, a hero, an Earth God, and a God of Nature. The male figure is replete with sensuality and energy for life. He thrives among the fantastic environments that are inspired by the beauty of nature, as one who is at peace with the world. He is open to introspective and meditative states of mind and to loving relationships. The male nude is never presented in my art in a state of oppression or mistreatment. Absence of violence in these artworks is obvious. The cosmos that is presented is a positive one.

# *Patriarchal Phobia of the Male Nude*

Censorship of the male nude from the female point of view frequently takes place within the art establishment. It is a facet of contemporary society that can be traced to early Medieval ages. The art world needs to face its own duplicity, and the issue must be further discussed and examined.[7] It is my hope that prevalent attitudes of censorship toward the male nude that has been created for the female gaze can be changed. The development of the female gaze is currently taking place, and our society is ready to accept it. A one-gendered point of view is no longer seen as a viable alternative for the existing social construct.

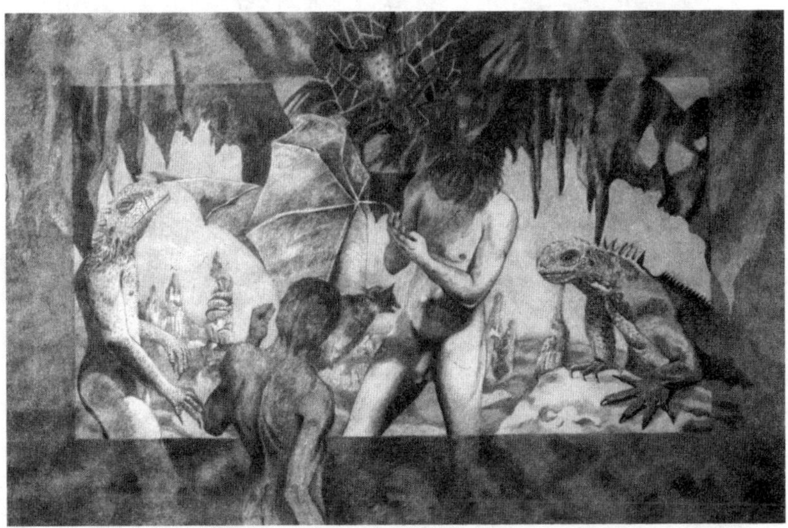

**5-4 Fauna's Satyrs** © Kyra Belán, 1975
Drawing, graphite and colored pencil, 27" x 40"

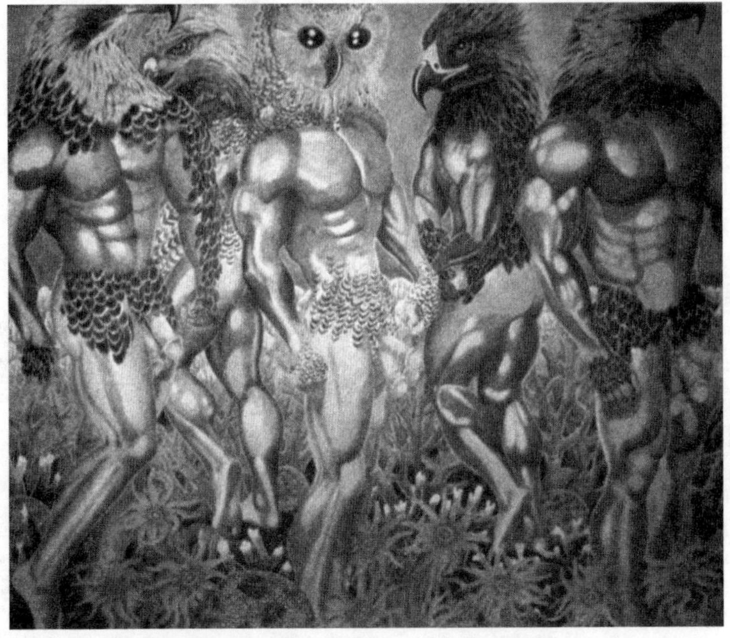

**5-5 Minerva's Warriors** © Kyra Belán, 1985
Drawing, colored pencil,, 40" x 48"

# 6

# *Earth, Nature, and the Eco-Feminist Vision*

In a conventional artistic vision, which reflects the dominant social system, nature is viewed as a territory to conquer and to tame. In fact, patriarchal society is structured according to a very specific hierarchical order. This organization can be visualized as a triangle or a pyramid, with the upper top portion reserved for the male God the Father, who also represents the heavenly realm. The male human is placed at the top of the earthly strata, followed by everyone and everything else that presumably exist at his service: woman, child, animal world, and the totality of nature. All that are located below man within the artificial structure of the pyramid are presumed to be in need of being tamed, conquered, controlled, and molded in order to accommodate to the one-gendered ideology and the desires and needs of the male. This hierarchy is assumed to originate as a divine sanction of the male God. Western cultural heritage is seen as the measure of all things, and it is placed above the accomplishments of other cultures by this Euro-centric order.

In my work, human beings are viewed as a part of nature and the Goddess is also our Mother Earth. Animals have the same privileges as human beings, and natural elements such as plants, underwater life, or flowers are also glorified as spiritual and sacred entities. Numerous artworks are dedicated to the creatures of the natural world that have been either persecuted or abused by andro-centric societies, or to whom negative mythology has been attached. They may also be endangered species. Peace, harmony, beauty, and joy are glorified in the artworks.Violence, subjugation, or terror is never the subject matter. My belief is that in order to heal the planet, our mind-set has to be changed, and positive images in art can help to effect this change.

At the dawn of the twenty-first century, our society is facing the possibility of self-destruction. For the past two thousand years, in particular since the Industrial Revolution, Mother Earth has been under siege. Dominant religious, philosophical, and ethical thinking has allowed the militaristic and status-conscious societies to systematically destroy our environment by polluting our atmosphere and our waters. Massive destruction of tropical forests and natural habitats that house numerous animals and plants has already caused total extinction of numerous species. In order for the planet to survive, each individual's value system must be sensitive to the need for a harmonious universe. Old religions and philosophies that proclaimed man as the master, conqueror, and destroyer of the planet and presented this dominator model of society as the only possible construct must be re-evaluated and changed. This change can occur: New visual images in the arts that represent the feminine values that glorify peace and compassion can help bring this change into our lives. Celebration of the inter-connectedness among all people and their environments as important and valuable can also help change the face of the planet, and visual images can accelerate this change.

For most of the twentieth century, contemporary art aesthetic disregarded the idea that content of a work of art could play an important role in art criticism. During postmodern times, the issue of content as an option constitutes an important argument for those artists who need to express their particular viewpoints to the public. It is my premise that content does not devalue art; on the contrary, it can add enormously to the complexity of a work of art. Since prehistory, content in art has been the motivational force.

It has successfully transmitted ideas that clearly reflected the value systems of the societies it served. In my works of art, social message is as important as the formal issues of the creation of an artwork.

I propose that the message presented in a work of art becomes clearer when expanded by a written explanation from the artist. This explanation, such as the one you are reading now, is the final stage of the completion of my art projects. Therefore, artificial barriers that were formulated to divide all the arts into tight compartments are erased. The boundaries of the beginning and ending of a work of art must be defined and determined by the artists themselves, rather than by previously established guidelines.

In my work, content emerges as a primary issue; the purpose of my art is to guide the viewer's mind set toward the goal of a positive future for the planet. Consequently, the aesthetic beauty of natural forms and animals is often my subject matter. The intention is to induce in the spectators a mental state of re-enchantment with their environment. The artworks are created with the purpose of re-awakening the love for Mother Nature that is already programmed into the genetic code of each human being. My goal is to help awaken the deeply embedded realization that animals are entitled to share this planet with human beings, and should not be abused, consumed, or exterminated.

My desire to convey these messages prompted me to produce several series of works, such as drawings and paintings, that tell the message of reverence toward nature: the *Shakti Series* depict plants, the *Kali Series* features birds or animals, and the *Floralia Series* explores the beauty, sensuality, and spirituality of a flower in a variety of permutations.

The *Shakti Series* consists of colored pencil drawings that depict luscious tropical environments. The style of the series is realistic, bordering on magical realism. The use of fine hatching technique with colored pencils produces a complex blending of colors. The composition is based on the balance, often radial, between positive and negative spaces. The artworks glorify the rhythms and harmonies that exist in nature.

## *Shakti, The Feminine Divine*

Shakti is the feminine divine principle of Hinduism. She represents the female active energy, as opposed to the passive male energy. Shakti is also the ultimate and original Mother God, and she is present in all the goddesses and gods of India. Today many philosophical/spiritual schools in the US recognize Shakti as the life force, or active energy present in human beings, animals, and plants, and believe that human beings can develop and enhance their Shakti through meditation for many positive results.

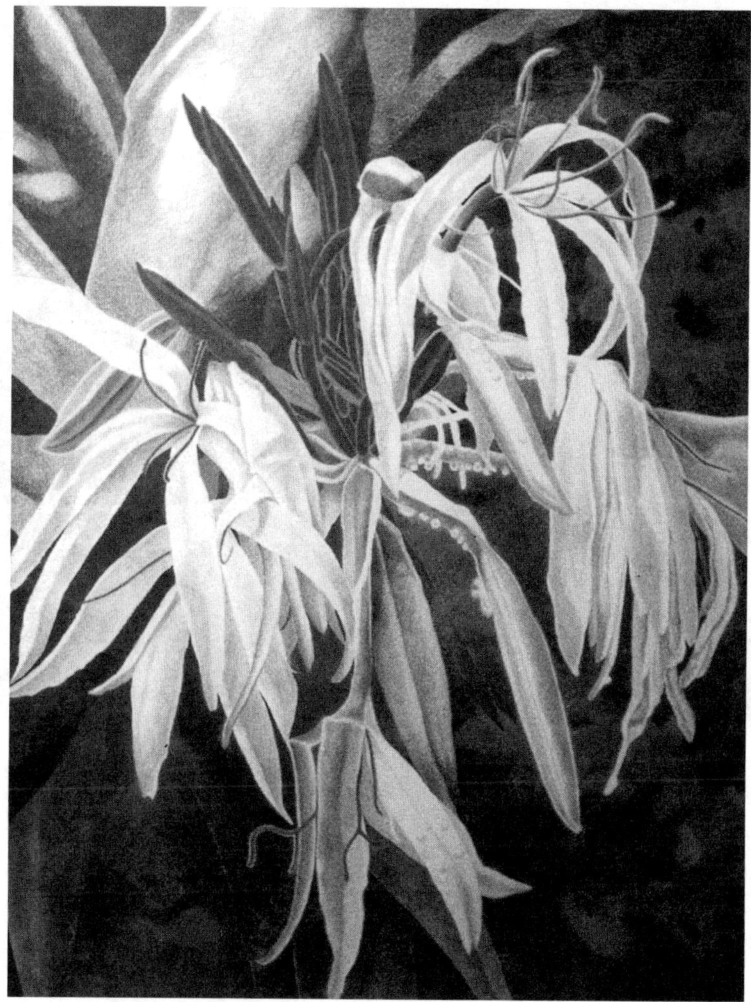

**6–1 Shakti I** © Kyra Belán, 1980
Drawing, colored pencil, 30" x 22"

The *Kali Series* consists of drawings and paintings of exotic birds, birds of prey, or animals. The objective is to focus upon the world of nature, endangered by the relentless encroachment of urban environments, pollution, and the systematic destruction of tropical forests. Although my technique has been developed by careful studies of nature and birds, the compositions for the works, like those for the figures and installations, emerge either from my dreams or a state of reverie. I sketch directly onto paper or canvas, sans preliminary works. One such work is a 40 inches x 48 inches colored pencil drawing, *Allegro Andante*. It is an interpretation of a group of interacting flamingos. They frolic throughout the middle ground, while a close-up view of a profile of a flamingo's head, visible in the foreground, confronts the beak of another flamingo. The flamingos are engulfed in lush, tropical, surreal vegetation. They live in a land where oceanic and terrestrial realms gracefully intermix to form a fantastic paradise.

## *Goddess Kali*

In India Mother Kali is worshiped in various temples dedicated to her. Kali is both the creator and transformer. She is the most powerful manifestation of transformative divine power, and can win over the most powerful gods. She is often represented as dancing passionately ; beneath her feet is the reclining God Shiva. She is seen as Mother Nature herself:: the life giver, life taker, and the cyclical principle of re-incarnation.

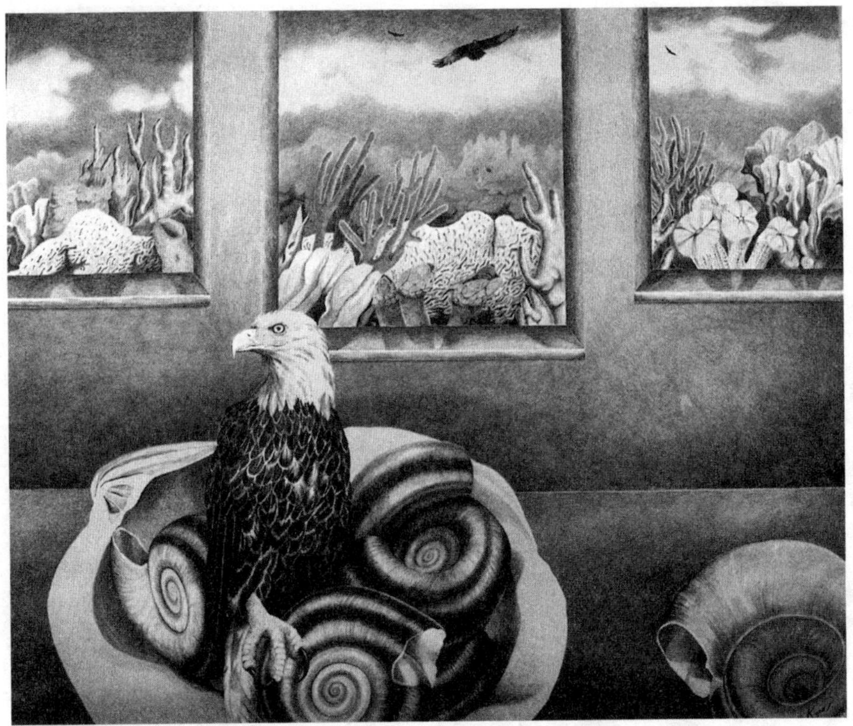

**6–2 The Dream** © Kyra Belán, 1979
Drawing, colored pencil, 40" x 48"

The American bald eagle has been the subject of many of my works, including the colored pencil drawing, titled *The Dream*..The title suggests that the image is an interpretation of a dream. A bald eagle, the main subject of this work, is seated inside a giant sea shell, which contains several oversized snail shells. Three windows open into a view of a fantasy landscape. The skies are alive with the presence of two eagles in flight. Colorful vegetation from a dream world, consisting of various types of corals and sea creatures, can be observed through the windows. Another drawing in colored pencil, a variation of the same composition, titled *Freedom* (1980), features two adult bald eagles and one eaglet in the foreground. The baby eagle is peering out of a large sea shell. The three windows open up into a deep space, where a luminous sky converges into a colorful and complex forest of the mind, inspired by an underwater realm. The sky is populated with several eagles in flight. Two green spheres of ambiguous origins seem to be floating through space. It is a world of abundance, where the eagles are free to explore their own safe universe.

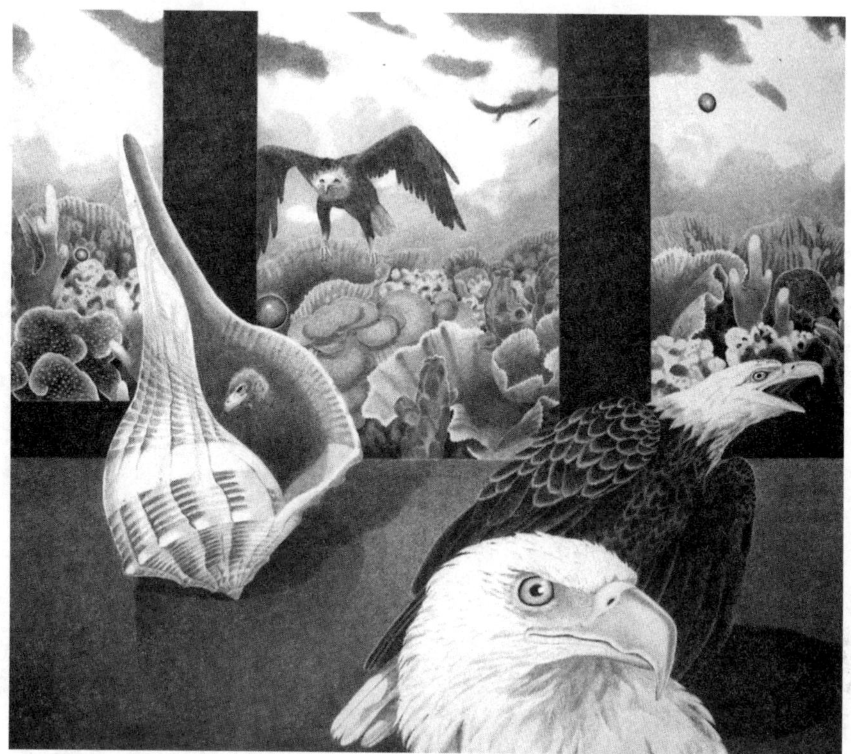

**6–3 Freedom** © Kyra Belán, 1980
Drawing, colored pencil, 40" x 48"

The eagle is the main subject of an oil painting, *The Other*. The bald eagle, surrounded by owls peering out of coral and sponge formations, is located within the bottom half portion of the work. The upper level of the bottom half shows anemones that recede into the sky. The heavenly realm is interrupted by a triangular "window." This triangle contains a flying white eagle. The two eagles can be interpreted as the earthly and spiritual selves, or the physicality and spirituality of the animal world and the planet itself.

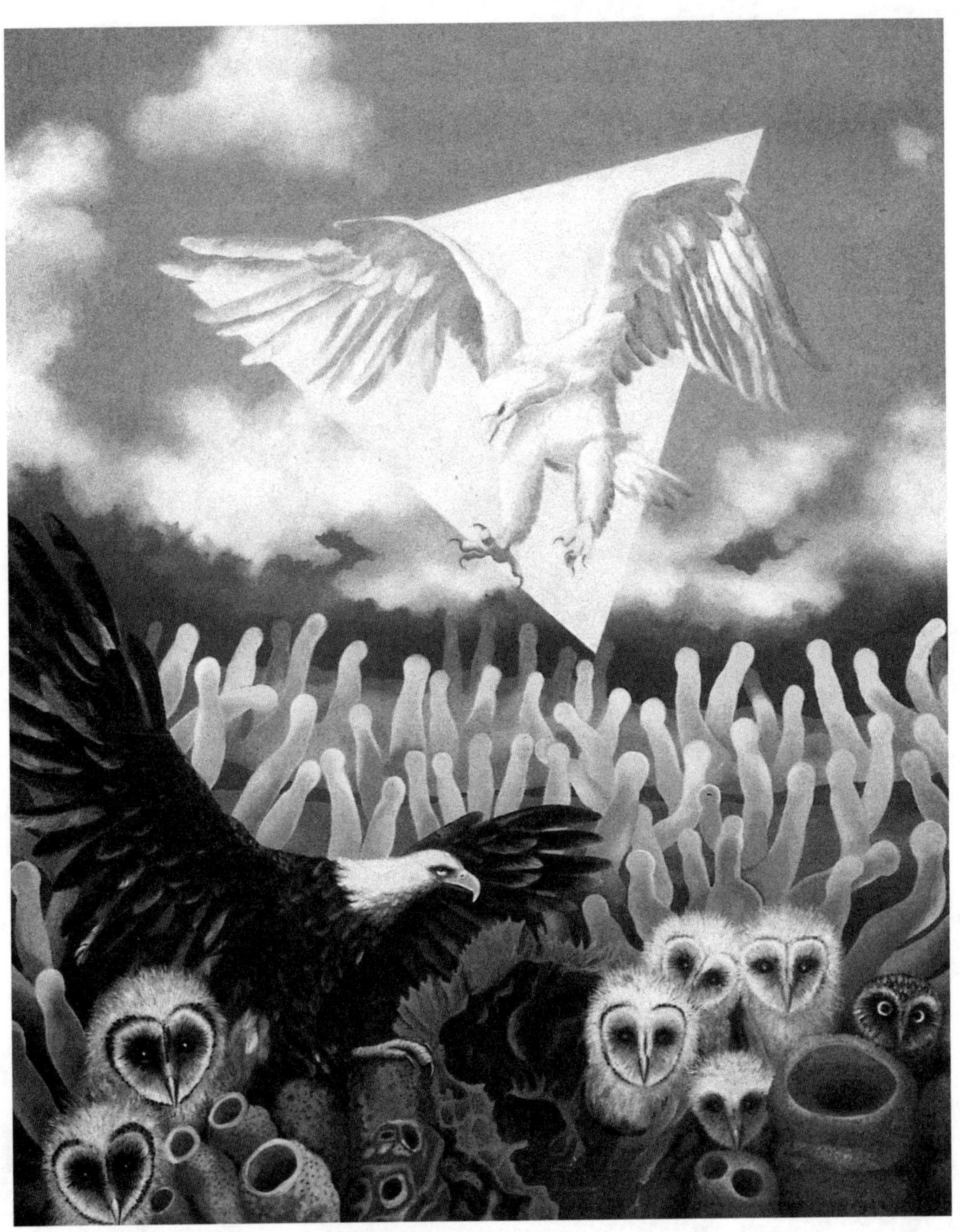

**6–4 The Other** © Kyra Belán, 1978
Oil painting, 50" x 38". Collection of Betty and David Owen

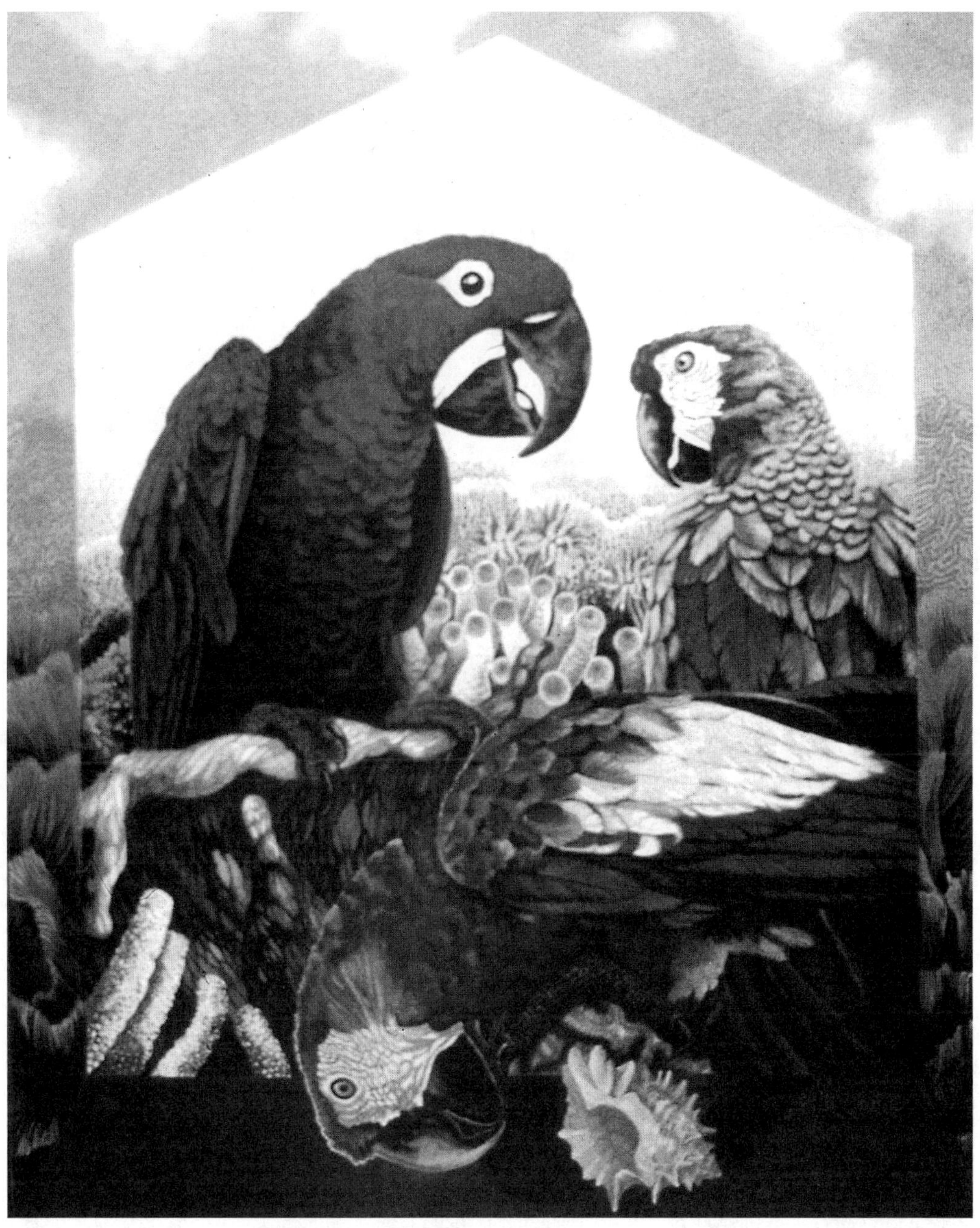

**6–5 Tropical Window** © Kyra Belán, 1984
Oil painting, 50" x 40"

Parrots or macaws are often the subjects of my two-dimensional artworks. They, like the eagles, coexist freely within a tropical and surreal environment. Two oil paintings, completed in the eighties, 50 inches x 40 inches each, titled *Tropical Window* and *Tao* (see Color Plate 15), confront the viewer with compositions that playfully include illusions of ambiguous spatial configurations. The parrots in these works can be identified as Hyacinth, Scarlet, and Military Macaws. The attention of the viewer is directed at the birds, while not precluding an examination of the combination of an underwater and a terrestrial world. The birds, as citizens of the realm, are the explorers of their fantasy environment.

## *The Floralia Series*

Named after Roman Goddess of spring, Flora, the *Floralia Series* consists of acrylic paintings on canvas; the series focuses on a flower, usually the hibiscus, as its subject matter. By narrowly limiting the subject, I create an infinity of colors, shapes and sizes of the artworks. The project also explores the concept that multiple units of the series can form numerous site-specific configurations. This series offers an extensive playground of "building blocks" for the arrangement and re-arrangement of various units of paintings into various environmental installations. Each individual painting is an adventure into an essence of a larger-than-life flower, which functions either as an independent and self-contained unit, or as a part of a larger whole. I do not hesitate to add a surreal element by exaggerating actual colors or creating new color combinations, some of which may be developed by horticulturists in the hybrids of the future.

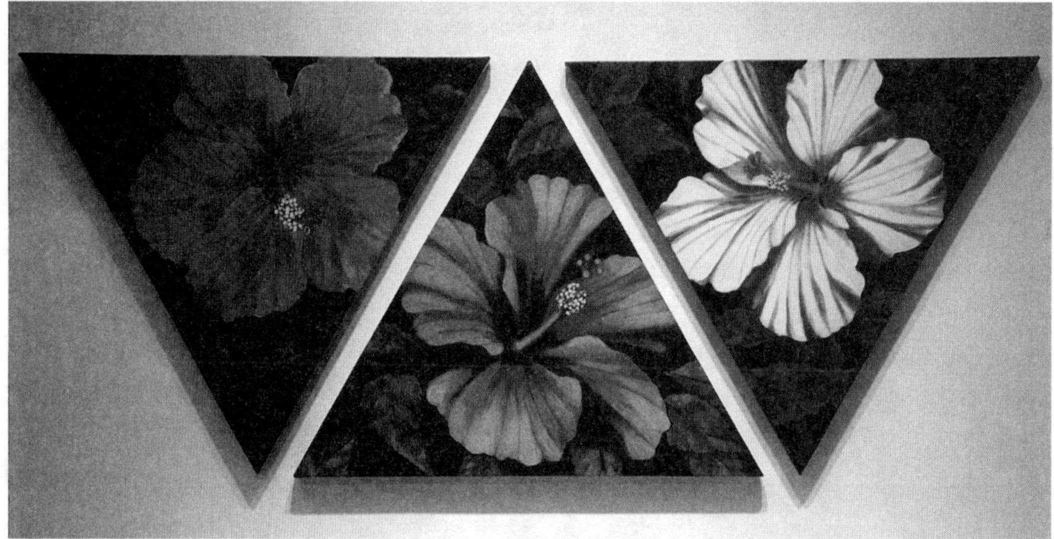

**6–6 The Pleiades** © Kyra Belán, 1995
Acrylic on canvas, modular triptych. Collection of Dianne Owen

This series express my belief that life can be playful and fun. This joy of life that I have discovered is expressed through the harmony of a flower. The series reflects my philosophy that a natural state of existence is a state of emotional well-being, and each human being can achieve this state with ease through a change of mind-set. The main purpose of these art works is to help this state of well-being to occur.

One example of *The Floralia* is an eight unit painting, titled *Changing Woman* (see Color Plate 6), created to honor the Earth Goddess of the Navajo Nation. Each unit is a 20 inches x 20 inches acrylic painting on canvas that depicts a close-up view of one flower; together they form a group of four red and four white hibiscus, yet each one of them is unique. There are various ways in which the multiple painting can be displayed either in a horizontal or vertical format. This work can be re-combined with other paintings to form a mural that would cover the walls and ceiling.

## *Symbolism of the Flower*

The flower has been one of the most prominent and frequently used symbols of the Great Goddess since ancient times. It has endured as a symbol for female spirituality and sexuality, a global phenomenon within numerous non-Western religions. Within Christianity, the Mother of God is also symbolically represented by a flower, which often displays five petals. Perhaps the most frequent use of a flower as symbolic of the omnipotent Mother God of antiquity can be found on the island of Crete.[8] Minoan civilization of ancient Crete is known as a major preserve of a pure state of matriarchal culture. It flourished peacefully among the newly patriarchal war-oriented societies that surrounded it.

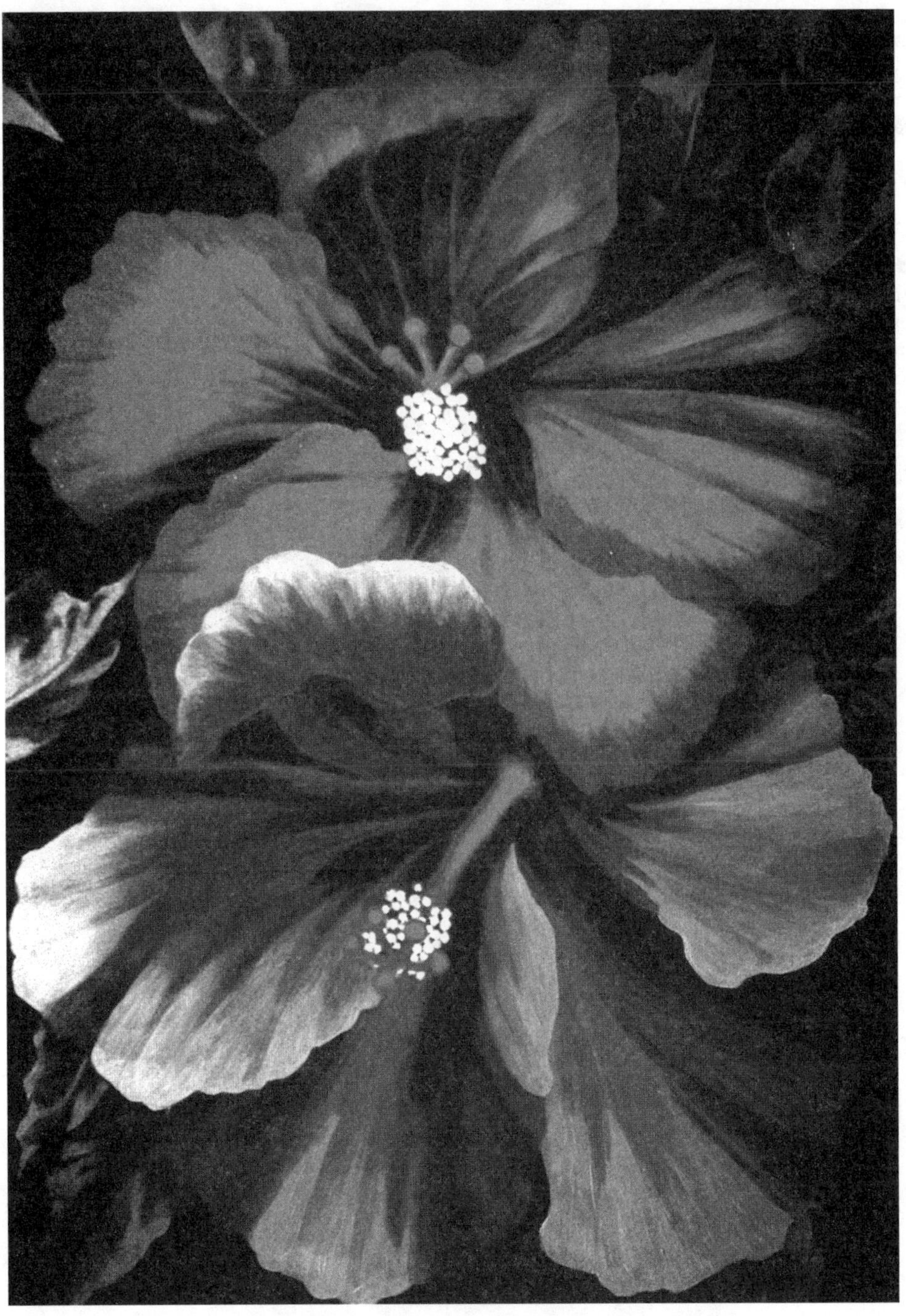

**6–7 The Floralia Series: Shakti** © Kyra Belán, 1995
Acrylic on canvas, 40" x 30"

As a long-time resident of Florida, I live among a variety of hibiscus flowers and have developed a special relationship with this tropical plant. The beauty of flowers has attracted numerous artists of the past. Some artists, like the great Baroque still-life painter Rachel Ruysch, dedicated their entire artistic productions to the exploration of flowers as their main subject. My decision to develop the series is, in part, a tribute to the genius of Georgia O'Keeffe, who created over a hundred flower paintings during her extensive career. My contributions to the floral genre include the concept of creation of groups of works designed to fit within a particular interior space and of multiple units of interrelated, but never identical, flower shapes.

Natural environment is the focus of my concerns. As a follower of the proponents of the Gaia hypothesis,[9] I believe that planet Earth is a complex living organism, imbued with the energy of life and spirituality. The purpose of my art is to examine and explore this magnificent vitality and beauty of our planet, and to bring nature closer to the heartbeat of an urban population. Ultimately, my goal is to help heighten the pro-ecological convictions of the general public.

# 7

## *The Artist as Shaman*

Since the dawn of civilization, when humans invented their first religion, the purpose of art was to generate and perform numerous religious rituals of humanity. Matristic societies of the prehistoric epoch dreamed up their first Mother God, and ever since, her ancient images have populated the archeological sites and the museums of the entire globe. From the available data of the most recent research, we can safely assume that the artist often doubled as the shaman-priestess-priest of this religion. This same tradition is still followed among contemporary tribal societies, whose shamans, or medicine men and women, also create sacred images that symbolize or represent their divinities. Therefore, images of Mother God, and later also of Father God, together with the multitude of ritual objects, were created for many millennia and are still created today. My personal choice, as a postmodern artist, has been to incorporate some elements of shamanic traditions of the world into my art. Inspired by numerous religions of the past and present that do not separate the earthly and the heavenly realms, I create ritual performance art that can touch the public with its messages about the importance of interconnectedness, love, reverence for nature, and the unity of the spiritual and the earthly realms. Performance art helps me to convey the idea of the sacredness of all the beings that populate our Mother Earth.

Current study of the cultures of the past can distinguish two societal models: the long-lasting matriarchal society that spanned many thousands of years, seemingly beyond 70,000 BCE, and the patriarchal model, dominant for over 2,500 years. The matriarchies, although peaceful, circular, and egalitarian structures, gave some preference to the female gender, yet allowed the male sex to occupy many important positions. The supreme creator of these societies was visualized in female form. A priestess and/or queen was often also the benevolent ruler of these social paradigms. The patriarchies are, as a rule, war-oriented and retain rigid hierarchical structures. A supreme male divinity is worshiped by every andro-centric social model. The main source of power of these structures is their obsessive domination of women. Even within some contemporary patriarchies, drastic measures are taken to enslave the female sex. These societies often condone legalized physical abuse and genital mutilation of women. Male-gendered religions are still used today to subjugate women's bodies and spirits, and the effect of patriarchal religious dogma is a powerful tool that is used to control women's minds and bodies.

Some sociologists, philosophers, and futurists believe that there is a way to form a society in which both genders are equal, a belief that I share. New religious and philosophical systems that promote traditionally female values of peace, love and care, nurture and respect for Mother Earth, would have to form a brand-new structure for this future social paradigm. Riane Eisler, in her book *The Chalice and the Blade*, calls this possible society a partnership model. I believe that, in spite of the current backlash against women and eco-feminist values, both women and men are discovering their feminine side and are learning to respect it. The only way for the human race to continue its existence and for our Mother to survive as a life-sustaining planet, is to learn to discover our feminine selves, and to respect our matristic values by integrating them into our social structures. There is a need to explore the feminine viewpoint in all aspects of our society; half the world's population is now struggling to have a voice in the making of the future of this planet, and the arts must reflect this new force. The visual image can carry a powerful message, but only if it is understood.

All humanity—women and men—must rediscover Earth-based spirituality and its sacred feminine principle. The female component of the Creator must re-emerge from the dark recesses of human psyche with the help of contemporary visual images. Although I create art because I enjoy doing it, the flow of images and messages is a result of the collective consciousness of this historical time. They reflect the emerging consciousness that is forming within the genetic make-up of our bodies.

This new human consciousness that pervades global culture is the beginning of a future that will generate harmonious relationships between the genders and among the races and cultures of the planet. The new world civilization will not be patriarchal or matriarchal, but a culture that will embody positive qualities of humanity. I see my work as one of the initial steps that will help lead us in that direction. While I simply convey my own messages, formed through my personal experience in this world, they reflect a change that global culture is beginning to undergo. For that reason, my art's message can help disseminate the seeds of the new vision of the future.

It is not my purpose to simply imitate the matriarchal past, but to extract from it the symbols, archetypes, and visions that best express my concepts. One of the concepts explored in my art is the idea that art has magical power, and that each artist is a visionary and a shaman. This individual supplies the world with images and messages that are interpretations of archetypes, symbols, and myths, relevant to the particular culture or cultures during the appropriate historical time. The term "shaman" is used to describe any person who "has the fire" within his or her subconscious, a flow of mythical and supernatural life of a community. The shaman must be in contact with the spiritual side of the earthly realm. Although shamanism is practiced today in many subcultures, the dominant patriarchal culture has long forgotten and excised this practice. Shamanism can be traced to the beginning of human civilization, a time when religion first took shape in human minds. Recent research into prehistoric and ancient matriarchies points in the direction of the theory that the first priests/shamans were women. Therefore, it seems natural for a woman artist to introduce an art form that is inspired by shamanic rituals into the mainstream of contemporary society.

Contemporary art is not a religion, and I see my exploration into the shamanic realm as a purely artistic expression that evokes the rituals of the past and present. This activity can be, if desired, extended into contemporary life on many levels. My hope is that my work will inspire others to engage in benevolent shamanic/ ritual activities that may be joyful or healthy for their spiritual, emotional, or intellectual development. My ideas surface from my subconscious mind and my knowledge of prehistoric, ancient, Pre-Columbian, Native American Nations, and other Western and non-Western cultures. My main vehicle of expression for the ritual aspect of my work is performance art. I decided to include ritual performances into my *Magic Circle Series*.. I chose to start a life-long project by honoring the Native Americans, since they are the true foremothers and forefathers of American contemporary culture.

## *Magic Circle Series: Performance Art*

The first performance of the *Magic Circle Series* was a public event that took place as the highlight of the opening of the exhibition in summer of 1978 at the Grove House Gallery in South Miami. It consisted of an installation that included drawings of goddesses and gods of ancient religions, rendered with colored pencil on paper. The floor installation featured "feather trees," formed of dried and trimmed tree branches and colorful feathers. The size of the "trees" varied between three and five feet. They were arranged in a semicircle, within which there was a "magic circle," a floor sculpture of six feet in diameter, surrounded by tree bark, shells, and painted rocks. Two video screens showed images of the beginning of the performance, which took place in a wilderness of Florida. In this performance, after assuming the role of a shaman, I was shown gathering the various materials for the future installation: the large dead tree branches and the tree bark on the ground. These excess materials were discarded by nature herself, to be recycled as art. Simultaneously, in front of the viewers, I was forming, out of colored sands, an image of a thunderbird within the circular sculpture. My "shamanic" costume consisted of a Cherokee feathered headdress, which, for this ritual, acquired the symbolism of peace and attunement with nature. The design of the sand painting was inspired by numerous recurrent dreams about a life as a Pueblo medicine woman, during the fifteenth century. That territory is now a part of the state of Arizona and northern Mexico. These dreams were so lucid that I consider them a possible remembrance of a previous lifetime. The completion of the sand painting signaled the end of the first performance of the series.

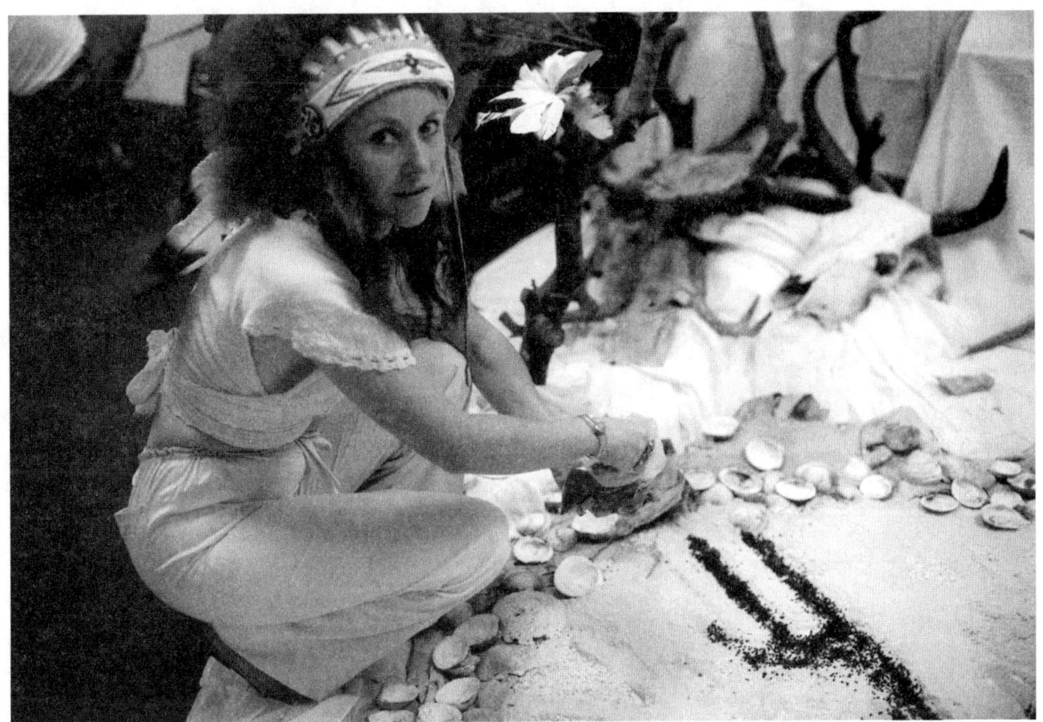

**7–1 Magic Circle** © Kyra Belán, 1978
Detail of installation, artist in ritual performance
The Grove House Gallery, Miami, Florida. Photo : GL Sullivan

The second *Magic Circle* performance took place in North Miami at An Alternative Gallery. The gallery walls displayed images of pagan divinities, while the center of the gallery space was occupied by a colorful sand painting, dedicated to Great Goddess Isis. Assuming the role of a priestess/shaman, I wore an elaborate feathered headdress, a feathered mask and a red dress. Two other women, dressed in white and also wearing feathered masks, played the roles of priestesses. The ritual was initiated with the process of completing the design around the circle. I arranged a border of feathers while the two other "priestesses" sat next to the sand painting. The process continued with a candle-lighting ceremony and the ritual walk around the circle, which concluded the performance.

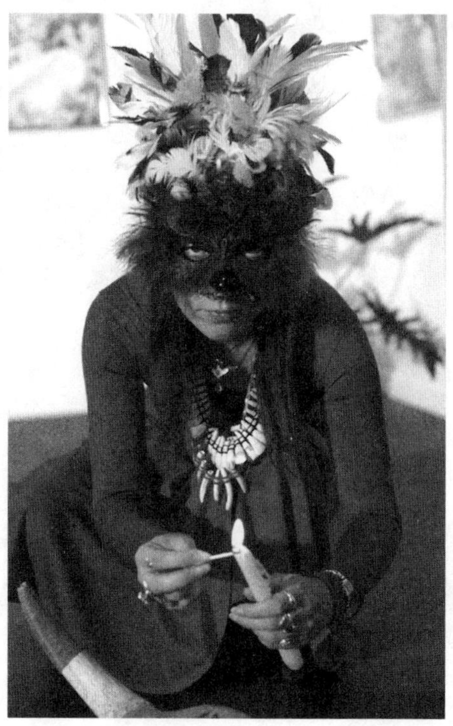

**7–2 Magic Circle II** © Kyra Belán, 1979
Artist in performance
An Alternative Gallery, North Miami, Florida. Photo : GL Sullivan

Numerous subsequent performances took place within completed site-specific installations. One constant element of these multimedia environments is the presence of a circular floor sculpture or installation, which is a universal symbol of the sacred feminine. In my work, the circular shape is also an icon for the re-emergence of Mother God within the human psyche. A part of the ritual always takes place around the circle and may include one to fifty people. Choreographed ritual walks, dances, sounds, and chanting take place within, around, and outside the installations. The sounds vary extensively from performance to performance. They can be exclusively percussive or include chants or consist of a mixture of percussion and music composed for the performance by professional musicians. The costumes designed for each artwork also vary, but each item of clothing or ornament has a symbolic significance.

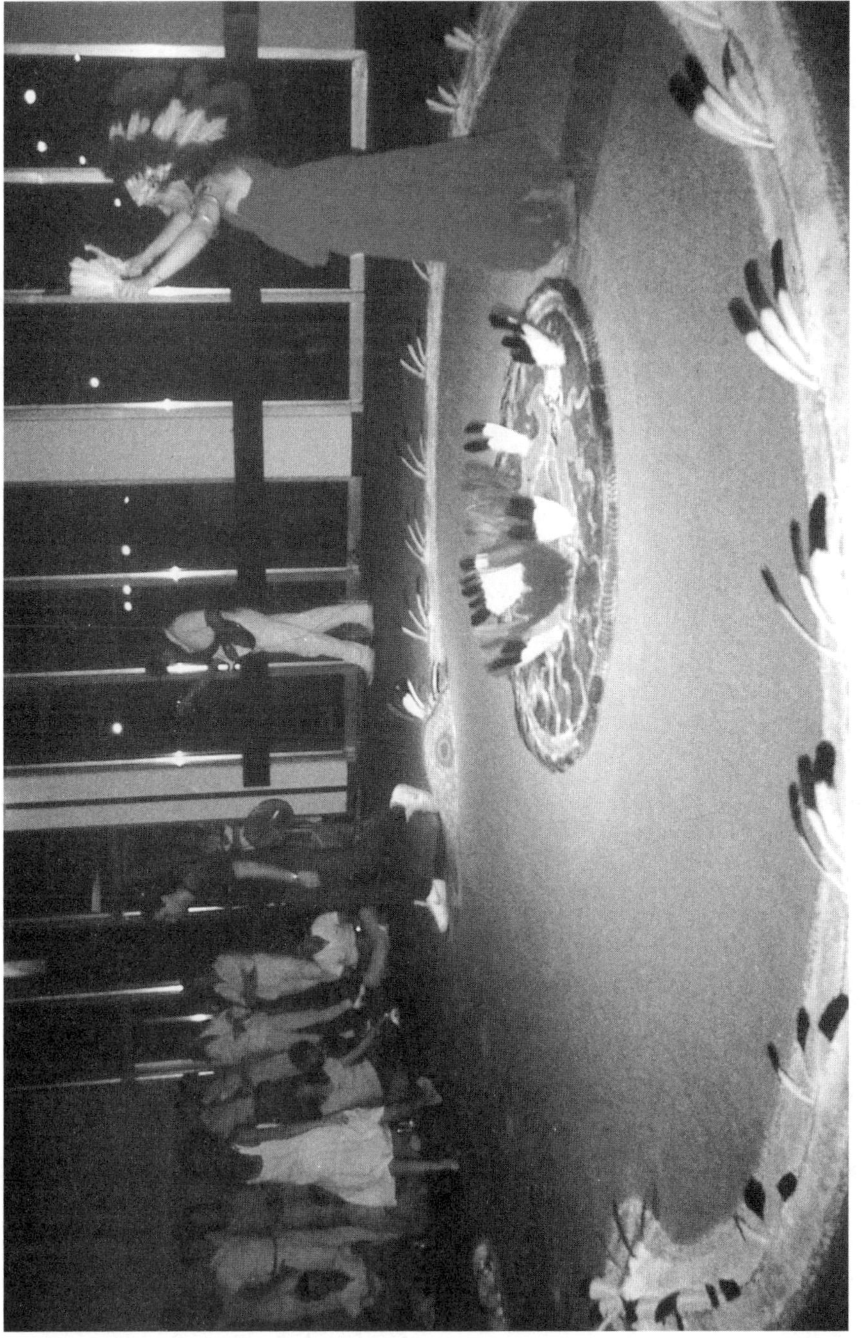

**7–3 Great American Goddess Coatlicue: Magic Circle VIII** © Kyra Belán, 1984
Detail of installation, ritual performance
Fine Arts Gallery. Broward Community College
Davie, Florida. Photo: GL Sullivan

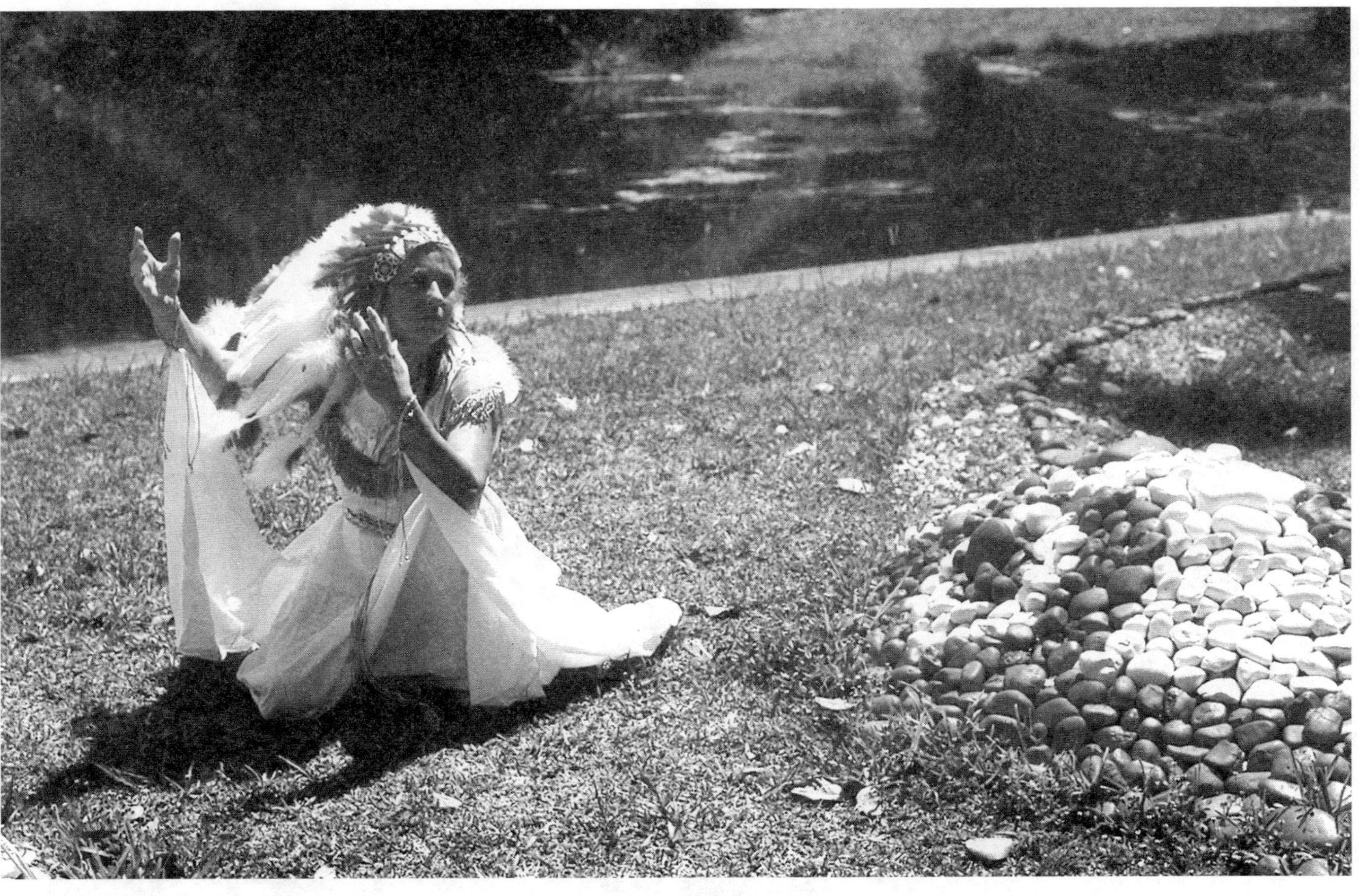

**7–4 Nature Goddess Sekhmet:**
**Magic Circle XII** © Kyra Belán, 1987
Detail of earthwork, artist performing
Miami Site, Key Biscayne, Florida. Metro-Dade Arts in Public Places
Photo: GL Sullivan

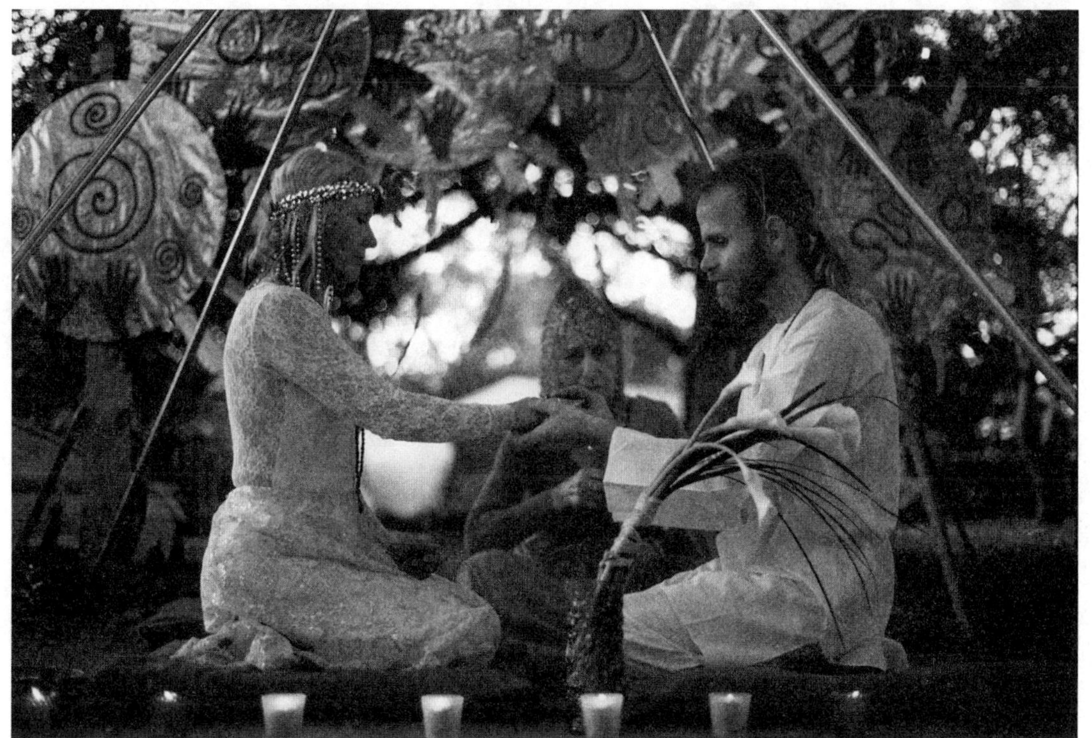

**7–5 Celebration for Goddess Juno:**
**Magic Circle XXII** © Kyra Belán, 1993
Detail of the installation and the wedding ritual
Left to right:Kyra Belán, Swami Naranda, and Charles Martin
Sri Naranda Yoga Center, Hallandale, Florida

## *Symbolism of the Circle*

The meaning assigned to the circle is extremely important in shamanism and numerous religions of the world. During the vastness of the prehistoric times, the circle was a universal symbol for Mother God, representing her powers of creation and destruction. It represented the cyclic nature of Mother Earth and explained the circularity of space, time and nature herself. The circle is still one of the most powerful symbols of the numerous Eastern belief systems such as Tibetan, or Native American religions. Native American Nations revere the sacredness of the archetypal circle that represents the flow of life of Mother Earth. Numerous Native American ceremonies take place around the circle, and it is also represented as the medicine wheel. During the recent patriarchal era, the circle has been regarded as a symbol of perfection and male spirituality.

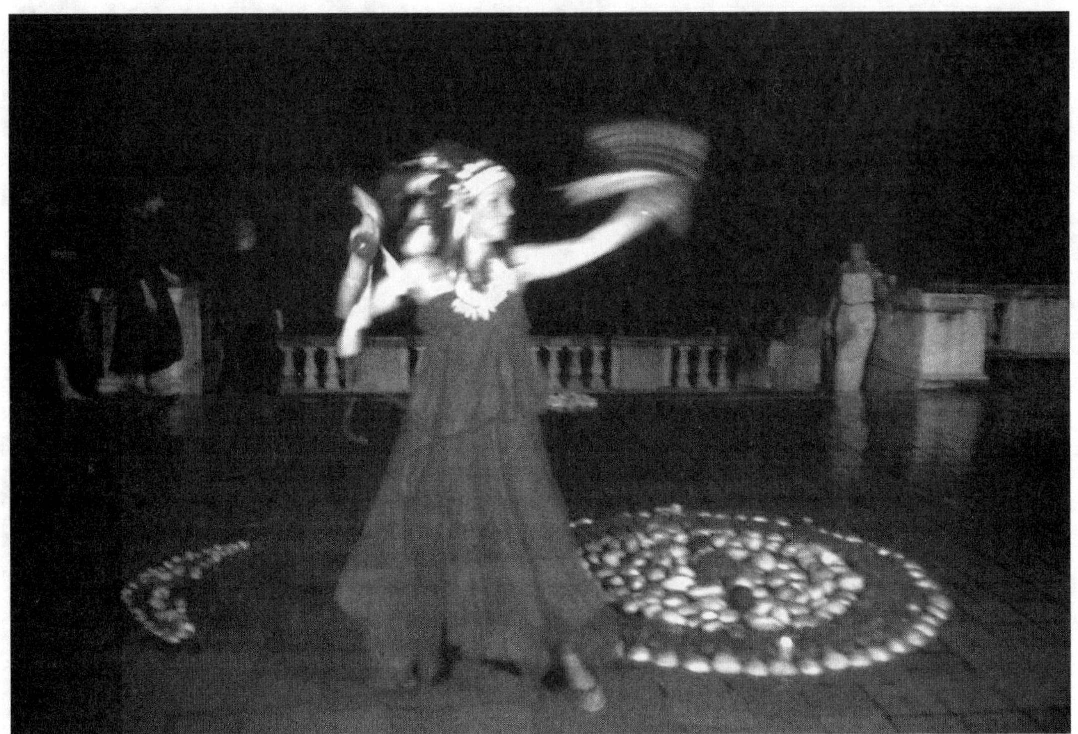

**7–6 Great Goddess: Magic Circle X** © Kyra Belán, 1985
Detail of the ritual performance and the symbolic circular environmental sculpture. Metropolitan Museum and Art Center, Coral Gables, Florida. Photo: GL Sullivan

In 1985, I designed a temporary outdoor sculpture for the Metropolitan Museum and Art Center in Coral Gables. Painted rocks, in red and yellow colors, formed the circular sculpture that was assembled on a large open platform of polished coral, located on top of the steps that led to the main east entrance of the museum. On each side, two crescent shapes were arranged with silver and blue rocks and shells. Wearing a long red robe, I led the "priestesses" who wore either white or black. The colors of the garments commemorated ancient traditions by evoking the Mother as the Creator of light, darkness, and the terrestrial realm. The ritual dance was performed around the circular "sun" sculpture and the two crescent "moon" sculptures. A circle of lights was generated by the candles around the "sun" sculpture during the conclusion of the ceremony.

One more instance of a performance work that took place around a circular installation, one that I developed for the Fine Art Gallery at Broward Community College, Davie, Florida in 1986. The large circular sculpture, of about 15 feet in diameter, was also "sun" shaped. The exhibition was dedicated to the celebration of all the Sun Goddesses of present and past religions of the world (see Color Plate 9). Yet another circular sculpture that dominated the rest of the installation took place at Sri Naranda Yoga Center in Hallandale, Florida in 1993. This time the earth art was located in the midst of large trees, surrounded by the vivid greens of the grass. Suggestive of both the Sun and the Earth, the painted quartz rocks were arranged into a circular pattern of reds, blues, yellows and golds (see Color Plate 13).

## *Prehistoric Ritual Processions*

We can trace the ritual processions and dances back to the beginnings of prehistory, when early matriarchal civilizations were first formed. Ritual movements were used then to celebrate or evoke the presence of the Great Mother. Some anthropologists assume that the arts of ritual dance, percussion, and chants preceded the arts of making ritual objects. It is likely that, led by the head shaman/priestess and the rest of the female priesthood, both genders participated in the sacred rituals.

In my performance pieces, when possible, both females and males participate. These people are enthusiastic volunteers of a variety of ages, from infants carried by adults to individuals in their eighties. The viewers are offered an option to participate and thus become a part of the artwork.

The participatory nature of these works lets the public experience a different perspective of art. This form of art reaches out to people, erasing the boundaries between art and life itself. Everyone becomes a part of the artwork by assuming roles within this temporal dimension of an artistic production. Moreover, the public becomes actively involved with the spatial configurations of the work. Multiple vantage points are experienced by those who walk through the negative spaces of the installations. Performances allow the public to become involved with the concept of the work and to enhance the discovery and presence of female spiritual consciousness.

Philosophically, ritual performances are an integral part of my own life as an artist. I believe that they must spill over, overlap, and fuse with the reality of my existence as an individual. I see my artistic production as an extension of my persona. Art became a very important event of my personal life during the opening performance for my earthwork and installation called *Magic Circle XXII: Celebration for Goddess Juno.* My wedding ceremony was incorporated into the ritual performance, completely erasing all the boundaries between art and life; they became one and the same. A very important commitment between two human beings was ritually confirmed and bonded to an artistic creative force. A commitment of marriage is perhaps the strongest bond of life; the nuptial ceremony is the ultimate celebration of the cyclic nature of human existence (see Color Plate 13).

The need to experiment with ritual continues to be an aspect of my art making. The spontaneity, sincerity, and rhythm of a ritual can lead the spectators into a meditative state that is healthy and thought-provoking. Since the seventies, the nature of our technology-oriented society has become increasingly more automated and impersonal. Ritual, as an art form, can communicate messages directly to the subconscious mind. Our ancestors spent thousands of years on ritual activities, which induced various states of emotional, intellectual, and spiritual awareness. Postmodern ritual art can be a mind expanding experience. The freedom with which various art forms may be recombined to form a ritual artwork dissolves the boundaries established by the rigid, hierarchical, and patriarchal outlook on what the art process is or may be. The ritual approach within my art making has given me the freedom to change and extend traditional art systems and values. It has allowed me to create unconventional artworks and to travel on a new freeway of conceptual thinking.

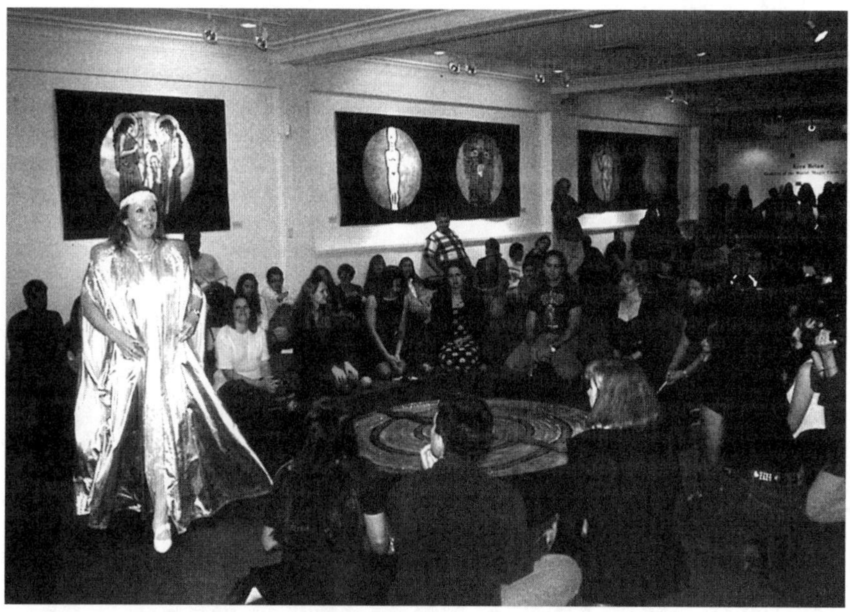

**7–7 Goddess of the World: Magic Circle XXVII** © Kyra Belán, 1997
Artist in performance, detail of site specific installation
Art and Culture Center of Hollywood, Florida

# 8

## *Site Specific Art: A Journey Into the Twenty-First Century*

The discipline of art history, as we know it today, was formulated during the Italian Renaissance. This model has served as a blueprint for the direction in which art historical research has been conducted. Consequently, visual artists have been influenced and restricted by the traditional rules that their academic environment and historical research have imposed upon them. The rules of academia routinely devalued or excluded the accomplishments of the entire female gender. Many of these academic rules have been broken or altered by the women and men artists of the twentieth and twenty-first centuries. During the postmodernist era, further ventures into new visual territories have been made.

Art has immense and yet unexplored capabilities to become integrated into the physical surroundings and every day lives of a community. My aesthetic philosophy has brought me to explore these possibilities. The degree to which my work can transform specific environments is determined according to the particular circumstances: the size, shape, and volume of the space involved; the use of that space beyond aesthetic purpose; and the population that will be exposed to the space the artwork occupies. A very important issue is whether the space will house a work of art on a temporary or permanent basis. These considerations are carefully evaluated before the work begins. I do not wish to confine my projects to traditional gallery or museum environments. I enjoy bringing my work into the community in order to allow a more direct relationship between the art and the public. This philosophy is consistent with my belief that my creations must have social and educational functions that could help direct our society closer to the goal of a peaceful, nurturing, and spiritual paradigm. The resulting art must also satisfy my technical, creative, and aesthetic standards.

My preoccupation with the environment, and my socio-ecological concerns increased my interest in performance and installation art. Planning of the installations that would house both the performances and the general public within them, made me aware of the many levels of reality: physical, cultural, emotional, and spiritual. As I design the work, I attempt to involve the public in the exhibitions and installations on more than one level: as spectators, participants, and as students of matristic and multi-cultural mythologies, archetypes, and icons.

Motivation to bring my art projects into the community prompted me to utilize a variety of spaces: interior or outdoor spaces of galleries, or both, and unconventional interior spaces that do not usually house artworks, such as a church or yoga center. I have utilized outdoor urban space, outdoor historical space, and wilderness space. I have also explored imaginary or future environments for the series of proposals for earthworks, monuments and temples dedicated to the celebration of the sacred feminine. These proposals honor the Great Goddess, the Great Mother, or Mary, who is perceived by the Westerners and Americans as the Mother of God and Queen of Heaven.

I consider all the possibilities available to me in these spaces. Within architectural interiors, I may use the walls, the floor, and the ceiling. My artworks, from drawings and paintings to earthworks, are designed to function as either single units or as parts of larger constructs. The installations and the earthworks are usually designed for temporary locations. Often parts or most of them must be destroyed, while some sections or components may be salvaged and worked into other installations or earth art. The symbolism of recycling the materials and portions of earthworks agrees with my goal to promote eco-consciousness.

My earthworks must carry the message that our natural environment has to be deeply respected. This often forces me to choose complex or difficult methods for my artistic production. Nature itself is often invited to participate, as an integral part of the artwork, whenever the circumstances allow this to happen. The de-installation of each earthwork is always carefully orchestrated to avoid any damage to the natural environment.

A series of acrylic paintings, *The Floralia,* is an exercise of adaptability that allows many possible outcomes. Individual paintings can be used to form innumerable arrangements within different wall configurations of each individual space. They are designed to be used as single works or to be recombined into vertical, horizontal, symmetrical or asymmetrical formations to adapt to a particular space. This is possible because of the rhythmic and repetitive combinations of sizes and the theme explored (the hibiscus flower), while never duplicating the same flower. The cyclical nature of Mother Nature is reaffirmed by this choice of organization for *The Floralia* series.

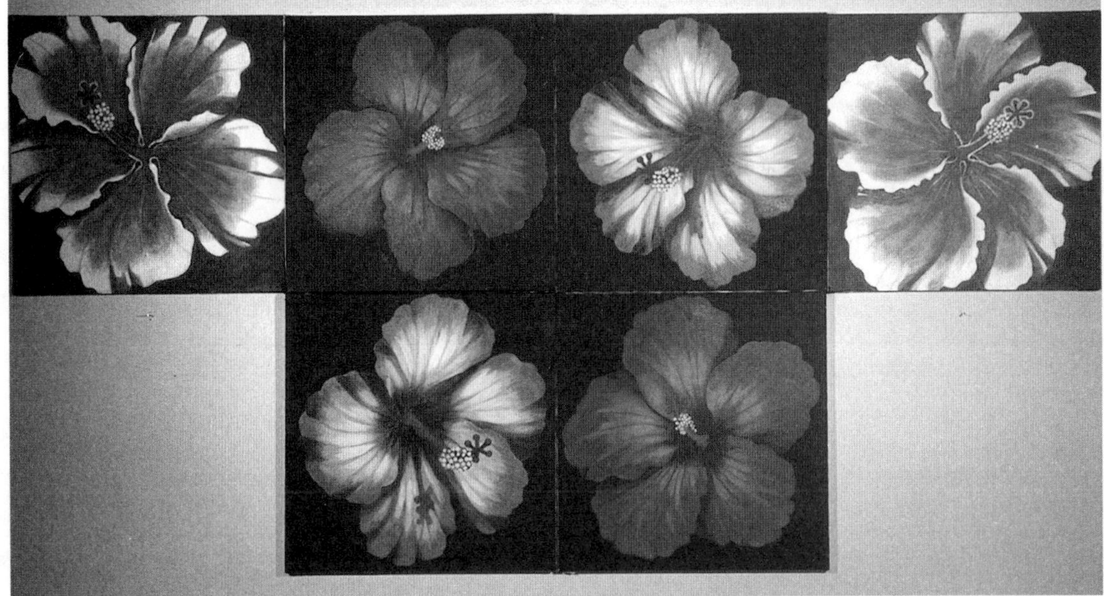

**8–1 The Floralia Series: Iris** © Kyra Belán, 1995
Acrylic on canvas, 6 units 20" x 20" each

Numerous possibilities for indoor and outdoor installations are built into the concept behind the *Magic Circle Series*. The exhibition spaces within which this series is housed help determine the media and the materials to be used. I have designed numerous installations to exist within a particular location for a limited amount of time, later to be almost completely destroyed, with the exception of the recyclable components or materials. To produce my site-specific exhibitions, I utilize many techniques, from traditional to mixed media. Current technology, such as video, pre-recorded sounds, projected or computer generated images also finds its way into being a part of this work.

## *Traveling Exhibitions*

One constant element that endures throughout the series is the production of works on paper. Since the *Gallery 621* solo exhibition, titled *Mother Earth, Mother God*, I have been producing more works on paper I decided to continue this production in a way that would permit the images to be adjusted for any type of interior space. This allowed me to decrease the amount of loss of the components of the exhibition each time it was de-installed. The modular nature of the works makes it easy to redesign each show for each new space. This project is easy to package and transport to new locations. Therefore, it is ideal as a traveling exhibition with many options for arranging some or all of the components into a new whole. The ease with which this exhibition can be installed, de-installed, and transported increases the possibility of showing it more frequently. The presence of the works on paper does not preclude the continuation of other techniques or experimental methods, such as the creation of outdoor site specific projects or earthworks; they continue to be a part of the series (see Color Plates 11, 12, 13, 14 and 15).

This traveling exhibition of works on paper in acrylic and mixed media is usually shown with additional components, such as feathers and painted or natural rocks or wood. A ritual performance usually takes place within the installation's space. Yet the series, designed for interior space only, can be shown alone, and the final decision about other materials or regarding the nature of the performance is made to fit the needs of a particular museum, gallery, or alternative space.

The exhibition includes a variety of artwork: three works 52 inches wide by 36 feet long, titled *Plumed Serpent One*, *Plumed Serpent Two*, and *Plumed Double Headed Serpent*; two works 52 inches wide by 36 feet long, titled *Tree of Life One* and *Tree of Life Two*; a 106 inches x 106 inches work on paper to be used as a part of a floor installation, titled *Magic Circle*; and numerous images of Goddesses, each 52 inches x 73 inches, that can be arranged in different configurations. These images are inspired by the prehistoric, ancient, and historical images of female God worshiped in caves, sacred sites, stone temples and other structures.

The number of Goddesses featured in the traveling exhibition is growing. These images of the Creator are painted in acrylic paints, iridescent acrylics and a mixture of acrylic and glitter paints on black paper. The images are inspired, to various degrees, by the images of the Great Mother that appeared all over the globe throughout the ages, from prehistoric to contemporary times. Some of them are interpretations of very familiar historical art works, and some are personal renderings, yet all tap into the archetypical symbology of the numerous Goddess religions of the world. Christian Mother of God, Mary, although a shadow of her former divine self, is also included. She is the highest-ranking female figure within Christian dogma. Still, for millions of people, she alone represents the feminine divine principle. Her origins have been traced to the matristic religions of the past that celebrated her as God. The exhibition, by introducing the public to numerous faces of Mother God, prepares them for spirituality of the future, and educates them about the rich and extensive heritage of the millennia of the past, when the sacred nature of female gender was fully acknowledged.

Although most people are familiar with some aspects of world mythology, I have decided to primarily include matriarchal and non-Western versions of the myths that correlate with the images of the divine feminine that form the *Magic Circle Series*. These visions of the Mother represent the needs of the people of the new millennium to recognize, enjoy and see within themselves the sacred feminine aspects of humanity..

## *Site Specific Installations, Earthworks, Performance Art*

The 52 inches x 73 inches images of the goddesses from the *Magic Circle Series*, in acrylic on black paper, can be arranged into numerous configurations for each location where they are to be viewed. The one requirement is that this portion of the series must be placed inside of an architectural setting. Other components of the series can extend into outdoor spaces, or be designed for outdoors only. The flexibility of the concept behind the series allows me to adapt it for many types of spaces. The scale and the complexity of the artworks also vary according to the particular needs of the specific locations and their demographics. Several of the works consist of outdoor installations with emphasis on negative space to be used for a public performance. The location, in this situation, becomes a significant factor. At times, performance art may play the most important role and even become the sole component of the work. The temporal nature of the artworks demands that a permanent record must be made through the use of technology—of video, photography, computer, and written word.

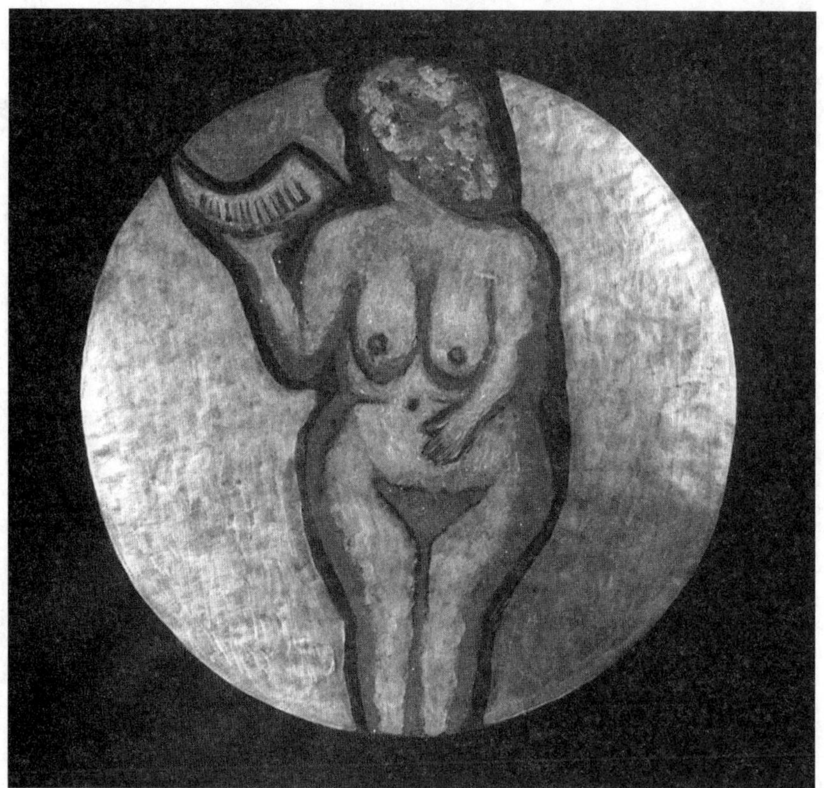

**8–2 Mother God of Laussel** © Kyra Belán, 1993
Acrylic on paper, 52" x 73", module
Inspired by the relief of Venus of Laussel, c. 20,000 BCE

## *The Myths and Archetypes of the Sacred Feminine*

The mythologies of the divine feminine are extensive, and new myths are often uncovered by the researchers. The studies of the sacred feminine take place across many disciplines, including anthropology, archeology, sociology, religions, philosophy, and art history, among others. The interest in female archetypes and their relevance to everyday life in the new millennium fuels a demand for these aspects of our multi-cultural heritage to be examined. The archetypal images have been created by me as recognizable portraits of the ancient, prehistoric, or current goddesses which function as a part of an installation, as individual works of art, or as both. The images of the sacred feminine form an extensive and long lasting heritage of humanity. I am fortunate that so much material is available to me for current and future research, and as an inspiration for artistic productions. I will share some of them with you in this chapter.

## *Mother God of Willendorf*

Goddess or Venus of Willendorf, believed to be the oldest image of God in existence, a small sculpture, perhaps as old as 70,000 BCE. She is an omnipotent creator and giver of life, fertility, and abundance (refer to image 2–1).

## *Mother God of Laussel*

This Mother God's original image is between 30,000 and 20,000 years old; she represents the omnipotent power of a Mother Creator, nurturer, and transformer of life and all that exists.

In her hand is the first known lunar calendar of thirteen months: the marks are obvious on the lunar symbol, a horn of plenty, relevant to the fertility and abundance giving Goddess.

## *Mother God of Cyclades*

This abstract and geometric image of the omnipotent Mother God was carved, usually out of white marble, on all the Cycladic islands, located between Greece, Crete, and Turkey. This Mother God was worshiped between 4,000 BCE and 2,000 BCE.

## *Mother God of Crete*

Inspired by the popular ceramic statue from the Palace of Knossos, Crete, this Great Goddess (see Color Plate 3) was the sole omnipotent divinity of the last major matriarchal civilization in Europe, looking over a very prosperous and rich society that peacefully existed among the warring cultures of antiquity, already predominantly andro-centric. The abrupt decline of this civilization, due to a devastating earthquake, began around 1,500 BCE.

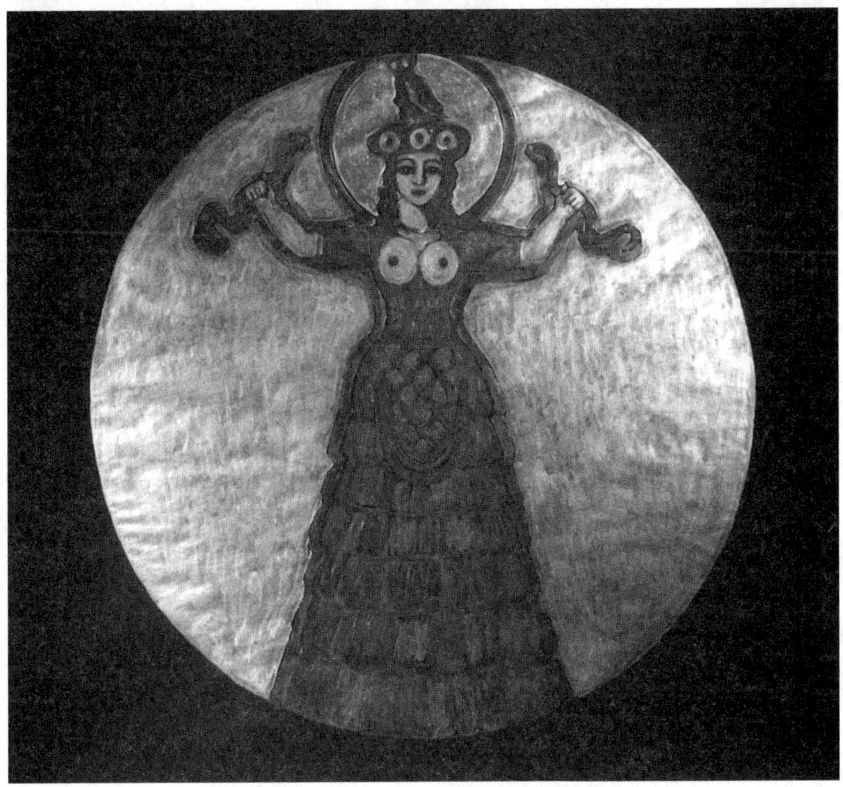

**8–3 Mother God of Crete** © Kyra Belán, 1993
Acrylic on paper, module, 52" x 73"
Inspired by the Snake Goddess, c.1500 BCE, Knossos, Crete

## *Mother God Sekhmet*

A lioness-headed solar divinity of ancient Egypt, she was recognized as the first and oldest god by the ancient Egyptians themselves. She is in possession of awesome powers and can be fiercely protective of her people. She usually holds an ankh, a cross that is a symbol for the life force and female spirituality. A lioness mask was inherited by Sekhmet from the omnipotent prehistoric Mother God. Sekhmet, according to another Egyptian myth, is an aspect of the Great Goddess Isis, interpreted as the Creator, Magician, and a Healer.

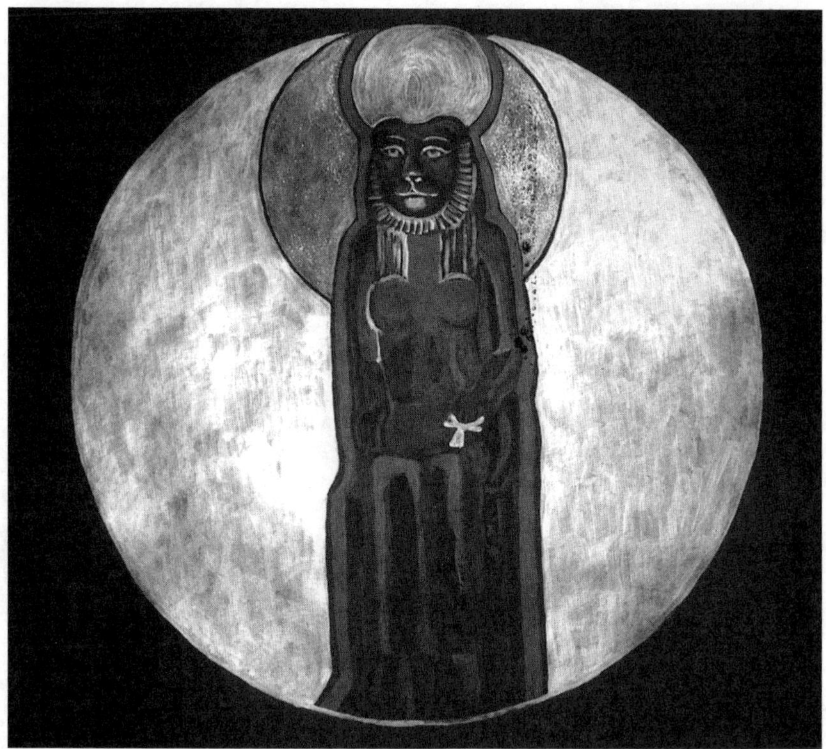

**8–4 Mother God Sekhmet** © Kyra Belán, 1993
Acrylic on canvas, 52" x 73", module
Inspired by numerous ancient Egyptian statues of Sekhmet

## *Mother God Inanna*

Inanna, an ancient Sumerian Goddess, whose religion dates as far back as 2000 BCE, is the subject of the first known writer and poet, Enheduanna; it is believed that she was one of Inanna's priestesses. Her writings about the Goddess were read for several thousands of years. The role of this Goddess is similar to that of Ishtar, Isis, Hathor and many others who were beloved by the people and whose powers were infinite. Inanna, often called the Queen of Heaven, descended into the underworld to meet with the Goddess Ereshkigal, her dark sister. Ereshkigal killed her, but ultimately Inanna resurrected, then emerged stronger than ever to regain her benevolent control of the Earth by restoring the abundance in nature, since while she was in the underworld, the Earth became barren. This is probably the earliest of many divine resurrection myths.

## *Mother God Isis/Hathor*

Hathor is the direct descendant of the prehistoric Egyptian omnipotent Mother God. Hathor and Isis are often interpreted as one. In fact, Isis is believed to be the oldest divinity; she is also a version of Sekhmet. Goddess Hathor is symbolized by the sacred Heavenly Cow, as she is seen as the creator and nurturer of the universe. The Milky Way in the sky is her "heavenly milk" for the humanity. Goddess isis was as supportive and loving of her people as Hathor; she is a Sun Goddess, a Moon Goddess, and is represented as winged. Within several patriarchal religions the images of angels are modeled after her. The religion of Isis lasted for nearly four thousand years and extended throughout the ancient world; then was weakened by the introduction of Mary into Christianity (who was perceived by the people as the aspect of the feminine divine) and went underground as an occult religion. There is a new trend to re-establish the reverence for Isis in our society (refer to image 2–3).

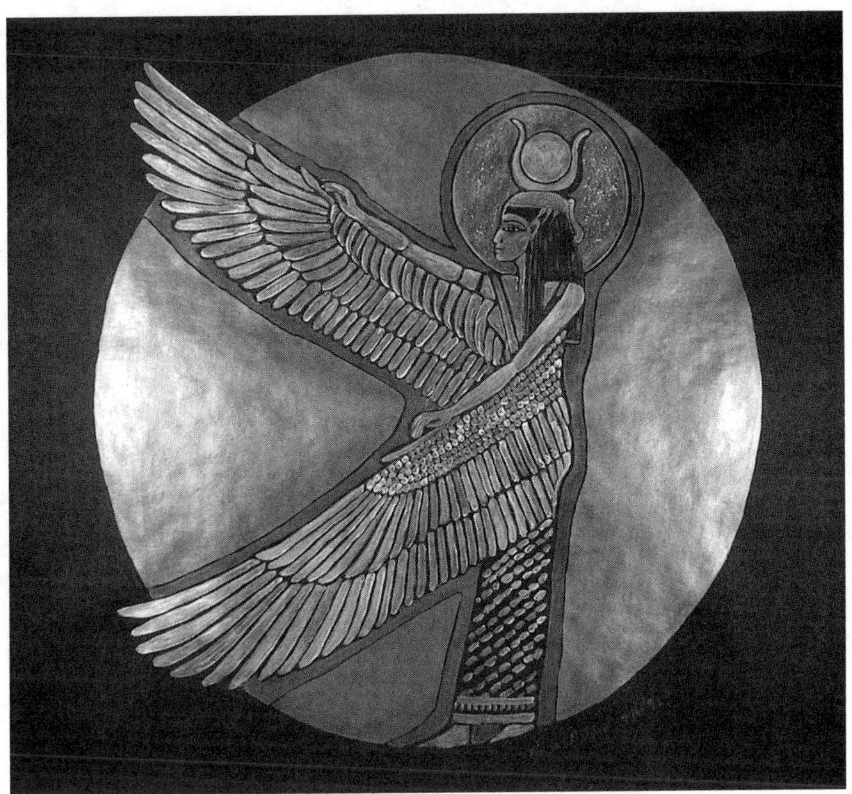

**8–5 Mother God Isis** © Kyra Belán, 1993
Acrylic on paper, 52" x 73", module
Inspired by the ancient Egyptian images of Isis

Various symbols of the Great Goddess of remote prehistoric times were passed on for millennia to many goddesses of early patriarchy, and then absorbed into the patriarchal male God iconography in some form. These universal symbols of the divine feminine include The *Ankh*, a cross with a loop on top, symbolic of the Goddess and of the universal life force. The *inverted triangle* (also a v) universally represented the divine feminine. The Goddess *Trinitiy of* prehistoric trinities included the triple Goddess as the Virgin in her role as the Creator, the Mother in her aspect as the Nurturer, and the Crone as the Transformer. These were followed by mixed gender trinities during early patriarchal times, and finally by all male trinities during fully patriarchal times. *The Chalice* is the symbol for the Goddess, the divine feminine, or the mysterious Holy Grail of Christianity.

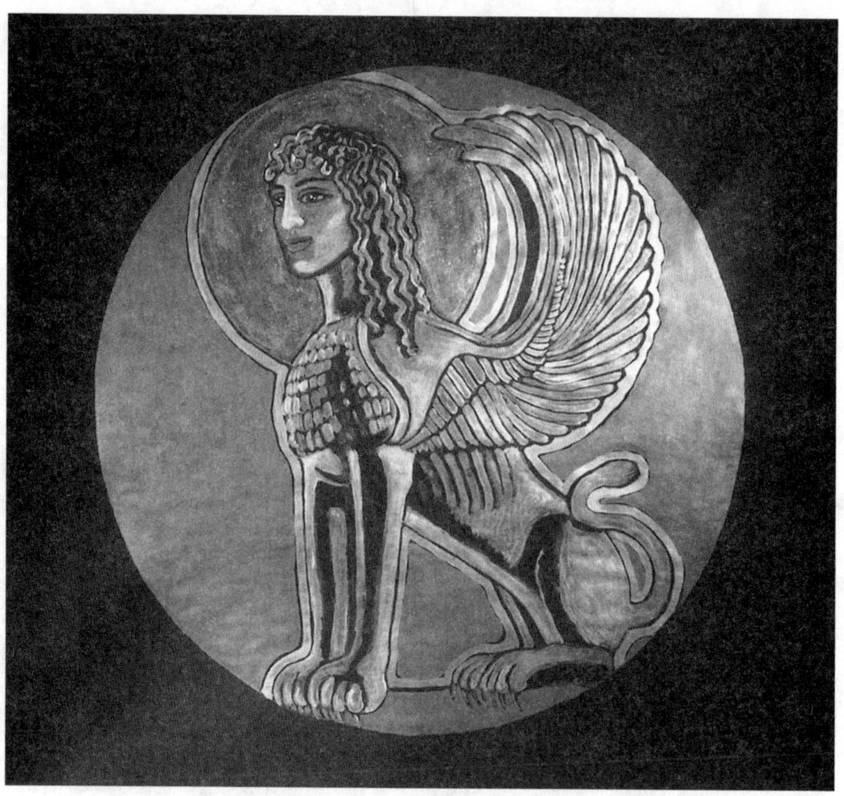

**8–6 Mother God Sphinx of Immortality** © Kyra Belán, 1993
Acrylic on paper, 52" x 73", module
Inspired by the ancient Greek Sphinx of Naxos

## *Mother God Sphinx of Immortality*

This image is inspired by the sphinxes of antiquity. They are ancient images that represent the Great Mother of the Greeks. They came to Greece from older times, most likely through Egypt, where the Great Sphinx, a symbol of Hathor, still stands. The sphinx is the Goddess as the giver of life and immortality, or eternal life within earthly and spiritual realms.

## *Mother God Demeter and Daughter God Persephone or Core*

These Mother and Daughter Gods were worshiped in prehistoric and ancient Greece for three thousand to four thousand years. The rituals for Demeter and Persephone or Core, some of which were secret, were among the most complex and life-altering of the world. All Greek people, who also worshiped other divinities, female and male, belonged to the "Eleusinian Mysteries." The secret rituals of the initiations, although practiced by thousands through the ages, were never revealed to outsiders. Mother God Demeter is a direct descendent of the Great Mother of prehistoric times, who was omnipotent and had a triple nature: the Virgin, or the creator; the Mother, or the nurturer and giver of abundance; and the Crone, whose role was that of the transformer and the taker of life, as well as the giver of wisdom. Demeter is the maternal aspect of the Goddess, which sustains life; Persephone is her creative aspect that awakens nature in spring; and Hecate, the Crone-transformer, is also included in the Mysteries, which primarily concentrate on Demeter and Persephone. Demeter is seen as the Earth Goddess and the creator of agriculture, together with her beloved daughter Persephone. The daughter God disappears underground in winter, only to resurrect in spring as nature's creative principle that promotes its growth and abundance (see Color Plate 19).

## *Mother God Artemis/Diana*

The Greek Goddess Artemis, or Diana to the Romans, was a descendant of the omnipotent creator Mother God; she was the Goddess of Nature and Earth, and a special protector of children. She remained a virgin, which meant in antiquity that she remained single. Artemis was independent and complete in herself. She was also the protectress of animals.

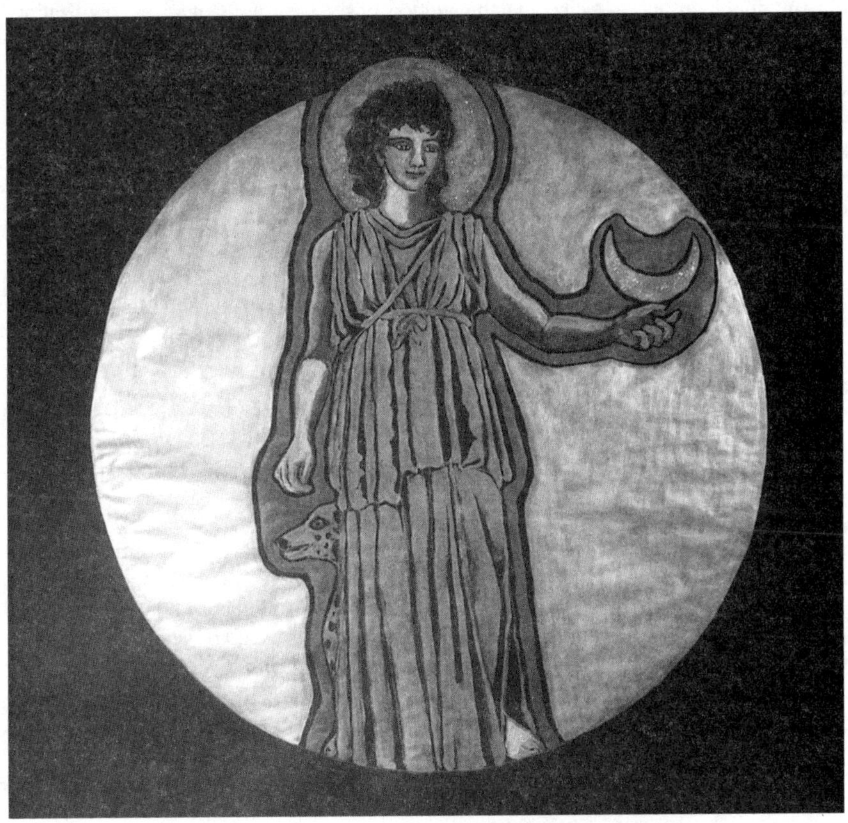

**8–7 Mother God Diana /Artemis** © Kyra Belán, 1993
Acrylic on paper, 52" x 73", module
Inspired by the ancient images of
Diana and Artemis of the Ancient Romans and Greeks

## *Mother God Athena/Medusa/Minerva*

Minerva was the name that Romans gave to this Goddess. Athena and Medusa were two aspects of the same Mother God, another descendant of the omnipotent creator of prehistoric ages. Athena was the protector of all the ancient Greeks, especially of the warriors. She was also the Goddess of wisdom, the arts and culture. The Parthenon, her temple located in Athens, housed a forty-two-foot high statue of the divinity. It is considered to be perhaps the most perfect temple that ancient Greece ever produced. Athena is celebrated today by American Neo-Pagans in Nashville,[10] where a true-to-size reproduction of the Parthenon (see image 3–1) and the statue of the Goddess herself is located.

## *Mother God Juno*

Similar to Demeter, this ancient Roman Goddess of Agriculture is also a descendant of the prehistoric creator, the Great Mother God. Juno was regarded as the giver of light, or Sun Goddess. She is a special protector of families and lovers.

One of her holidays was held on February 14, the day dedicated to women and men who wished to find their soul mates, and to the lovers who wanted to reinforce their relationships. Unable to eradicate this Goddess and the celebration in her honor, Christian fathers replaced her with Saint Valentine as the new patron of the lovers, preserving February 14th date and making the transition from sacred feminine to masculine possible. Thus, the mission of erasing the memory of the Goddess was accomplished, while the holiday itself was kept intact.

## *Mother God Coatlicue*

The most powerful divinity of the Aztec people, the builders of the great pre-Columbian civilization, Coatlicue is the omnipotent Great Mother of all the goddesses and gods. She is the creator, giver of life and of abundance, the Earth Goddess and the transformer. She takes human beings out of the earthly realm into the realm of afterlife.Today, Coatlicue and Tonantzin, her Earth Mother aspect and daughter, are worshiped through the icons of her Christian version, Nuestra Señora de Guadalupe. This dark Madonna is the official patron of the people of Mexico and the Americas (see images 4-4, 4–5).

## *Magna Mater*

Magna Mater, or Great Mother of Ancient Rome, was another descendant of the omnipotent Cosmic Mother. She was one of the most worshiped divinities of the Romans — the Great Mother, the Earth Goddess, and the nurturing and forgiving Lady who was there for those who needed her. She is another prototype for the future Queen of Heaven of the Christians, The Virgin Mary.

## *Mother God Tara*

In the Orient, the concept of Tara precedes that of Buddha. Originally worshiped as the mother of all Buddhas, She is the Mother God of Compassion, and the underlying divine energy of all that is. Goddess Tara is currently worshiped in Tibet and other countries in Asia, and also in America. This mother of humanity is also the Goddess of introspection, meditation, healing, and harmony in life. Numerous works of art were created by artists through the centuries to celebrate Tara. Many museum in the US have statues of Tara of exquisite quality. Today artworks depicting Tara are mass produced to satisfy the demand from the public. Many myths of Tara celebrate various powers and aspects of this goddess; particular favorites are the Green Tara and the White Tara.

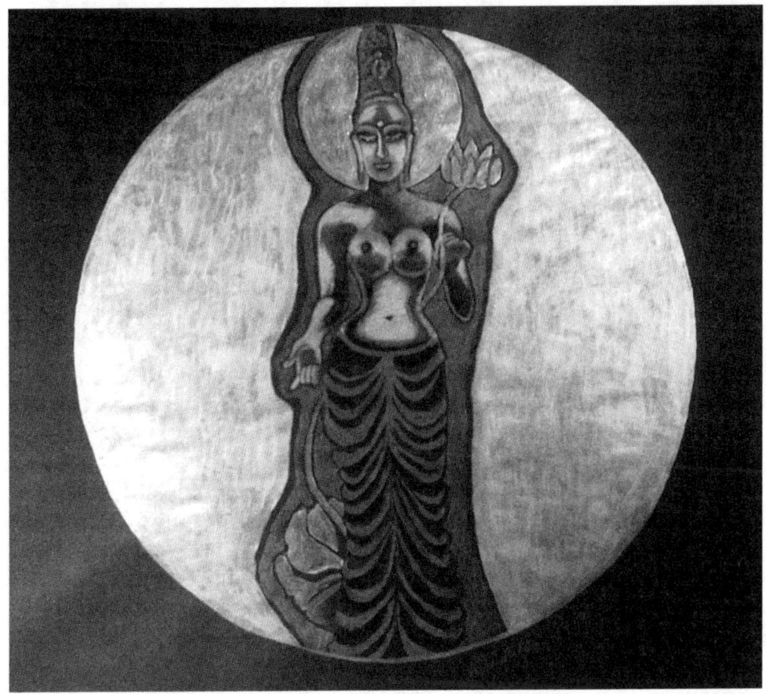

**8–8 Mother God Tara** © Kyra Belán, 1993
Acrylic on paper, 52" x 73", module
Inspired by the Tibetan and Oriental ancient and contemporary images of Goddess Tara

## *Mother of God, Nuestra Señora de Salud*

The Virgin Mary is a former Goddess who was incorporated into Christianity as a major figure during the sixth century. Mother of God and of the Church, Mary is deeply venerated throughout South America and other territories around the globe that practice Catholic religion. In Central and South America, the Virgin Mary is often associated with the Native American Great Mother God or the Earth Goddess, such as Pachamama of Peru or Coatlicue of Mexico. She is the compassionate, gentle, loving, and forgiving Mother of humanity (see Color Plate 20). Mary is strongly linked to the Holy Spirit, seen in early Christianity as the female aspect of God, and symbolically represented by the dove, formerly the symbol of numerous goddesses.

## *Mary Magdalene*

Mary Magdalene, wrongly labeled as a prostitute by the Pope Gregory I for many centuries, and depicted in art as such for that reason, was also believed to be the divine feminine of the sacred couple she formed with Jesus. The new research indicates that Mary Magdalene was a powerful companion and supporter of Jesus, likely his bride/spouse, and has spend a part of her life in France. In my book, *Madonnas from Medieval to Modern* (Parkstone, 2001) I mention this possibility, which is covered more extensively by Margaret Starbird and Lynn Pinknett, among others, in their books. The many shrines dedicated to Mary Magdalene in France have the statues of the Black Madonnas, also associated with Goddess Isis and Virgin Mary. These Madonnas are believed to be miracle producing. One of the attributes or symbols of Mary Magdalene is the chalice, a traditional symbol of female divinities, and it is often called the Holy Grail.

## *Mother God Lakshmi*

Lakshmi's powers within Hindu religion are unlimited; she represents the active divine energy. One of the most endearing goddesses worshiped in contemporary India, she is also regarded as the giver of abundance and prosperity (see Color Plate 18).

## *Mother God Akua Ba*

This Mother God of life-giving powers is worshiped by some of the people of Africa. The figure resembles a sun disc attached to a cross-like figure. The sun disc is also an abstraction of a human face. Akua Ba's stylized figure is also reminiscent of an ankh, a looped cross that symbolizes life, immortality, and the energy of the goddesses of ancient Egypt.

## *Mother God Yemaya*

This Goddess is from West Africa and is currently worshiped in America, particularly by those people who practice Santeria. Yemaya is the Goddess of creation. She gave birth to fourteen Yoruban goddesses and gods. She is perceived as a protector and a comforter and is often equated with the Virgin Mary. She is also the creator of the waters of the world.

## *Mother God Kwan Yin*

Kwan Yin or Guan Yin is the Goddess of Compassion and the all-loving Mother of Humanity to the Chinese: she is the forgiving Buddhist Goddess of Mercy and Healing. The images of Kwan Yin have been produced in abundance in China, particularly through the middle ages. Currently, the interest in Kwan Yin is on the increase in Asian countries and in America. Kwan Yin is often depicted riding a dragon and/or surrounded by dragons. the dragons are mythical animals that represents good fortune. It is believed that Kwan Yin's compassion, love, and her powers to help human beings have no limitations. There are several interesting myths about Kwan Yin, and her incarnation on earth in order to help her people, as she is the Saviour figure.

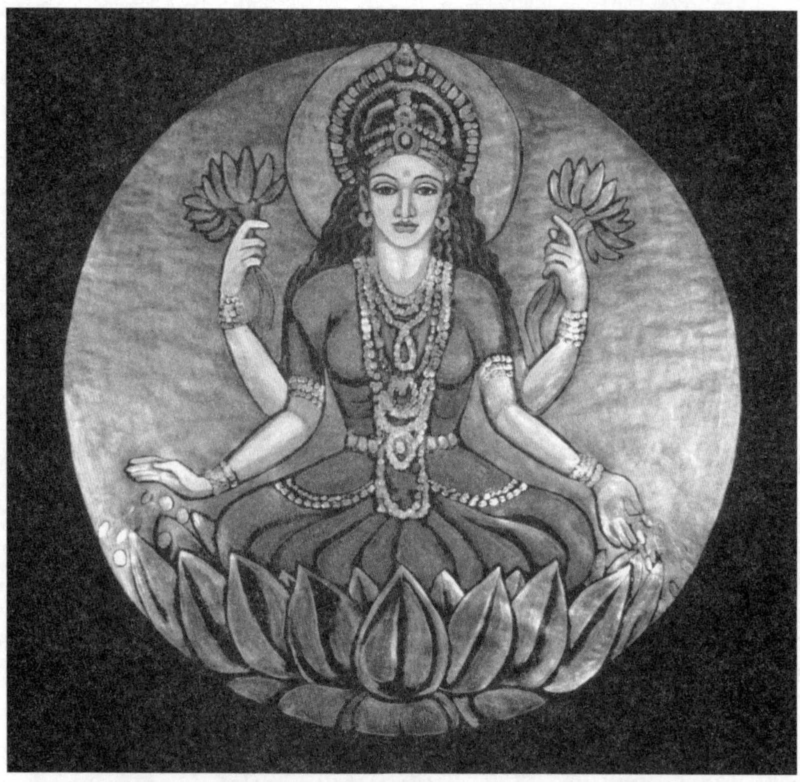

**8-9 Goddess Lakshmi: Magic Circle XXV** © Kyra Belán, 1994
Detail of installation: acrylic on paper, 52" x 79", module

# *Proposals for Site-Specific Projects*

The series of *Proposals for Site-Specific Projects: Celebration of the Divine Feminine* consists of drawings for numerous earthworks, monuments, and temples dedicated to Great Mother God. This re-introduction to the sacred feminine attempts to fill the existing gap in our culture, which routinely celebrates the divine masculine while ignoring the feminine side of the world's spirituality. The materialization of these art works would help to replenish this void. I contend that a society that celebrates only the masculine and minimizes or denigrates the feminine is not a complete or harmonious paradigm. My belief is that only a balanced society works well for all its citizens; both genders and all cultures must participate in the creation of this new social structure.

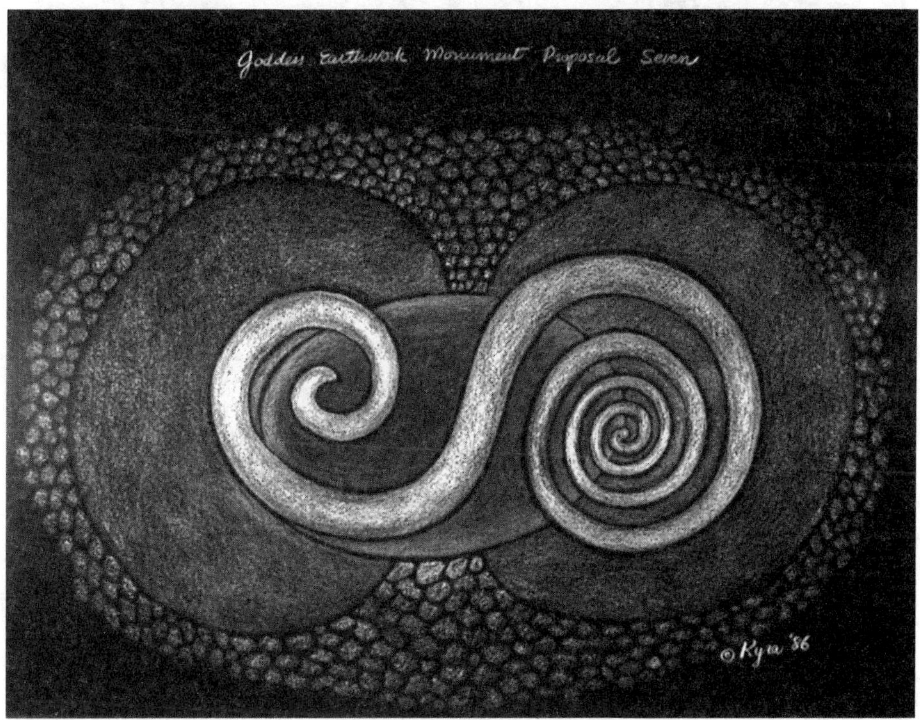


**8–10 Goddess Earthwork Monument Proposal Seven** © Kyra Belán, 1986
Drawing, colored pencil on paper, 15" x 20"

The proposals for the earth art monuments and temples that are dedicated to the Goddess are drawings on paper, rendered with colored pencil. The proposed works are always depicted as surrounded by natural landscapes that may include bodies of water. This would help establish a strong connection between the proposed monuments and the concept of earth-based spirituality. A drawing, *Goddess Earth Art Monument Proposal Seven*, depicts an oval-shaped artificial lake surrounded by two low, grass-covered, round mounds. All three are encircled by a platform of boulders embedded into the soil, forming a larger oval. Spanning over the lake and partially the two mounds is a concrete structure shaped into a double spiral, one of the most ancient symbols for the Great Mother God. The low, curved slopes of the spiral structure would allow people to walk over the surface and contemplate the surrounding nature. The lake would be stocked with fish and embellished with aquatic plants such as water lilies (the flower and the fish are also ancient and contemporary symbols for the divine feminine). The monument would be a participatory experience. Land, water, and sky are included in this composition. This design would allow the spectators to be surrounded by the natural beauty of Mother Earth.

Another monument proposal, titled *Goddess Earth Art Monument Proposal Eleven*, also includes an artificial lake, which is circular. The surrounding terrain is green with vegetation, and a serpentine spiral form encircles the lake. It could be made of concrete or rock, and it appears to submerge into the ground and re-emerge from underneath the earth surface. The "face" of the serpent enters the lake, and its head is visually completed by the presence of a spherical shape, which could also be created of concrete or natural rock. The sphere is partially submerged in the waters of the lake. Two more spheres, also emerging from the lake, are located on each side of the crescent-shaped serpent's head. They form a visual triangle around the serpent. The sculpture's shape is a complex interplay of Goddess symbology: the spiral, the serpent, the circle, the triangle, the sun, and the moon. A participatory sculpture, it can be walked on over the "body" and the "head" of the serpent. The emphasis on close relationship with the natural environment is obvious in this proposal; it would encourage the spectator to meditate on nature.

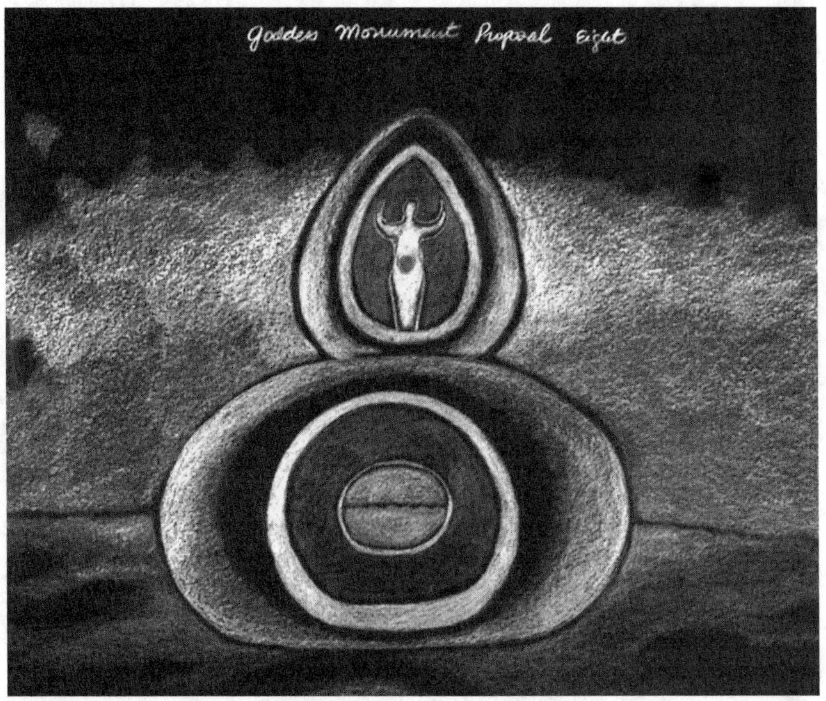


**8–11 Goddess Monument Proposal Eight** © Kyra Belán, 1986
Drawing, colored pencil on paper, 15" x 20"

Other proposals for monuments do not include water but emphasize a strong connection with the natural environment. *Goddess Monument Proposal Eight* (1986) is a colored pencil drawing that shows a natural landscape covered with green grass, in the center of which is located a two-tier biomorphic form. The bottom section of the sculpture consists of an oval, containing within it a circular tunnel that opens into a view of nature. The top layer is a natural form reminiscent of a sliced fruit that contains another shape within, like a fruit pit. In the center of the "pit" is an abstracted Goddess figure. Her arms are raised, and a red oval is painted on her lower torso, symbolic of her life-giving powers. The colors of the sculpture range from yellow to hues of reddish brown; all are earth tones that suggest that this Mother God is a part of the Earth itself. This monument can be easily made out of concrete or natural-colored rocks, such as colored marble or granite. The proposed sculpture could be from 15 feet to 40 feet in height, and would offer four distinct views: two similar side views and two different frontal views, with the Goddess figure visible only when the viewer faces east, while the opposite side is shaped into a likeness of a biomorphic "fruit." An observer who is facing east would have the opportunity to contemplate the rising sun through the "tunnel." This panorama would enhance a feeling of spirituality and connectedness with the planet, and may induce a state of meditation.

Another monument proposal, a drawing in colored pencil, is titled *Goddess Tlazolteotl*. The monument was proposed as a temporary structure for an art park; therefore the original dimensions are modest. The work could easily be created for a permanent location on a much larger scale. The monument celebrates an Aztec divinity and therefore is inspired by the shapes used by that pre-Columbian civilization: the serpent and the pyramid. This proposal for an outdoor structure has a five-layered pyramid in the center; the outer layer would be made of rocks in red, yellow, and blue colors. It is surrounded by an annular form, also covered by a layer of painted rock, in blues, reds, and yellows. The next layer is shaped into a double-headed serpent. An entrance between the heads invites the public to walk into the space between the serpent and the inner ring, in order to observe the pyramid from a closer point of view. The sculpture could occupy a center of a neighborhood park. Several benches could be installed to allow people to rest between or outside the serpent.

## *Proposal for a Goddess Temple and Environment*

My current project is a proposal for a site-specific environment that would help effect the transition between the old paradigm and the new model of the future, a society of balance between feminine and masculine values and spirituality. At this time, it exists only in my mind or on paper, and it is my hope that this work will materialize in the future. Since the oppression of the female sex is justified by the absence of the divine feminine within our dominant culture, there is a need to re-insert female spirituality in order to free both genders from the andro-centric society. As one step in that direction, I see the need for a cultural center dedicated to female spirituality. I propose a temple dedicated to the contemplation of the images of the Great Mother. The architecture of this temple would be based on circular, spherical, or geodesic forms, that suggest the shape of our planet. A permanent collection of fine art, dedicated to the divine feminine and created by contemporary artists, would provide visual stimulation for those who may be meditating or praying to the Great Mother. The nature of the collection would be multi-cultural; artists of both genders and all races would be proportionally represented. The temple would be surrounded by acres of natural environment. Sculptures and earthworks, dedicated to the celebration of feminine spirituality, would be placed throughout this park. All these artworks would be environmentally friendly . An art museum dedicated to artworks that celebrate all aspects of female spirituality would accumulate art in any media and from all historical periods and cultures. Indoor and outdoor space would be available for performance art. All forms of art technology, such as digital art labs and video studios, that would produce art projects dedicated to the re-establishment of the divine feminine, would be located in the building near the art museum. Housing for visiting artists and artists-in-residence would be included in this cultural complex.

A university would also be connected with this cultural center. It would be dedicated to research on the history, sociology, anthropology, psychology, and theology of matristic cultures and to the re-interpretation of the existing patriarchal religions. Research that would lead to the formation of a new concept of earth-based spirituality, suitable for the future non-hierarchical social order, would be of high priority to this university. This research would facilitate the emergence of a new, universal, and all-encompassing religion and culture that will emerge out of the combination of the old matriarchal and recent patriarchal religions and values.

One of the probable futures for our planet is that a new society would eventually emerge out of the blend of the ancient and the contemporary matristic undercurrent and the benevolent aspects of recent patriarchal culture. This new model would consist of human beings whose consciousness is imprinted with a harmonious combination of the nurturing matriarchal and the best of the patriarchal values. These future people would be able to develop their psychic skills, while also utilizing their rational and physical abilities. This idea may be classified as utopian, but a simple change in current mind-set would achieve a painless transformation from one state to the other.

A work of art can affect both inner and outer environments: the inner space of a human mind and the physical space itself. Through art, it is possible to initiate a change in our lives and to imprint the world with a new value system that will lead into a future of positive values and earth-based spirituality. This spirituality can elevate human beings above the old personal quests for power through control and oppression of others into the realm of a peaceful coexistence with other human beings and the planet. These transformed human beings will be able to enjoy spiritual awareness and inner peace. Within the new system, emotional, physical and spiritual benefits of love, cooperation, nurture, and interconnectedness will be highly valued. Wars, violence, or the misuse of power will not be acceptable. I have no illusion that art alone can achieve these goals for our society, but it can make a contribution toward these outcomes. Our current paradigm is undergoing an evolution: more and more people are becoming involved in a gradual, but substantial social change toward a humanistic and pacifist society.

# 9

# *Digital Art in the New Millennium*

The new millennium is best defined by the presence of a rapidly evolving computer technology. Clearly, our lives are controlled by the artificial intelligence of the computer. Digital technology is an integral part of our school and college systems, transportation, employment, government, national defense, and global communications. It is natural that artists, as keen observers and social critics, have become interested in the computer as a means of creative expression and have been utilizing digital technologies to generate art for over two decades. Consequently, new art forms created on the computer have emerged and are constantly evolving. While during the late twentieth century artists usually had insufficient access to computer lab, in the new millennium digital technologies of quality became easily available.

One of the direct predecessors of computer-generated art is video art. It sprang into existence during the late 1960s and early 1970s as a record of performance art since, thanks to instant replay, both the artist and the audience could immediately review this ephemeral art. Artists who had access to a video production studio were able to edit their performance footage or create and manipulate images. I have been involved in both of these new media arts since the late 1970s. Prompted by desire to record my performance art on tape, I also explored video art as a separate medium.

Just as a portable video camera allowed artists to record performance art, a personal computer had become complex enough by the late 1980s to allow them to be creative. For fine artists who attempt to create innovative work using computers, Apple products are often the answer. During the late 1990s, Apple introduced iMac and the Macintosh G3 and G4, all designed to entice the graphic industry. Macintosh G5 followed these in the twenty-first century. Consequently, numerous graphic applications were developed, including Adobe Photoshop, an extremely versatile program that seems perfect for my own artistic needs. My philosophy is to create work on the computer as a pure form of artistic expression. I believe that, at this time, digital technology can be a perfect medium for an artist. Art can be created using an infinite variety of media, and I propose that, for the artists of this millennium, computer technology is as natural as a brush and a canvas were for Impressionist painters like Mary Cassatt or Vincent Van Gogh.

My interest in the computer was first kindled in 1980 when I produced several artworks using scanned images of my drawings and photographs, transformed on the primitive computer into textural black and white surfaces. I cross-hatched over them with colored pencils, and added some elements of collage to complete the compositions. Yet technology was not usually available to me; therefore, it was only at the end of the last millennium that I was able to produce a substantial body of digital artwork. I created my art using Macintosh G3 and G4 computers and then printed out the images in various sizes, on paper or canvas. Recently my interest expanded toward experimentation with web art technologies. Digital photography also plays an important role in my current artistic production. As an established artist who experiments within the new media arts and postmodernism, I incorporate digital technologies and multimedia as a means to convey my messages of eco-feminism and multi-culturalism. In order to maintain a philosophical continuity, I often transform and manipulate parts of my previously created body of work with the aid of the computer and incorporate them into my electronic art production, thus maintaining visual connections among my various series and themes.

The *Spirit Circle Series*, my first body of electronic works, was exhibited at The Art Gallery, Broward Community College, Pembroke Pines, Florida, from November 1999 through January 2000. Arranged into a site-specific configuration on the walls of the gallery, it was integrated into an installation that extended from the floor and into the wall areas. The exhibition was also designed to accommodate two ritual performances. This digital series consists of works on paper or canvas.

Unlike traditional media, this new art-making technology allows me to resize, modify, and reprint each component of the series on the computer and a plotter. Therefore, a variety of spaces – conventional or alternative – can show these artworks, often re-born in new formats and configurations. Therefore, each show becomes site-specific.

One of the unifying factors of the series is its emphasis on the beauty, vitality, and vastness of nature. The Grand Canyon of Arizona became a background setting for some of my mythological themes, which represent a diverse and multi-cultural heritage of the Americas. A huge and breathtaking gorge, it is still regarded as an important sacred space by the Native American tribes, and it is an embodiment of an archetypal representation of the womb of the Great Mother Earth, a symbol for the creation of life.

*Grand Canyon Akua Ba*, a digital artwork, evokes two powerful spiritual archetypes from two continents and cultures: the ancient Cycladic civilization of the Mediterranean, and contemporary Africa. Akua Ba, an abstract female figure and a sacred image of the Asanti (see chapter 8), is located in the center of the image. She represents the Great Mother Creator, believed to be the giver of abundance and fertility. The shape of this mother figure is in a form of a cross, an ancient symbol for spirituality in many religious mythologies, including those originated in Africa. Her large round head is reminiscent of a sun disc, thus explaining that this Earth Mother is also a Sun Goddess. She is seen surrounded by a circle of golden glow. Two Cycladic figures, representing Mother God of old Europe, are located on each side of Akua Ba. All three are shown as slightly transparent, an effect indicating that these time-bending figures may be apparitions from another dimension, apparitions in the midst of the exuberance of nature (Color Plate 21).

A digital artwork designed in vertical format, *Canyon Spirit Shield*, was printed on canvas. It was created as a tribute to the ancient Native American Anasazi civilization. In the background, rocky surfaces of the Grand Canyon recede into the vastness of space, while in the foreground, the centrally located circular shield displays three universal Native American symbols for the Goddess and spirituality: the cosmic egg, spiral, and hands.[11] Placed immediately behind the solid shield are two transparent shields, which seem to dissolve into the recesses of the canyon. The concept of a shield as a repository of personal and shamanic powers is inspired by Native American cultures. The artwork was created with the intent to celebrate the contributions of these original Americans to the heritage of the world (Color Plate 22).

The iron-rich rocks of Sedona, in the northwestern territory of Arizona, inspired me to create a number of electronic works, including *Our Lady of Red Rocks* (color plate 23). This image depicts a mountain rising into a bright blue sky. In the center, the icon of Our Lady of Guadalupe is standing inside an arch propped up by two columns. Immediately below is a figure of a woman dressed in red whose arms are raised. Another image, that of the Aztec Goddess Coatlicue, is visible above and behind the figure. The Aztec Goddess is symbolized by the double-headed serpent inspired by the well-known stone statue of the Goddess located at the Museo Antropologico of Mexico City (she is frequently reproduced in art history texts). Goddess Coatlicue was believed to be the Mother Creator of the Aztec people, and one of her aspects was perceived as Tonantzin, the Earth Goddess (see chapter 4). In Mexico, a syncretic religion, based on the combination of Christian and Native traditions formed during the sixteenth century. According to these syncretic beliefs, Mary, the Christian Mother of God, was understood to be, simultaneously, the Earth Goddess Tonantzin and the Creator Goddess Coatlicue. This fusion of beliefs and traditions from two civilizations soon produced a state of stability and lasting peace between the Aztec peoples and the Spanish *conquistadores*.. Syncretic beliefs, rituals, and ceremonies are still practiced in Mexico today to celebrate Our Lady of Guadalupe.

One of the European predecessors of Our Lady of Guadalupe is the ancient Roman Goddess Juno Lucina. Juno, like Our Lady, is associated with both solar and earthly powers. The artwork, *Sedona Juno Lucina*, is a tribute to this female solar divinity. Sedona is located in a sun drenched region of exquisite beauty in northwestern Arizona. The majestic Goddess is shown standing among the red boulders of a mountain and occasional blotches of emerald colored pines. A circle of light and flames surrounds her figure, and her head is circumscribed by a star-splattered halo. She is holding a snake in her left hand, which is regarded as an archetypal symbol for the Earth Mother. Like many ancient Europeans, Native American tribes from the area ritualize the serpent, a symbol of the divine feminine and of Mother Earth.[12]

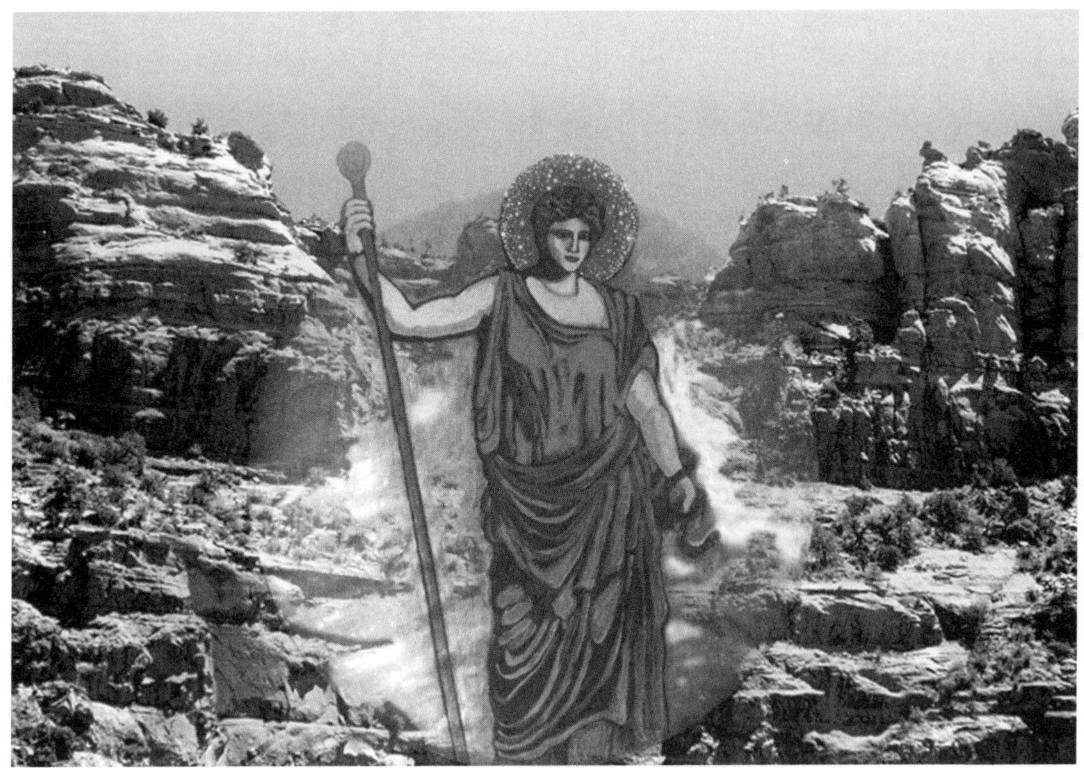

**9-1. Sedona Juno Lucina.** © Kyra Belán, 2000
Digital art

Another powerful Native American symbol is the Thunderbird. It is one of the oldest tribal symbols and totems. This stylized eagle often represents the Earth Mother and divine spirituality and power. In my electronic artwork, *Canyon Eagle Circle*, this archetype is seen as if suspended over the vast expanse of the Grand Canyon. The image was first assembled out of rocks and colored sands, then photographed and scanned into the Mac computer, then altered and painted in Adobe Photoshop. The image of the Grand Canyon was also altered, and the sky painted in Photoshop. Transformed by various stages of digital production, the image is about spirituality, beauty, and perfection of nature.

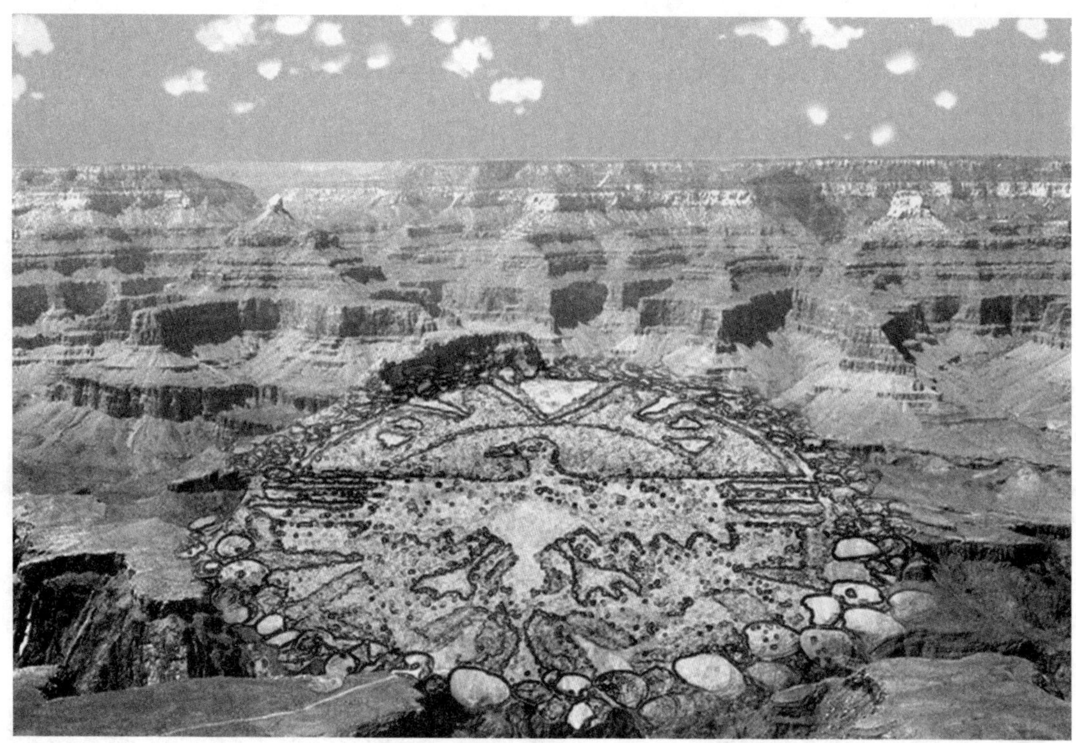

**9-2. Canyon Eagle Circle** © Kyra Belán, 1999
Digital art

In some cases, the theme of an electronic work may be inspired by a previous artwork, created in a traditional medium, such as a drawing or painting. The artwork titled *The American Goddess* consists of a fusion of a scanned drawing, a scanned painting, and a substantial amount of computer-generated work. A colored pencil drawing, *Goddess Trinity Rising*, and an acrylic painting, *Mother God of Laussel,* were used to create a theme similar to the previous motif, yet the original meaning was further enriched. The drawing was partially repainted using Photoshop software, and the painting was also electronically reworked. Then I manipulated the images and created a background space. The iconography of this image is multi-layered: The Goddess on the spectator's left represents the Egyptian Goddess Isis (see chapter 8), an omnipotent divinity. On the right, Goddess Diana of the ancient Greeks (see chapter 8) as the Goddess of Nature and Earth Mother can be observed. In the center is a figure whose starry blue cape is inspired by the attire of the Virgin of Guadalupe, while folds of her white robe are similar to those of the garment worn by the Statue of Liberty. Therefore, the figure represents two archetypal images of the Americas (see Color Plate 2). There is one more female divinity present: Mother God of Laussel, the prehistoric Creator divinity of old Europe, superimposed over the body of the Lady of Guadalupe. The new completed image represents a large span of the history of humanity, reminding us of the prehistoric, ancient, and American civilizations where the presence of the divine feminine is predominant. The reference to the Statue of Liberty is subtle, but important; she represents the right of the people to be free. She is also an occult Goddess within a contemporary culture which routinely celebrates the divine masculine, and which only recently has rediscovered its matriarchal roots and the divine feminine.

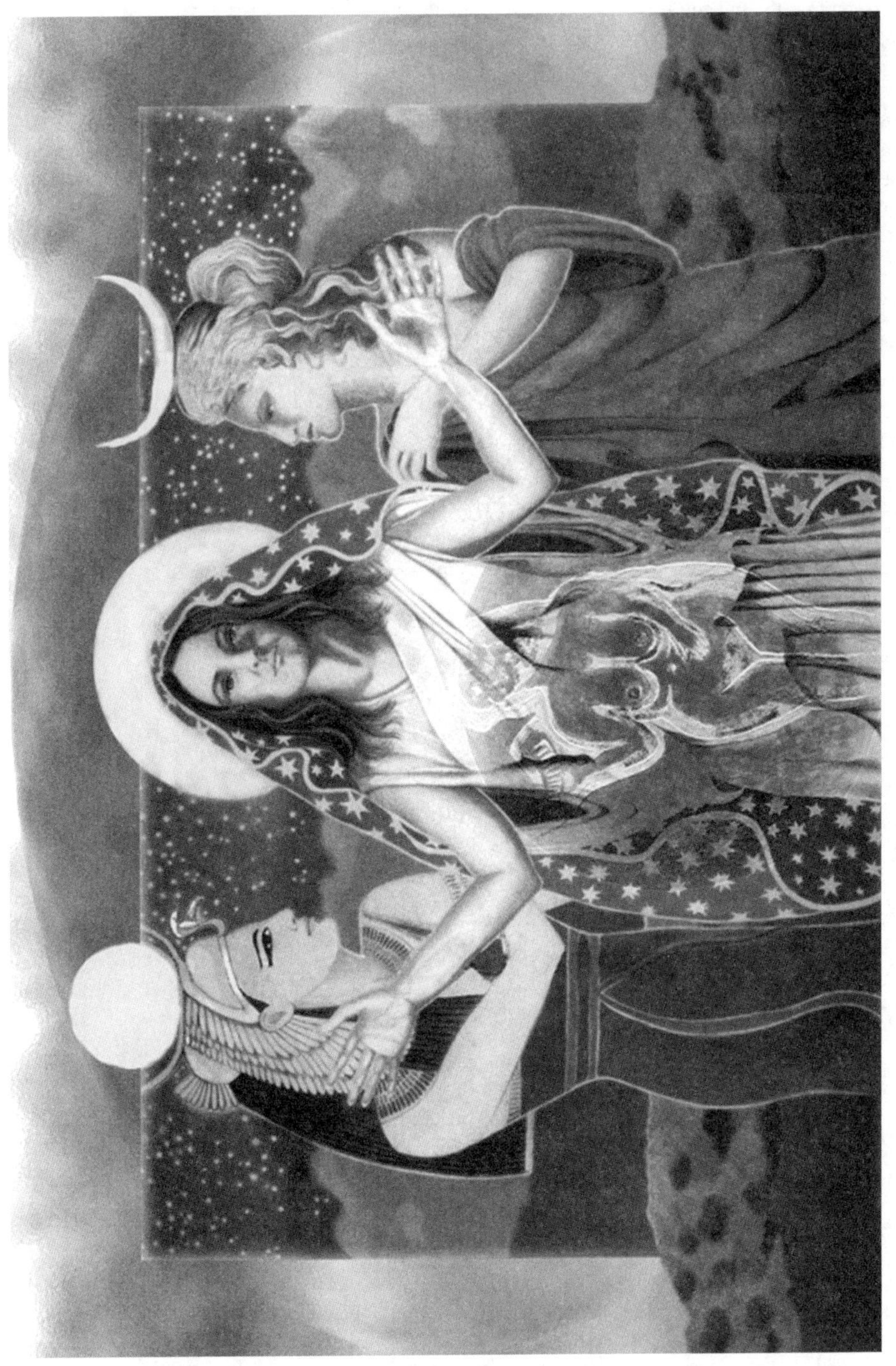

**9-3. The American Goddess.** © Kyra Belán, 2001
Digital art

## *Nuestra Señora de Guadalupe, American Goddess*

Our Lady of Guadalupe is both the Christian Mother of God and Aztec Goddess Tonantzin. The digital image of the figure, clearly resembling the image of the *tilma* located inside the cathedral dedicated to Our Lady of Guadalupe in Mexico City, is shown standing on a beach in front of an ocean. The body of water behind the Madonna symbolizes a life force of maternal love.

Nuestra Señora de Guadalupe, official patron of the Americas according to the Catholic Church, was named after the seventh-century image of the Black Madonna located in Guadalupe, Spain. The miraculous apparitions of Our Lady of Guadalupe, a syncretic blend of the Christian Mother and Aztec Mother Goddess, resulted in an enduring peace and the merging of the native and the conquering populations into a new culture.

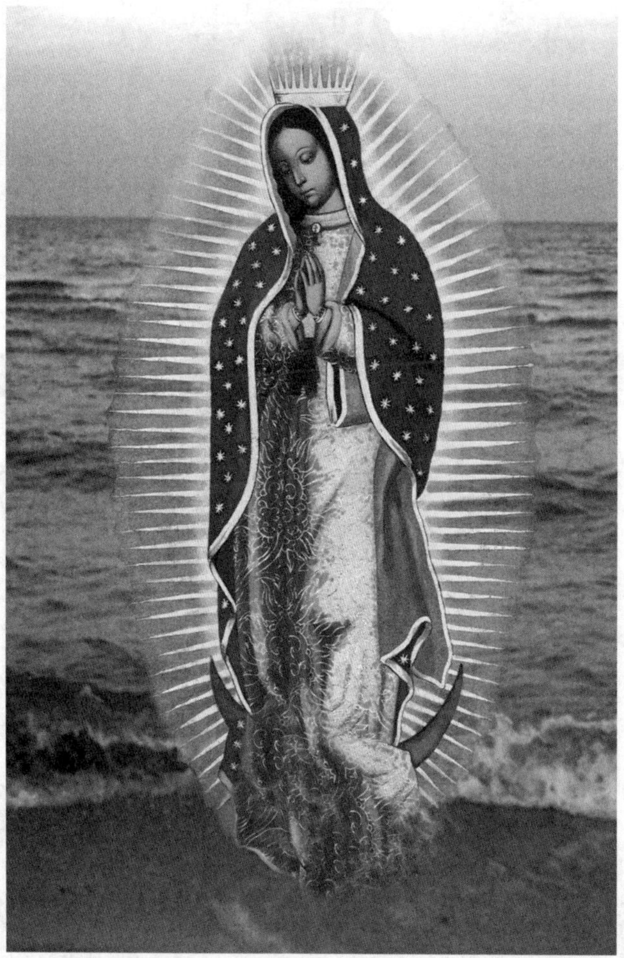

**9-4. Our Lady of Guadalupe.** © Kyra Belán, 2003
Digital art

The miraculous apparitions of Guadalupe were about a connection between the people and the essence of God the Mother. She identified herself as Tonantzin, Aztec Mother Goddess who gave birth to Teotl, the God of Truth. Guadalupe's child was quickly equated with the Christian Jesus in the minds of the church fathers. She, as Tonantzin, chose to appear to Juan Diego, an Aztec peasant who spoke only Nahuatl. This happened just ten years after the Spanish conquered Tenochtitlán, later to become Mexico City. The apparition of Tonantzin-Virgin Mary took place on December 9, 1531, on the hill of Tepeyac, the realm of the Aztec Goddess. The Virgin of Guadalupe in her aspect of a solar divinity is also equated with the omnipotent Aztec Goddess Coatlicue, the creator of hundreds of Gods and Goddesses as the stars of the Milky Way. As Tonantzin she was worshiped as the loving protector and lunar Goddess; the Moon was also associated with Marian iconography.

By appearing to Juan Diego, Guadalupe restored his dignity as a human being. Consequently, honor was returned to all the native people, and their hopes for better life were also restored. The official account of the event is believed to be written by Don Antonio Valeriano several years later, and is called the Nican Mopohua. Even though some years had elapsed since the miracles, the reliability of the account is high, considering that the traditional books of the Gospels were written between 70 to more than 100 years after the events of the New Testament initially happened, and they are also considered reliable. Guadalupe's request to have her cathedral built on the site of the old temple dedicated to Tonantzín further cemented the idea that the old and the new religions were amalgamated into a new syncretic cult.

The last Guadalupan miracle, the impression of her image on the *tilma,* a cape worn by Juan Diego, fully convinced the bishop and the local population of the supernatural nature of the apparitions. The tilma was a part of the attires of the peasants and was made out of agave or maguey plant, from the cactus family. This kind of fabric usually has a life span of about 20 years. Yet the image of Guadalupe-Tonantzín, imprinted on the tilma, is totally intact after over 470 years of life in spite of the changes of temperature through the years, the kissing and handling of the image by thousands of humans, and the constant exposure to the soot of burning candles. In 1791, after the image was finally framed, two workers accidentally spilled some nitric acid onto the tilma. The acid produced only a slight discoloration of the fabric, while its metal frame was destroyed. An even more dreadful incident took place at the old temple in 1921, after a bomb was stashed inside a vase located beneath the image. The explosion occurred at the end of the mass, damaging the surrounding area including the marble bas-reliefs on the walls. It also melted a copper and gold processional cross, which since has been displayed at the temple to commemorate the new miracle – the fact that the explosion did not damage the *tilma* itself. After this last incident it was enclosed under a bulletproof glass.

One of the most significant scientific investigations of the *tilma* took place in 1936 under the direction of American Nobel Prize-winner and scientist Richard Kuhn. Originally hoping to disprove the tilma's otherworldly qualities. Kuhn concluded that "the elements that produce the colored patches on the cloth are unknown to all research. Neither mineral, animal, nor vegetable, the image seems to have been painted without any brush or lithographic method" (Hanut, p.# 30). Kuhn and his team of scientists also noticed that the angel at Mary's feet and the golden rays of light that seem to emanate from her body were added later, painted in oil.[13] Our lady of Guadalupe has become a potent symbol for American spirituality on many levels, and her popularity as a female sacred archetype in on the increase.

## *Lady Liberty*

The Statue of Liberty is a symbol of freedom in America and, by extension, throughout the entire world. My choice was to depict the Lady Liberty standing in front of the Grand Canyon, a tourist attraction and natural phenomenon of grand proportions. Both are allusions to the divine feminine. The predecessors of Lady Liberty include Libertas, the Goddess of Freedom of ancient Rome; Goddess Athena of ancient Greece; and, further back in time, the Great Mother Goddess of old Europe. The Egyptian Sun Goddesses Hathor, Isis, and Sekhmet are also her predecessors, and her solar halo attests to that.

As an archetype the statue represents the divine woman who manifests in a variety of ways, according to the mythologies of various cultures. Since America is a melting pot of many civilizations, this colossal statue is very appropriate as her symbol. The statue is the largest sculpture of a female currently in existence on this planet rising from the base to the tip of the torch, according to the 1984 survey, at 152 feet and 2 inches. The Lady is made out of 310 riveted copper plates and is the creation of French sculptor Auguste Bartoldi. A gift to the American people from the people of France, she was inaugurated on Liberty Island on October 28, 1886.

Lady Liberty is firmly lodged in the human psyche; she appears with frequency in publications, ads, television, cinematography, and on the internet. I decided to take this image out of its original context of New York harbor and place her in front of a natural phenomenon, the Grand Canyon. The beauty of this womb of Mother Earth is undisputed; its panoramic spectacle enchants millions of observers every year. This juxtaposition of the two American icons shows how they interrelate as symbols: The Native Americans celebrated the sanctity of the Grand Canyon long before the Europeans arrived, while the Statue of Liberty is the result of the blending of ancient mythologies and archetypes of the old world. The impact of both is greatly enhanced by the renewed interest in the idea of democratic society, the individual's rights, and the inclusion of the feminine values of peace, nurturance, and respect for the natural environment. Currently, the preservation of our planet is more urgent than it was in the twentieth century, due to the increase in the world's population (see Color Plate number 24).

The view of the Lady Liberty, the American goddess, in front of the Grand Canyon suggests the unity between the people and their beautiful country.

## *The Digital Revolution*

These artworks demonstrate that the digital revolution has given the artists opportunities to express themselves in a new way. Computer technologies allow numerous options to create art, such as the ability to resize and modify the artworks with ease and in a short period of time. Other possibilities of artistic experimentation include the web, animation and various interactive technologies. The art establishment's rules have also been changed: Art can be shown on the internet, and thus exposure to the artwork is maximized. The world wide web offers many new opportunities to communicate, exchange ideas, concepts, and social messages. As electronic technologies keep improving, the future for global communication – and art is a form of communication – will result, I project, in a more inclusive global village. Technology, when accessible to a large portion of humanity, may help society to evolve toward a more balanced, equal, and multi-cultural world.

# Notes

1. Perhaps the most researched locations of the prehistoric and ancient worship of Mother God are Europe, the Near East, and Egypt. Besides the sacred monuments and temples that were dedicated to the Great Mother, a multitude of priceless works of art depicting the Goddess or her iconography have been unearthed from these regions. Many of these artworks are now on display in museums across the world. Recent research of Pre-Columbian civilizations is also yielding new sites, temples, and images of the Great Goddess. The most recent re-evaluation of the pyramids and temples of Teotihuacan, located near Mexico City, indicates that this culture was another Goddess-worshipping civilization, as stated in the Miami Herald article by John Noble Wilford (reprinted from *The New York Times*), published on January 4, 1993. New interest in travel to the sites of the numerous Goddess worshipping civilizations of the past and the present generate a new kind of travel literature and travel tours. An example of this new genre is a book by Aneli S. Rufus and Kristan Lawson, titled *Goddess Sites: Europe*. The newly re-discovered matriarchal civilizations of Mother Earth represent an extensive and inexhaustible artistic heritage and constitute a vast source of information on the mythology of humanity. This new wealth of information is our common cultural heritage. It belongs to all of humanity, and it is transforming our popular culture.

2. The original divine trinity was female. During prehistoric and ancient times, the Great Mother was perceived by human beings as triune. The three distinct aspects of the Great Mother were the Virgin, the Mother, and the Crone. The Virgin aspect of the Goddess represented her as the active universal creator, in particular as the initiator of the cycles of nature in spring and the originator of human life. The Mother symbolized the nurturing power of the Goddess. She was seen as the giver of abundance in nature during the seasons of summer and autumn. The Crone, or the Wise One, embodied the transformative powers of the omnipotent Mother, who continued the natural cycle of life into the cycles of death and afterlife. The Crone was responsible for the slowing down of activities in nature during the months of winter. The three aspects are described by Barbara Walker in her book *The Crone*. During the early stages of the patriarchal take-over of older matristic civilizations, the trinity was transformed into a mixed-sex trinity, such as the Egyptian divine family of Isis, her husband Osiris, and her son Horus. Ultimately, several major patriarchal religions adopted the all-male divine trinity. The Christian trinity of God the Father, God the Son and the Holy Spirit is the best known of all male trinities in the Western world, although recent re-interpretation are beginning to re-introduce the divine feminine element into this religion.

3. The temple and the Fellowship of Isis are located at Clonegal Castle, Enniscorthy, Erie. Several members of the fellowship publish books on the subject of Mother God that are distributed under Cesara Publications in England and can be obtained in the U.S. at some bookstores.

4. My resolution of the composition for the drawing, titled *The Phoenix* , required the use of three distinct background areas symbolizing the three aspects of the Mother God: the Virgin, the Mother, and the Crone. The Virgin aspect of the Goddess isolates her creative power and focuses on her gift of the season of spring to humanity: the creation and the awakening of life. The Mother aspect of the trinity represents her nurturing powers and the abundance of the seasons of summer and autumn. The Crone represents the advent of the winter season, as well as the transformative stage of her creative power, such as the slowing down and dying of nature, in order to be reborn again. Together, the three aspects represent the cyclical nature of life, and reinforce the concept of reincarnation that the mythology of the Phoenix already suggests.

5. Within a typical patriarchal system, male artists are considered to be the norm, and female artists are seen as an aberration of this norm. Only the male artists are believed, often on a subconscious level, to have the innate right to explore any subject matter, including the male nude. This is true in spite of the fact that, for the last two thousand years, many patriarchies disapproved of the presence of male nudity within the art establishment. Museum walls and art history books usually celebrate the achievements of artists of one gender and one race: white male.Michelangelo, considered by many as the greatest artist of all times, produced numerous male nudes, and he was rarely censored

for his "transgressions." While today's society does not feel comfortable with the male nude, a male artist has a much greater chance of getting his male nudes displayed at a museum or gallery than a female artist has. Contemporary American artist Robert Mapplethorpe is one example of this phenomenon. While several incidents of censorship of his work did occur, his photographs did not stay out of public view. Several books that documented his achievements appeared in bookstores, although the artist's content is seen as controversial by this culture due to his daring statements about gay sensibility and sexuality.

6. Female nudity has been part of the Western tradition in art for many centuries. Art museums and art history books are replete with usually passive, often reclining, nude young bodies, depicted according to the Western ideals of female form. College-level art students are bombarded by images of the female nude in the fine arts, while the contemporary commercial art world explores and exploits female nudity in order to advertise and sell products or to entertain men. Today's society provides men and women with frequent exposure to the female nude. Thus, only women, of all ages, must look up to the usually unattainable ideal female nude—a very thin, yet large-breasted figure. Consequently, women's lives are routinely altered by this fact, causing anxiety and prompting their dissatisfaction with their own bodies. A substantial number of women are subject to so much pressure from society to keep their looks appropriately in check that they suffer serious illnesses, such as anorexia nervosa, and bulimia which sometimes cause their deaths. Constant preoccupation with their appearance also leads women to submit to health-damaging diets, plastic surgery, breast implants, and the purchase of cosmetics to embellish their looks. Female artists are often so conditioned to female nudity that they continue to perpetuate the patriarchal vision of the female body as a sex object in their own artworks. Sometimes they are rewarded by the patriarchy for doing so. As a rule, art buyers of both sexes invest in a work of art while guided by patriarchal stereotypes. This fact often works against those female artists who may be trying to express themselves by bringing into their arts their gender-based experiences. There are indications, though, that a change is now taking place as the new social paradigm of partnership is beginning to take shape.

7. The purpose of this chapter is to introduce the important issues of the female gaze and the male nude. My studies into the dynamics that fuel the current bias against the male nude's presence within our culture are yielding interesting information about our contemporary society. A separate book, with a working title of *The Adonis Files*, is my project on this subject.

8. As symbols of the Great Mother, flowers often appear among the iconography of the frescoes and art objects of the Palace of Knossos and numerous other structures of the matriarchal Minoan civilization. This culture peaked around 1450 BCE on the island of Crete. Some of the flowers that appear on the walls of the palaces of Crete may be lilies; others may form decorative borders and may possess four or more petals. Besides the flowers, numerous other symbols of the Great Mother can be observed on the island as a part of her artistic traditions. Other frequently used images of Minoan art that are symbols of the Great Goddess are the butterfly, the double ax, the serpent, the bird, the sacred cow/bull and the dolphin. Abstract symbols of the Goddess that often appear in Minoan art are the spiral and the circle.

9. The contemporary scientific community is currently undergoing a transformative process of integrating and interrelating its previously compartmentalized scientific disciplines in order to serve our Mother Earth more effectively. Rachel Carson, in her famous book *Silent Spring*, started us on a voyage toward the goal of becoming an ecologically healthy society by making us conscious of the danger of chemical pollutants to the Earth's biosphere. Contemporary progressive scientists such as J. E. Lovelock and Elizabeth Sahtouris view the planet as an organically integrated system of interactive functions and forces, as a living organism. The urgency of saving the planet from pollution and disintegration due to human mismanagement of its resources is clear to most of us at this time. We are realizing that it is imperative for us to change our course of action if we are to survive as a species and let the ecosystem also survive. Mother Earth, as a life-giving and life-supporting biosphere, must continue to exist if humans, their cultures, their myths, and their arts are to survive.

10. The Nashville Parthenon is a nearly exact replica of the original temple dedicated to the Goddess Athena, located on the Acropolis Hill in Athens, Greece. The giant statue of the Goddess is closely inspired by the original, lost during the sixth century. Numerous religious groups that follow neo-pagan traditions have been using the Nashville temple for their ritual ceremonies. These rituals are not unlike those of the ancient Greek worshipers who have used the original temple in the past. Related festivities and games, also inspired by ancient Greek religious rituals, often take place on or near the site to celebrate the Great Goddess.

11. In Native American, European, African and Asian mythologies, the egg is usually the symbol for Mother Goddess the Creator. This cosmic or World Egg often appears in the arts of these civilizations. Ancient Egyptians'

sign for the World Egg was the same as the sign for the embryo in the mother's womb. The spiral represents the birth-giving Goddess, as Mother Earth. It is an archetype for the birth of humanity through the womb of the Earth. In the mythologies of the Americas, spirals also represent the birth-giving waters of the Earth Goddess. Since prehistoric times, human hands have appeared in cave art and as petroglyphs, representing the powers of creation, the Goddess as Creator, and later also male gods; many Native American tribes currently use these symbols in their rituals and as their artistic expression.

12. The snake has been, since prehistory, identified with the Great Goddess all over the world. She is the symbol for numerous goddesses, including Goddess Isis of the ancient Egyptians. When a matriarchal culture became a patriarchal society, or a mixture of the two, the serpent would then be used as a symbol for the new male gods, as well as for the goddesses. In other instances, when the changeover from matriarchy resulted in a complete patriarchy in which the women of that society would constitute a class of people deprived of human rights, the serpent was often vilified by that society and would become a symbol of evil.

13. Eryk Hanut, author of the book *The Road to Guadalupe*, quotes Dr. Kuhn's statement about the miraculous "unknown to all research" nature of the *tilma*. Other writers, such as Jeannette Rodrigues, author of *Our Lady of Guadalupe*, and Ann Castillo, editor of *Goddess of the America*, discuss the value of the new syncretic Guadalupan cult and how it promoted peaceful coexistence of two previously antagonistic and diverse populations, and their coming together to form a new country and *la raza*of Mexico.

# *Bibliography*

Austen, Hallie Iglehart. The Heart of the Goddess. Berkeley: Wingbow Press, 1990.
Awiakta, Marilou. Selu Seeking the Corn-Mother's Wisdom. Golden, CO: Fulcrum, 1993.
Belán, Kyra. Madonnas from Medieval to Modern. Paris, France: Parkstone, 2001.
Berger, Pamela. The Goddess Obscured. Boston: Beacon, 1985.
Beyer, Stephan. The Cult of Tara. Berkeley: Univ. of California Press, 1978.
Blavatsky, H. P. Isis Unveiled. 2 vols. Pasadena, CA: Theosophical Univ. Press, 1988.
Boucher, Sandy. Discovering Kwan Yin, Buddhist Goddess of compassion. Boston: Beacon Press,1999.
Budapest, Zsuzsanna E. The Grandmother of Time. New York: Harper & Row, 1979.
Campbell, Joseph. The Power of the Myth. New York: Doubleday, 1988.
Chadwick, Whitney. Women, Art, and Society. New York: Thames and Hudson, 1990.
Christ, Carol P. Laughter of Aphrodite. New York: Harper & Row, 1987.
Condren, Mary. The Serpent and the Goddess. New York: Harper & Row, 1989.
Daly, Mary. Gyn/Ecology. Boston: Beacon, 1990.
——. Pure Lust. Boston: Beacon, 1984.
Damian, Carol. The Virgin of the Andes: Art and Ritual in Colonial Cusco. Miami Beach: Grasfield, 1995.
De La Croix, Horst & Richard Tansey. Gardner's Art Through the Ages. New York: Harper & Row, 1986.
Devine, Mary Virginia. Magic from Mexico. St. Paul, MN: Llevelyn Publications, 1992.
Durdin-Robertson, Laurence. God The Mother: The Creatress and Giver of Life. Kildavin, Eire: Cesara Publications, Anno Deae Cesarae Hiberniae Dominae MMMMCCCII.
Eisler, Riane. The Chalice and the Blade: Our History, Our Future. New York: Harper & Row, 1987.
Fine, Elsa Honig. Women and Art. Upper Montclair, NJ: Allanheld & Schram, 1978.
Gadon, Elinor W. The Once and Future Goddess. HarperSanFrancisco, 1989.
Gardner, Laurence. Bloodline of the Holy Grail, Shaftesbury, Dorset: Element, 1996.
Getty, Adele. Goddess. New York: Thames and Hudson, 1990.
Gimbutas, Marija. The Goddesses and Gods of Old Europe. Berkeley: Univ. of California Press, 1982.
——. The Language of the Goddess. New York: Harper & Row, 1989.
——.The Civilization of the Goddess. San Francisco: HarperCollins, 1991.
Gore, Al. Earth in the Balance: Ecology and the Human Spirit. New York: Penguin Books USA, Inc., 1993.
Hanut, Eryk. The Road to Guadalupe. New York: Penguin Putnam, 2001.
Gould Davis, Elizabeth. The First Sex. New York: G. P. Putnam's, 1971.
Harris, Ann Sutherland and Linda Nochlin. Women Artists: 1550–1950. New York: Knopf, 1976.
Heller, Nancy G. Women Artists. New York: Abbeville, 1987.
Johnson, Buffie. Lady of the Beasts: Ancient Images of the Goddess and Her Sacred Animals. New York: Harper & Row, 1988.
Kanta, Katherine G. Eleusis. Athens: Kanta, 1979.
Lee, Scout Cloud. The Circle is Sacred. Tulsa, OK: Council Oak Books, 1995.
Leloup, Jean-Ives. The Gospel of Mary Magdalene. Rochester, VT: Inner Traditions, 2002.
Lippard, Lucy. Overlay. New York: Pantheon, 1983.
Lovelock, James E. Gaia: A new look at Life on Earth. New York: Oxford Univ. Press, 1991.
Mapplethorpe, Robert. Black Book. New York: St. Martin's Press, 1986.
McDermott, Rachel Fell and Jeffrey J. Kripal Encountering Kali. Univ. of California Press, 2003.
McLean, Adam. The Triple Goddess. Grand Rapids, MI: Phanes Press, 1989.
McGrath, Sheena. The Sun Goddess Myth, Legend and History. UK: Blandford, 1997.

Mookerjee, Ajit. Kali the Feminine Force. New York: Destiny Books, 1988.
Mylonas, George E. Eleusis and the Eleusinian Mysteries. Princeton, NJ: Princeton Univ. Press, 1961
Noble, Vicki. The Double Goddess. Rochester, Vermont: Bear & Company
Orenstein, Gloria Feman. The Reflowering of the Goddess. Tarrytown, NY: Pergamon Press, 1990.
Plaskow, Judith and Carol P. Christ. Weaving the Visions: New Patterns in Feminist Spirituality. San Francisco: HarperCollins, 1989.
Petersen, Karen and J. J. Wilson. Women Artists. New York: Harper & Row, 1976.
Picknett, Lynn. Mary Magdalene. New York: Carroll & Graff, 2003.
Pollack, Rachel. The Body of the Goddess. London: Vega, 2003
Radford Rueter, Rosemary. Sexism and God-Talk: Towards a Feminist Theology. Boston: Beacon, 1983.
Rinpoche, Bokar. Tara The Divine Feminine. San Francisco:ClearPoint Press,2001.
Rodriguez, Jeanette. Our Lady of Guadalupe. Austin: Univ. of Texas Press, 1994.
Rufus, Anneli S. and Kristan Lawson. Goddess Sites: Europe. San Francisco: Harper, 1990.
Sahtouris, Elizabeth. Gaia: The Human Journey From Chaos to Cosmos. New York: Pocket Books, 1989.
Schipflinger, Thomas. Sophia-Maria A Holistic Vision of Creation. York Beach, Maine: Samuel Weiser, Inc. 1998.
Sjoo, Monica and Barbara Mor. The Great Cosmic Mother: Rediscovering the Religion of the Earth. San Francisco: Harper & Row, 1987.
Slatkin, Wendy. Women Artists in History. Englewood, NJ: Prentice Hall, 1985.
Starbird, Margaret. The Goddess in the Gospels. NM: Bear & Company, 1998.
Stone, Merlin. When God Was a Woman. New York: Harvest/HBJ, 1978.
——. Ancient Mirrors of Womanhood. Boston: Beacon Press, 1979, 1991.
Straffon, Cheryl. Earth Goddess. UK: Blandford, 1997.
Streep, Peg. Sanctuaries of the Goddess. New York: Little, Brown & Co, 1994.
Teish, Luisah. Jambalaya. San Francisco: Harper & Row, 1985.
Tufts, Eleanor. Our Hidden Heritage. New York: Paddington, 1974.
——. American Women Artists. New York: Garland, 1984.
Walker, Barbara G. The Crone. San Francisco: Harper & Row, 1985.
——. The Skeptical Feminist. San Francisco: Harper & Row, 1987.
——. The Woman's Dictionary of Symbols & Sacred Objects. San Francisco: Harper & Row, 1988.
——. The Woman's Encyclopedia of Myths and Secrets. San Francisco: Harper & Row, 1983.
Walters, Margaret. The Nude Male. New York: Penguin Books, 1978.
Warner, Marina. Alone of All Her Sex. New York: Vintage Books, 1983.
Wilshire, Donna. Virgin Mother Crone. Rochester, VT: Inner Traditions, 1994
Wiltshire, Susan Ford. Athena's Disguises. Louisville, KY: Westminster John Knox Press, 1998.

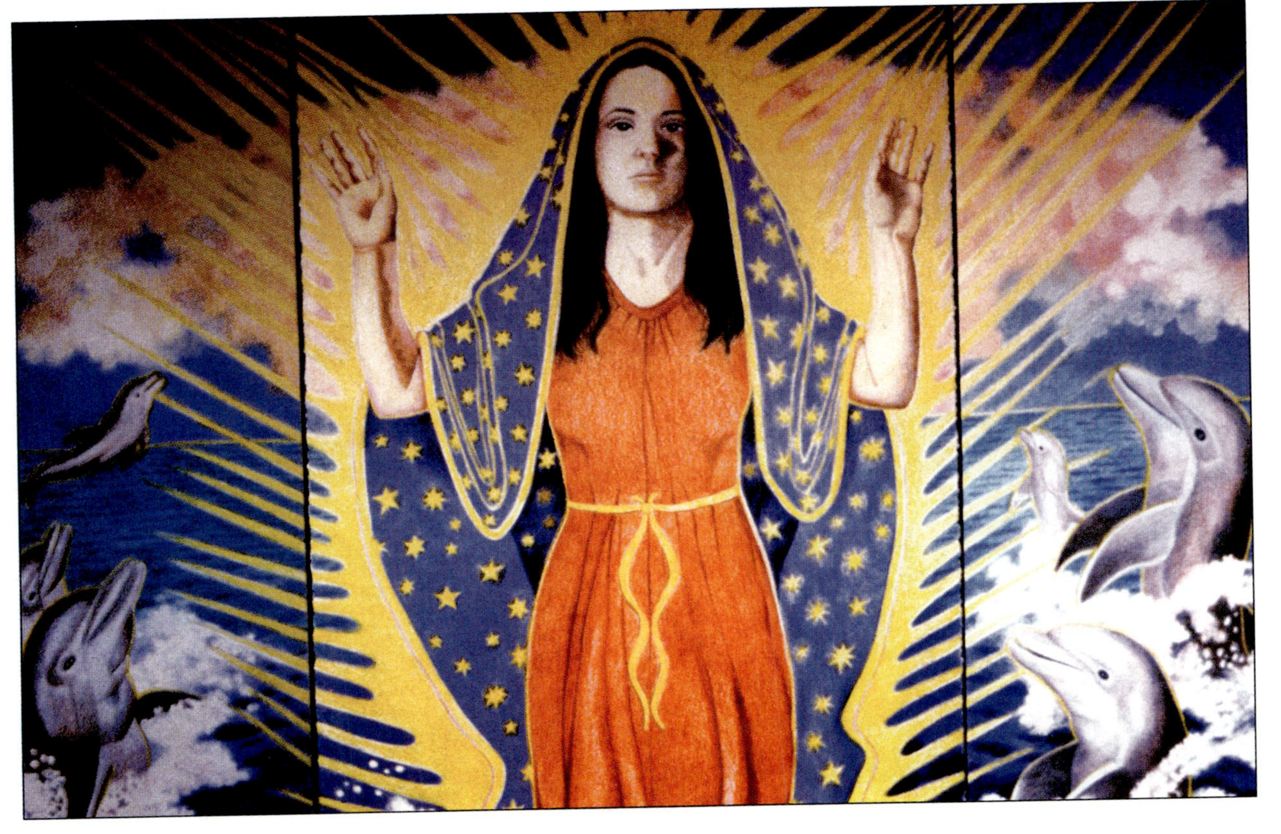

**1. Nuestra Señora de Florida** © Kyra Belán, 1991
Drawing, colored pencils, 30" x 44", triptych.
The Latin American Art Museum, Miami, FL.

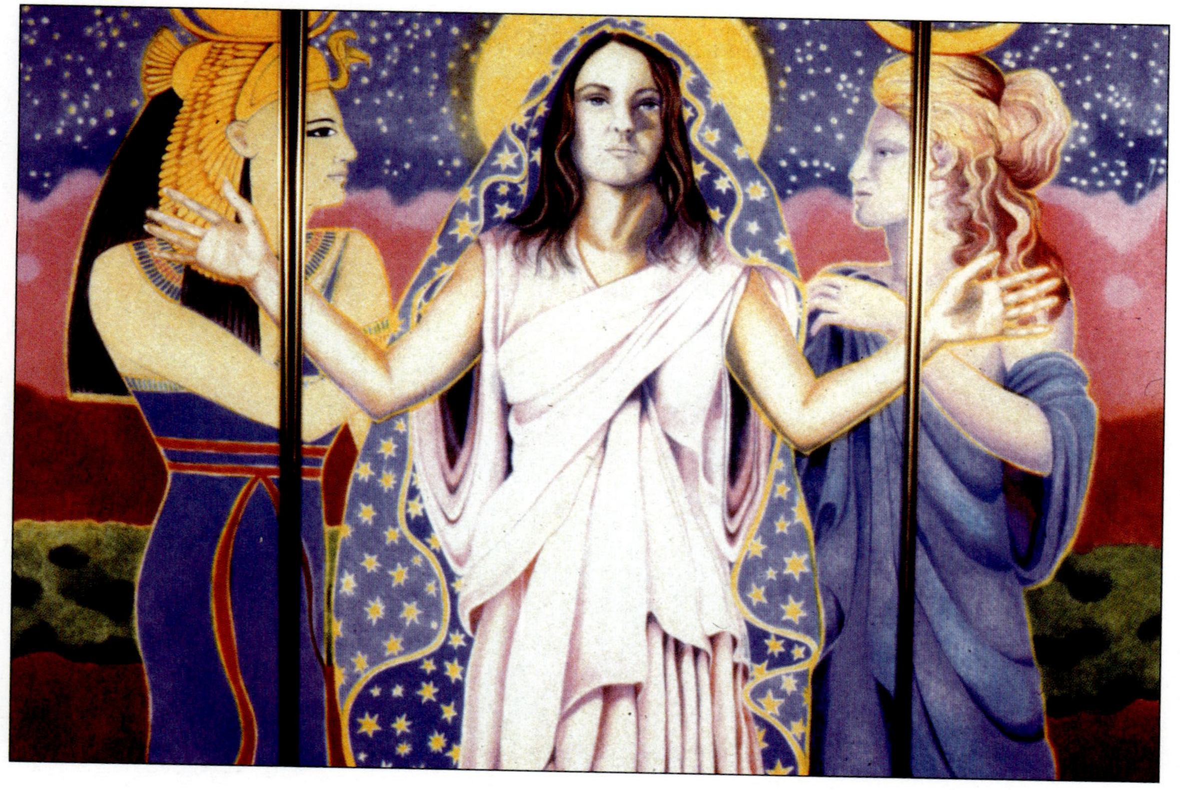

**2. Goddess Trinity Rising** © Kyra Belán, 1991
Drawing, colored pencils, 30" x 44", triptych.

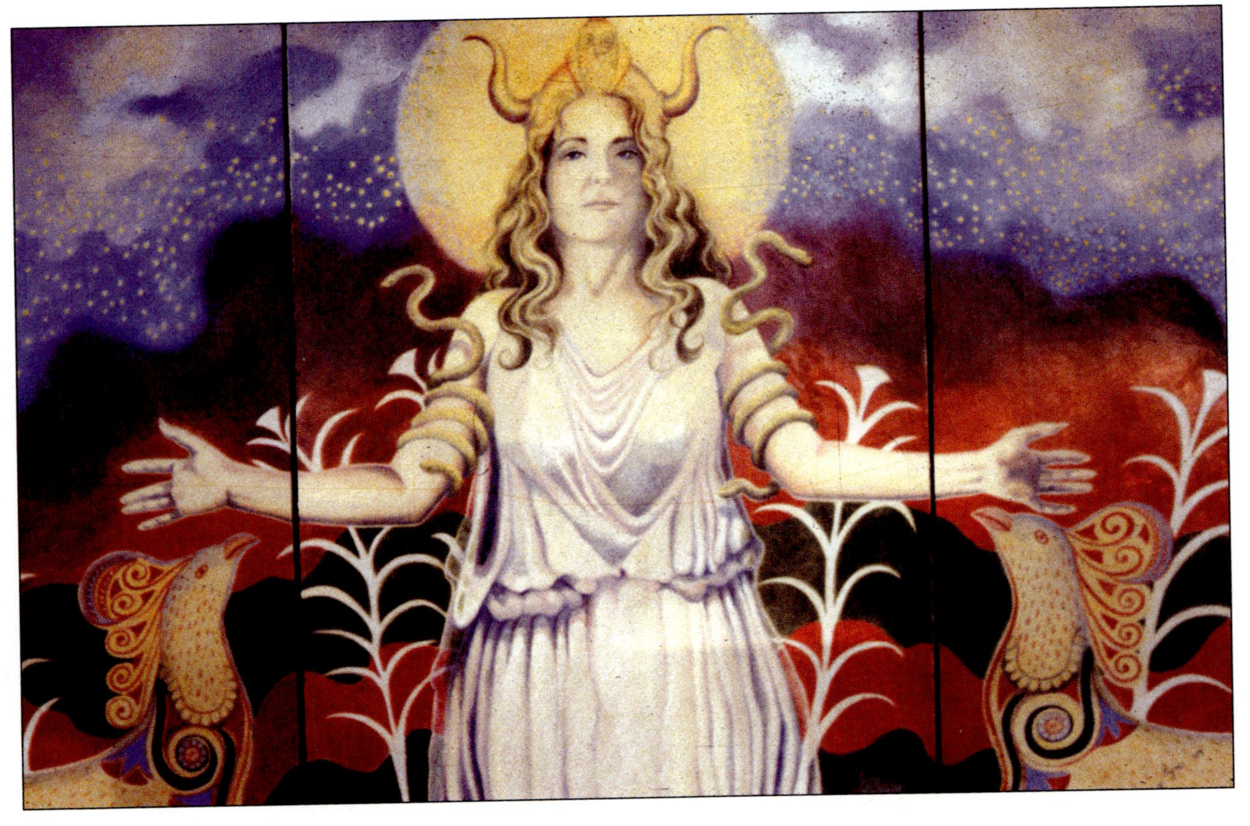

**3. Goddess Rhea of Crete** © Kyra Belán, 1989
Drawing, colored pencils, 30" x 44", triptych.

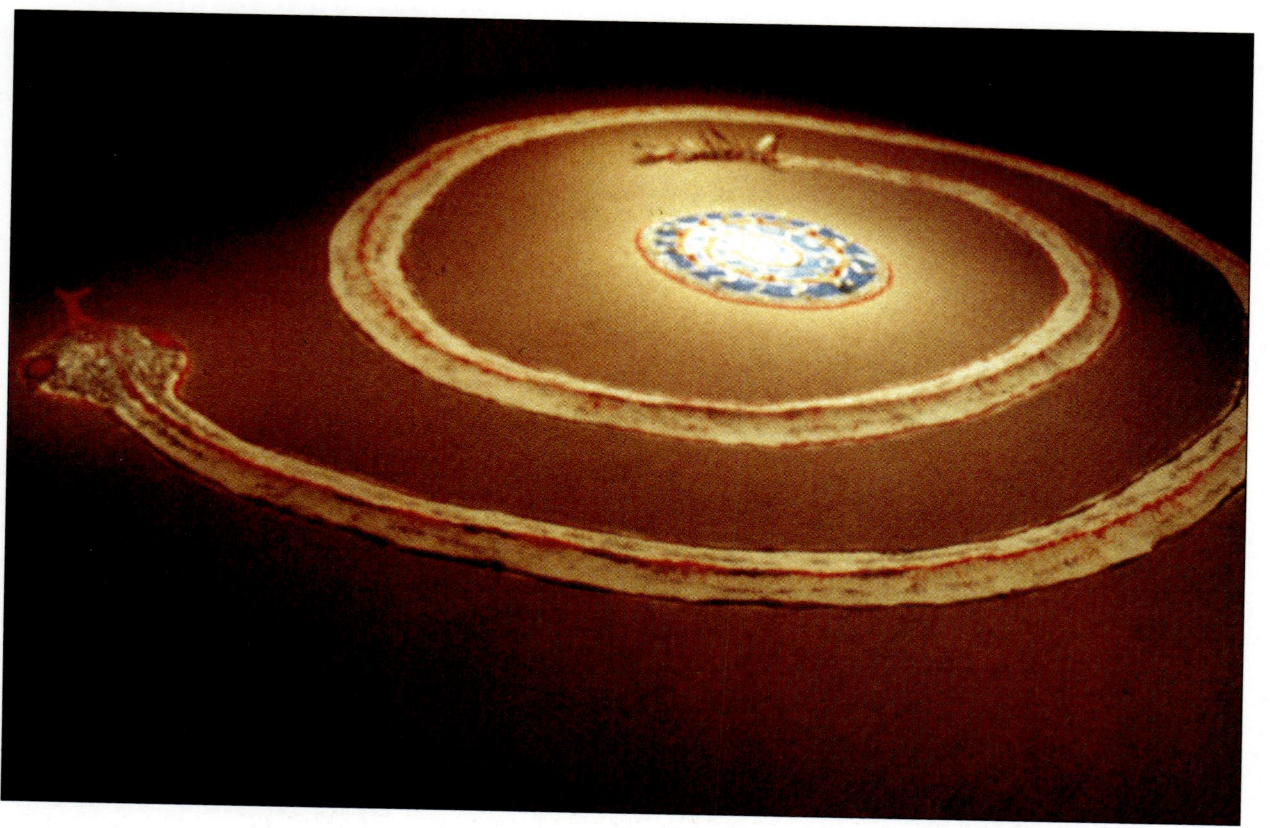

**4. Great American Goddess Coatlique:**
**Magic Circle VIII** © Kyra Belán, 1984
Detail of environmental installation.
Fine Arts Gallery, Broward Community College, Davie, FL.

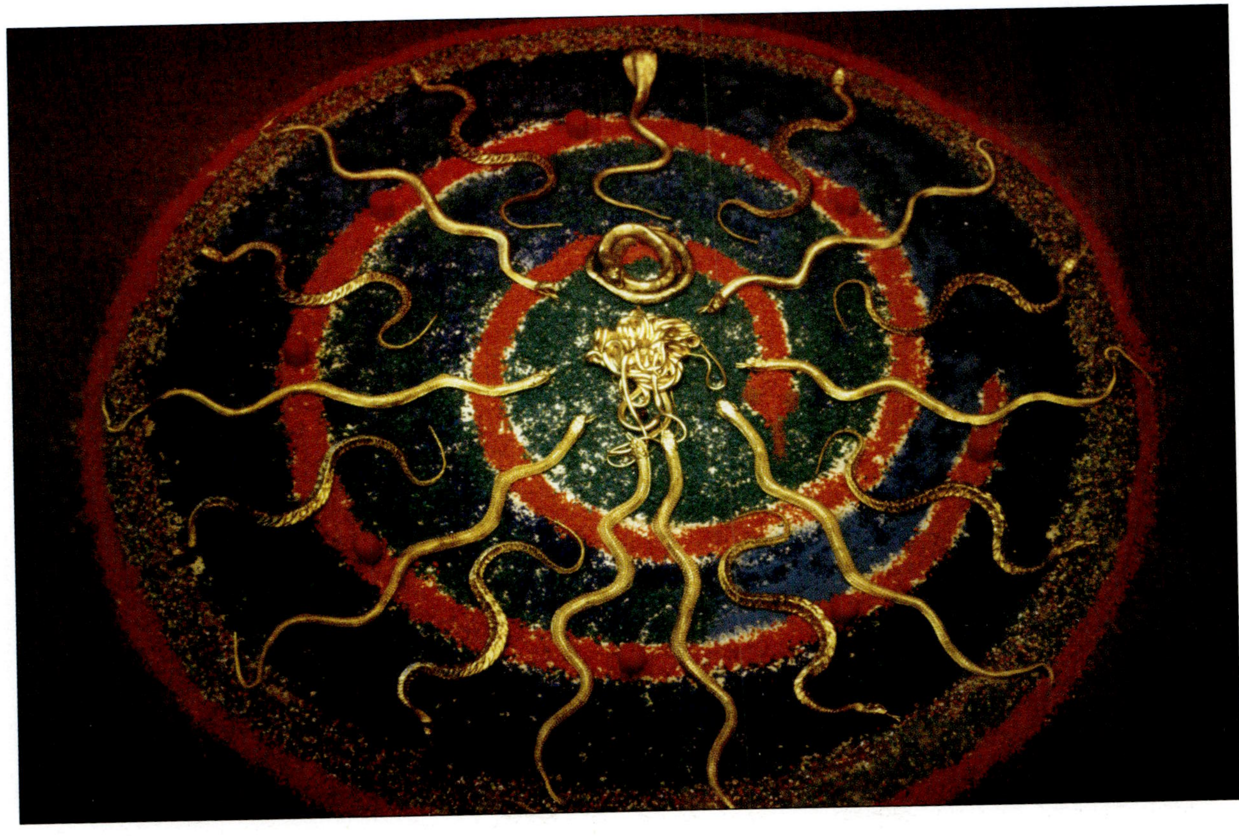

**5. Great American Goddess Coatlique:**
**Magic Circle VIII** © Kyra Belán, 1994
Detail of environmental installation.

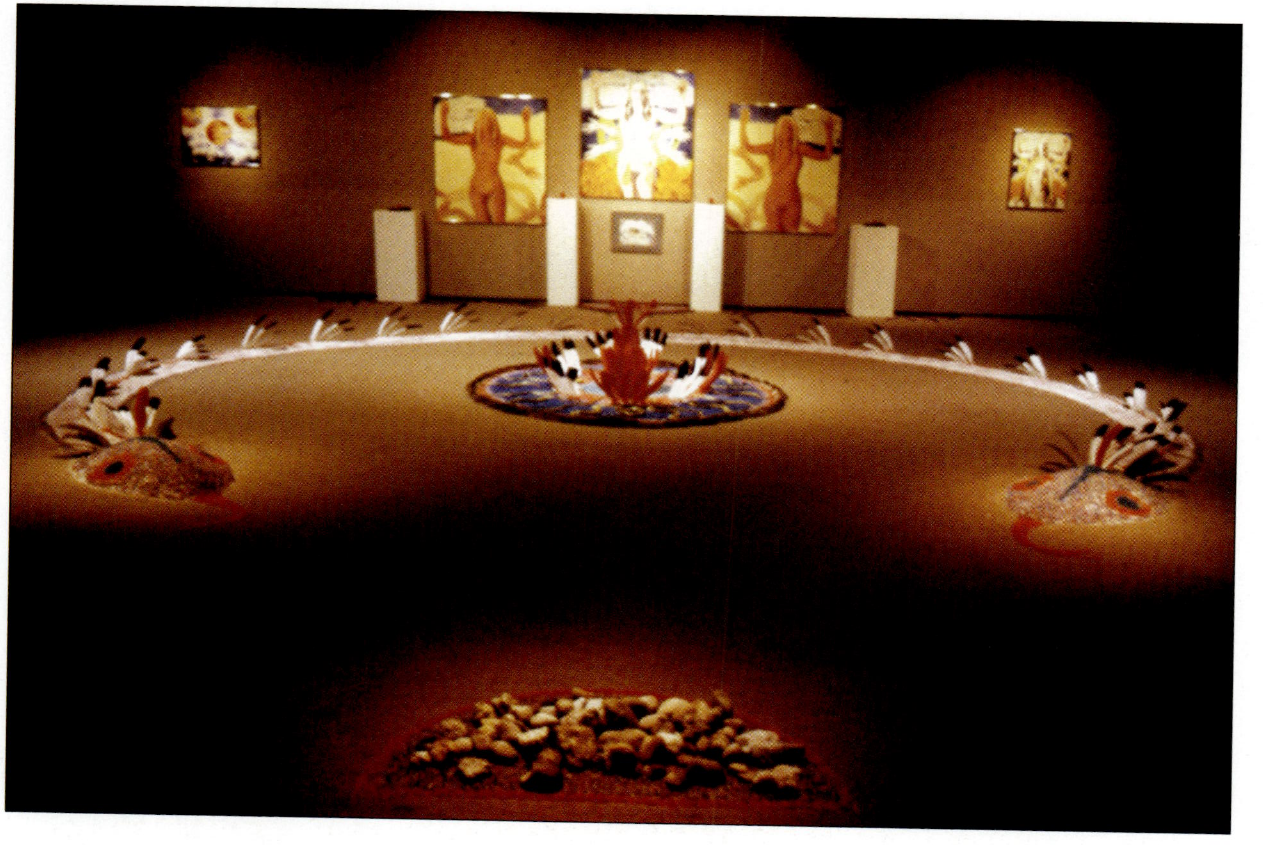

**6. In Quest of the American Goddess Coatlicue:**
**Magic Circle IX** © Kyra Belán, 1985
Detail of environmental installation.
Fine Arts Gallery, Broward Community College, Davie, FL.

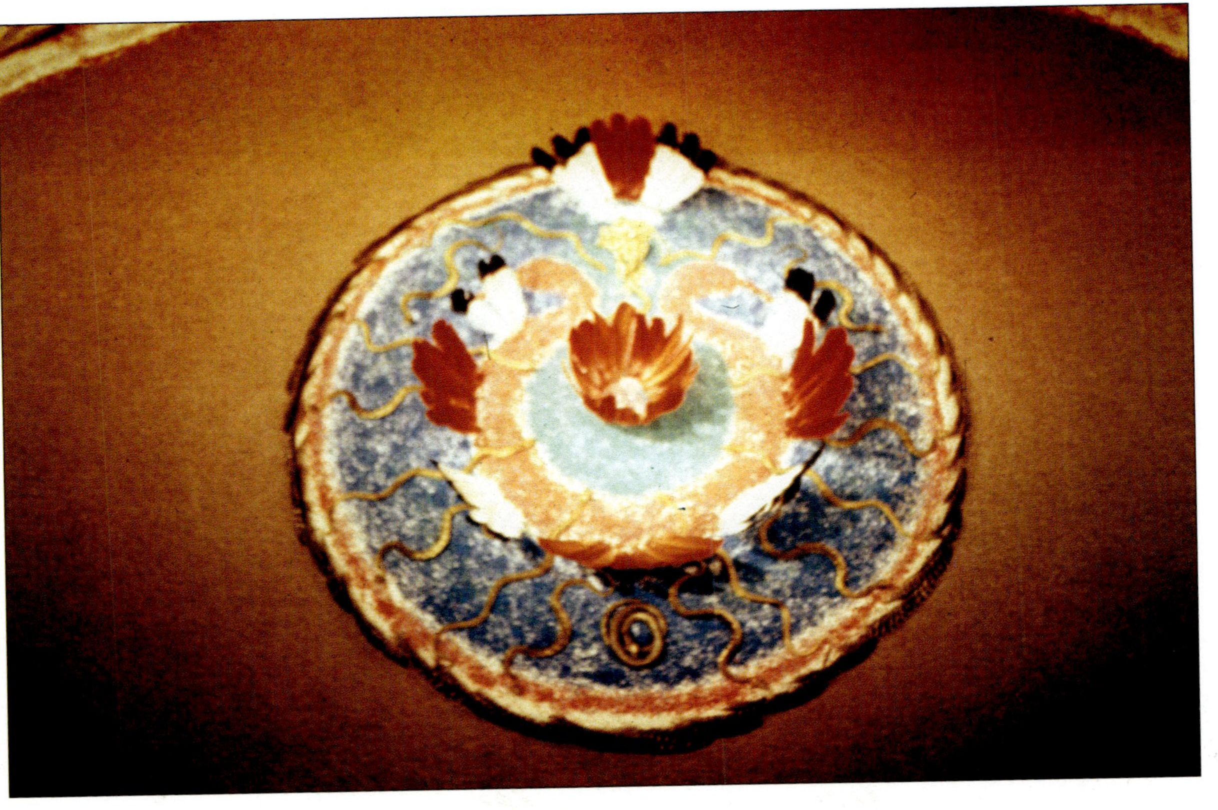

**7. In Quest of the American Goddess Coatlicue:**
**Magic Circle IX** © Kyra Belán, 1985
Detail of environmental installation.

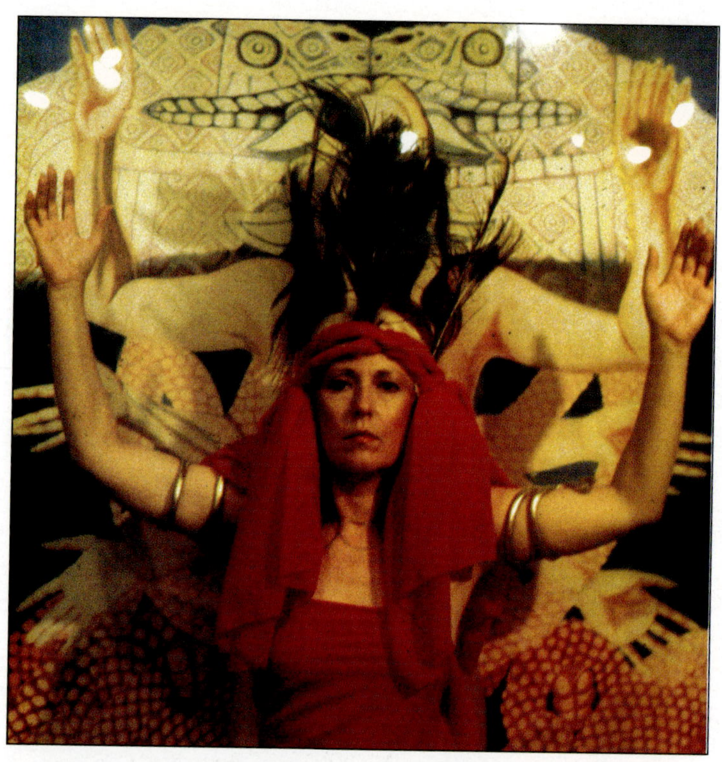

**8. In Quest of the American Goddess Coatlicue: Magic Circle IX** © Kyra Belán, 1985
Artist in performance, detail of installation.

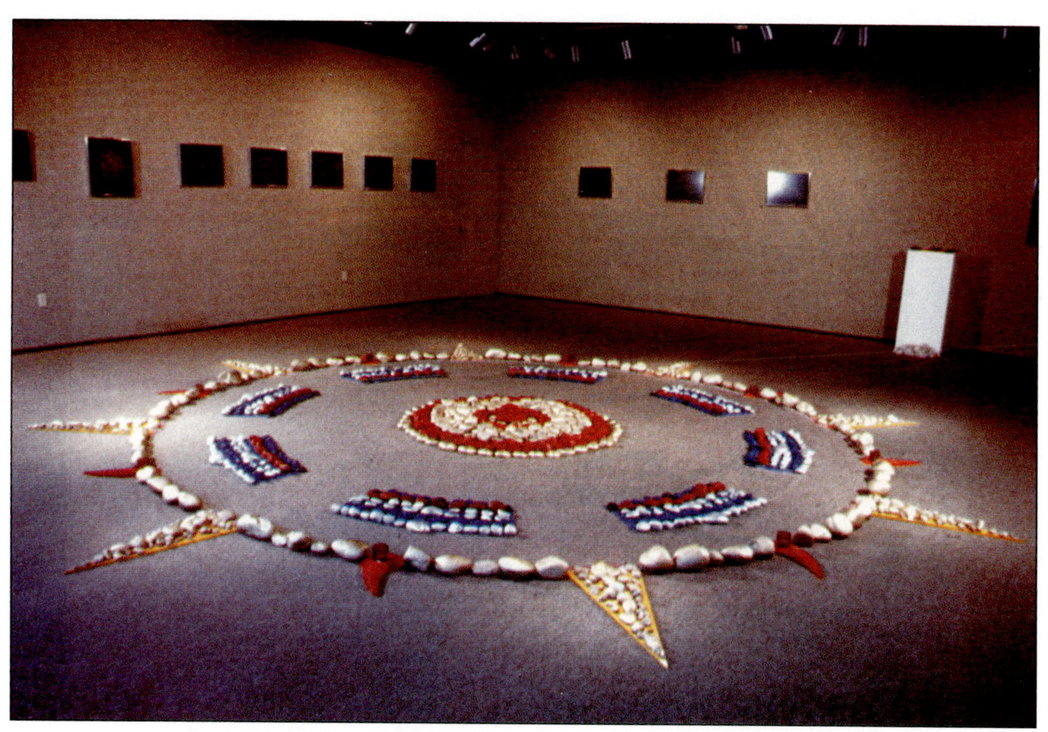

**9. Sun Goddess, Emergence of the Myth:**
**Magic Circle XI** © Kyra Belán, 1986
Environmental installation.
Fine Art Gallery, Broward Community College, Davie, FL.

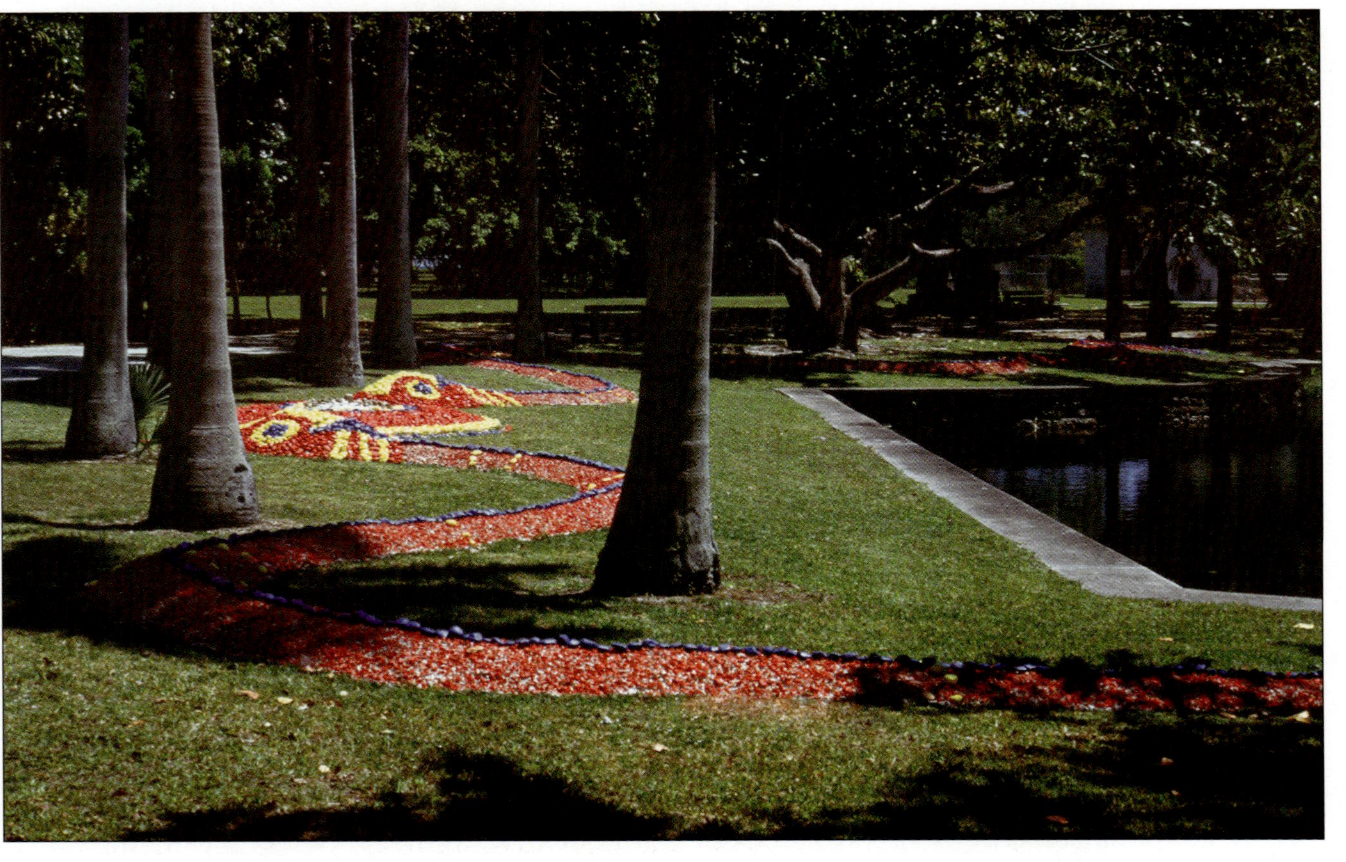

**10. Nature Goddess Sekhmet: Magic Circle XII** © Kyra Belán, 1987
Detail of earth art: painted quartz and coral rock.
Miami Site, Key Biscayne, FL.
Funded by Metro-Dade Art in Public Places.

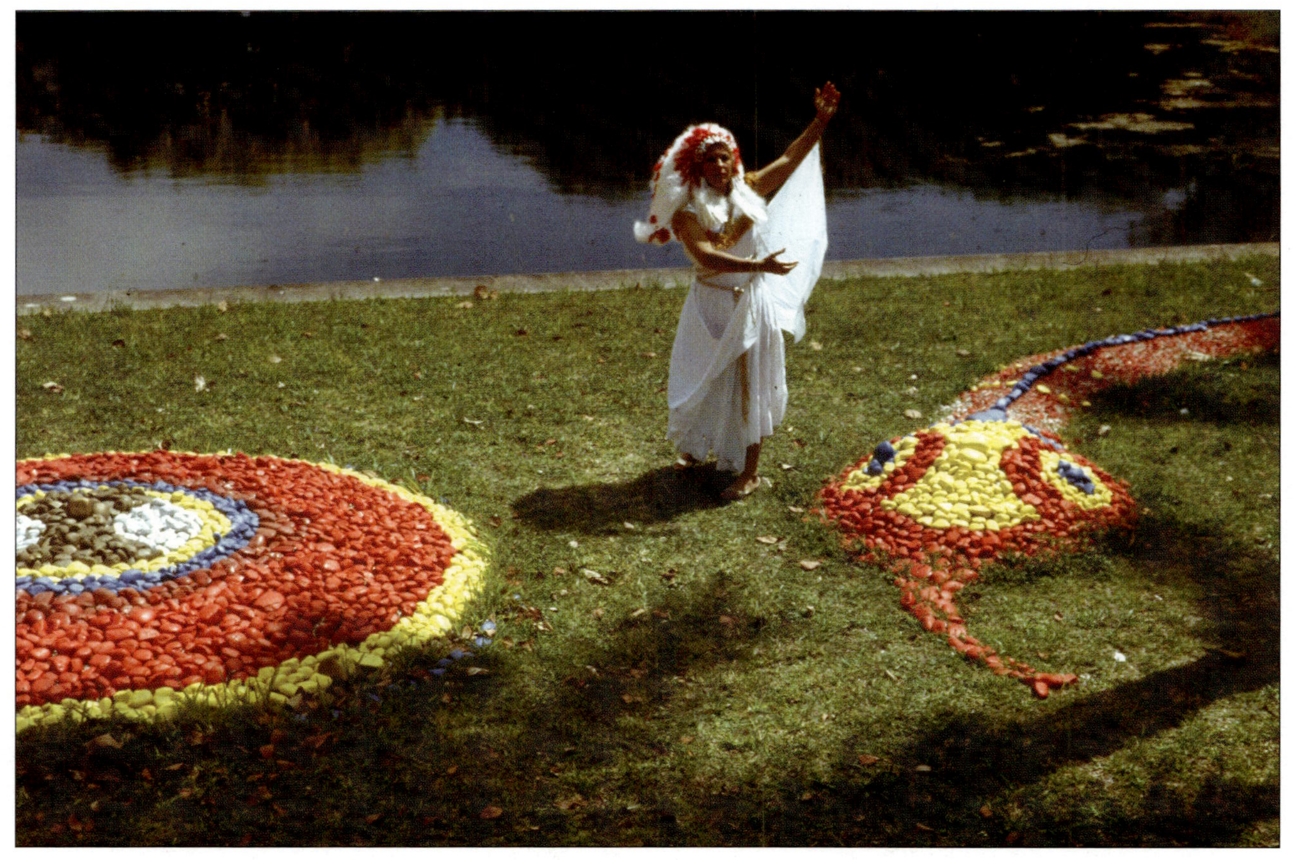

**11. Nature Goddess Sekhmet: Magic Circle XII** © Kyra Belán, 1987
Detail of earthwork, artist in performance.
Photo credit: GL Sullivan

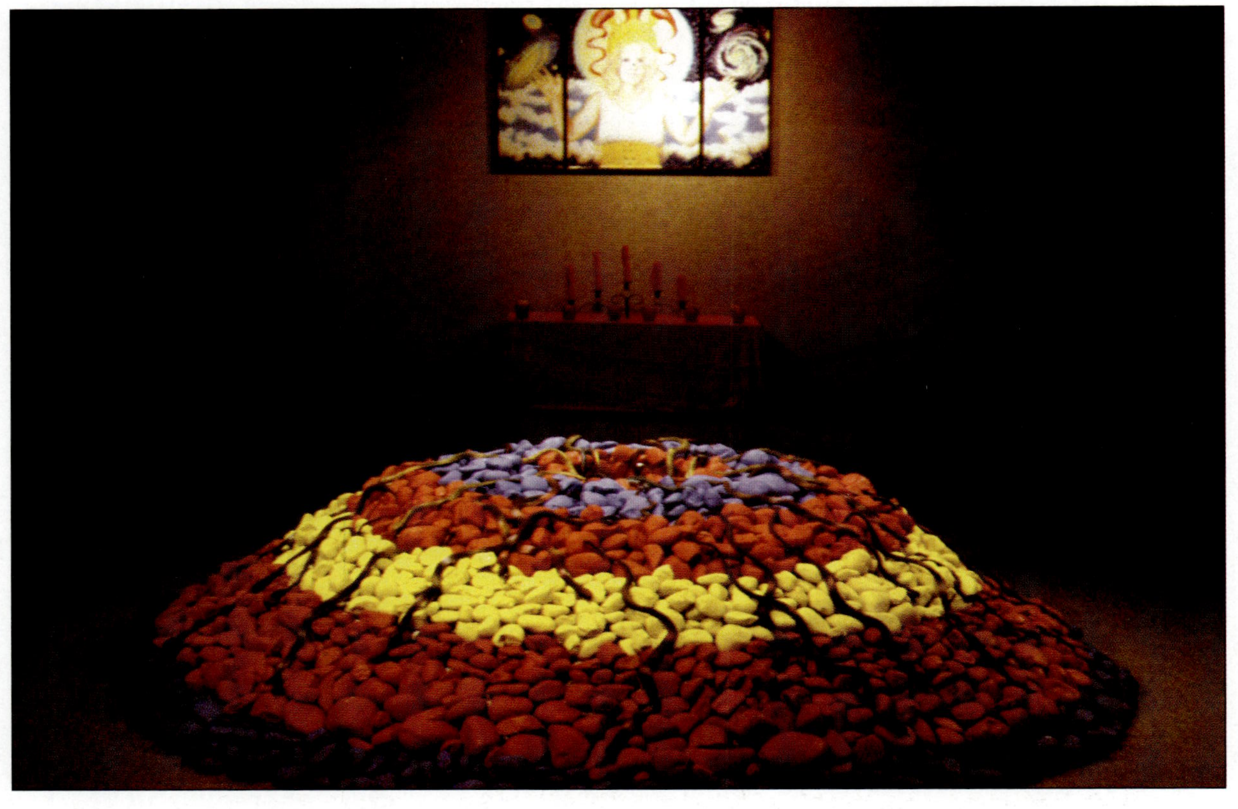

**12. Goddess Medusa: Magic Circle XIII** © Kyra Belán, 1987
Detail of environmental installation.
Fine Arts Gallery, Broward Community College, Davie, FL.

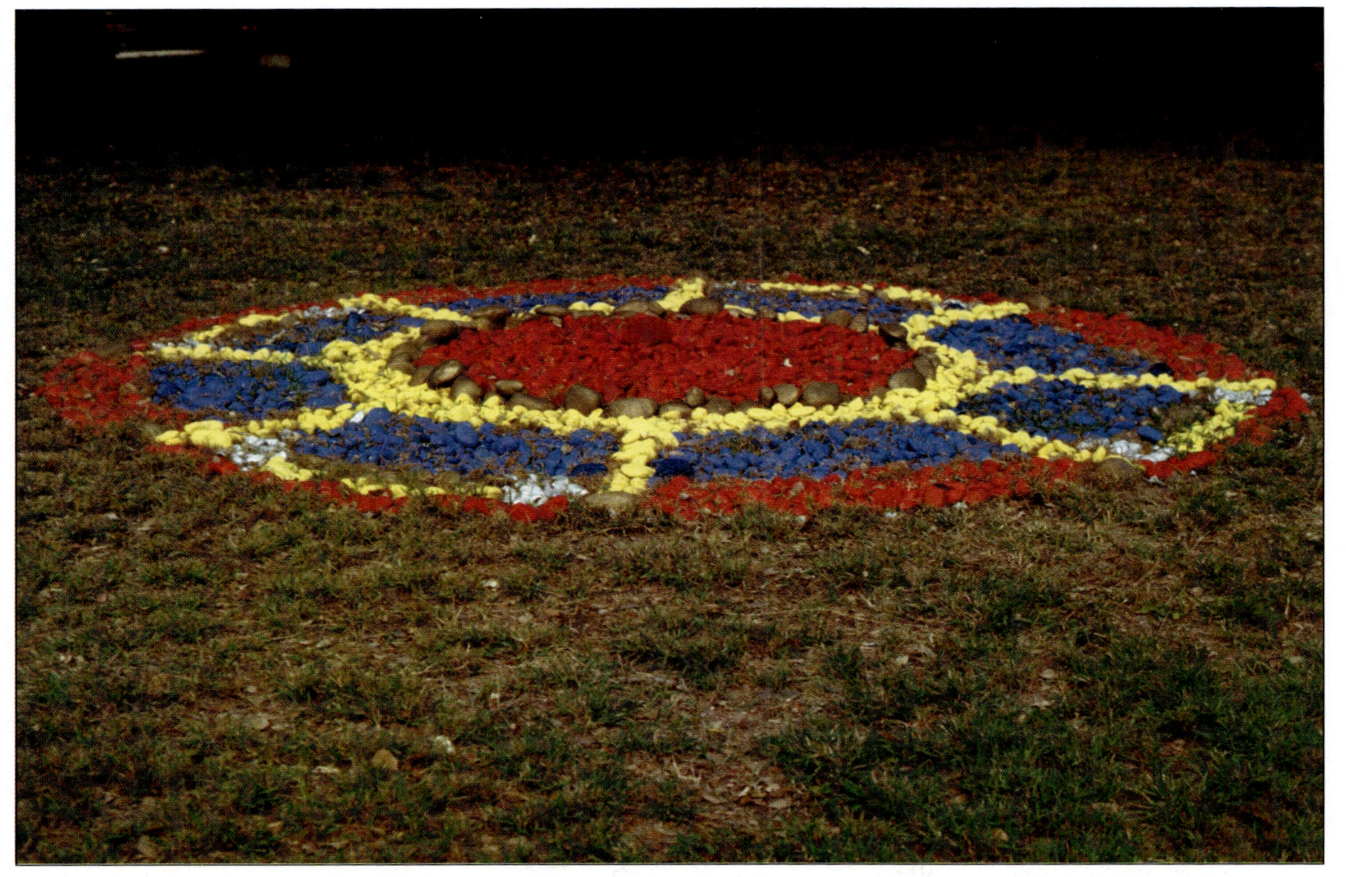

**13. Celebration for Goddess Juno: Magic Circle XXI** © Kyra Belán, 1993
Detail of earthwork, painted quartz.
Sri Naranda Yoga Center, Hallandale, FL.

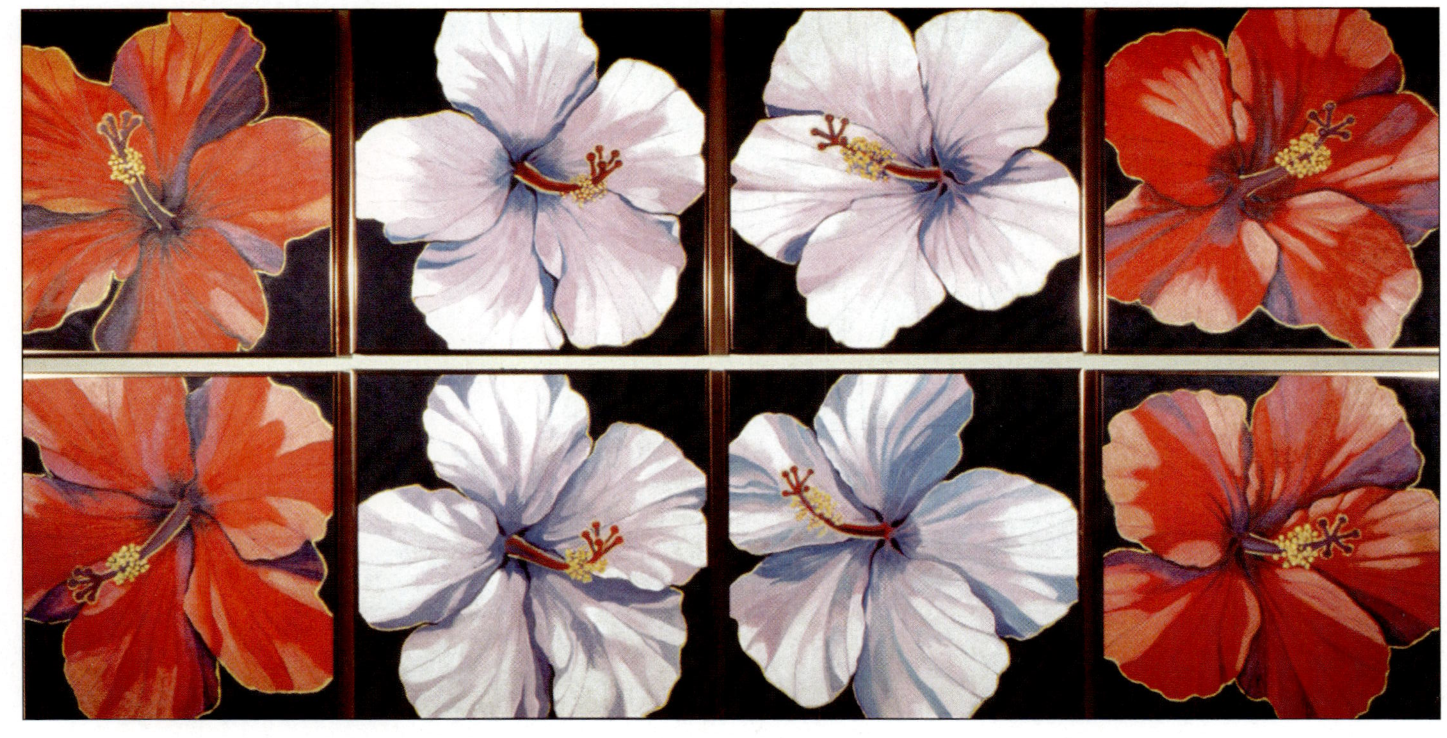

**14. The Floralia Series: Changing Woman** © Kyra Belán, 1995
Acrylic on canvas, 42" x 86", modular, detail of site specific installation.
Art and Culture Center of Hollywood, FL.

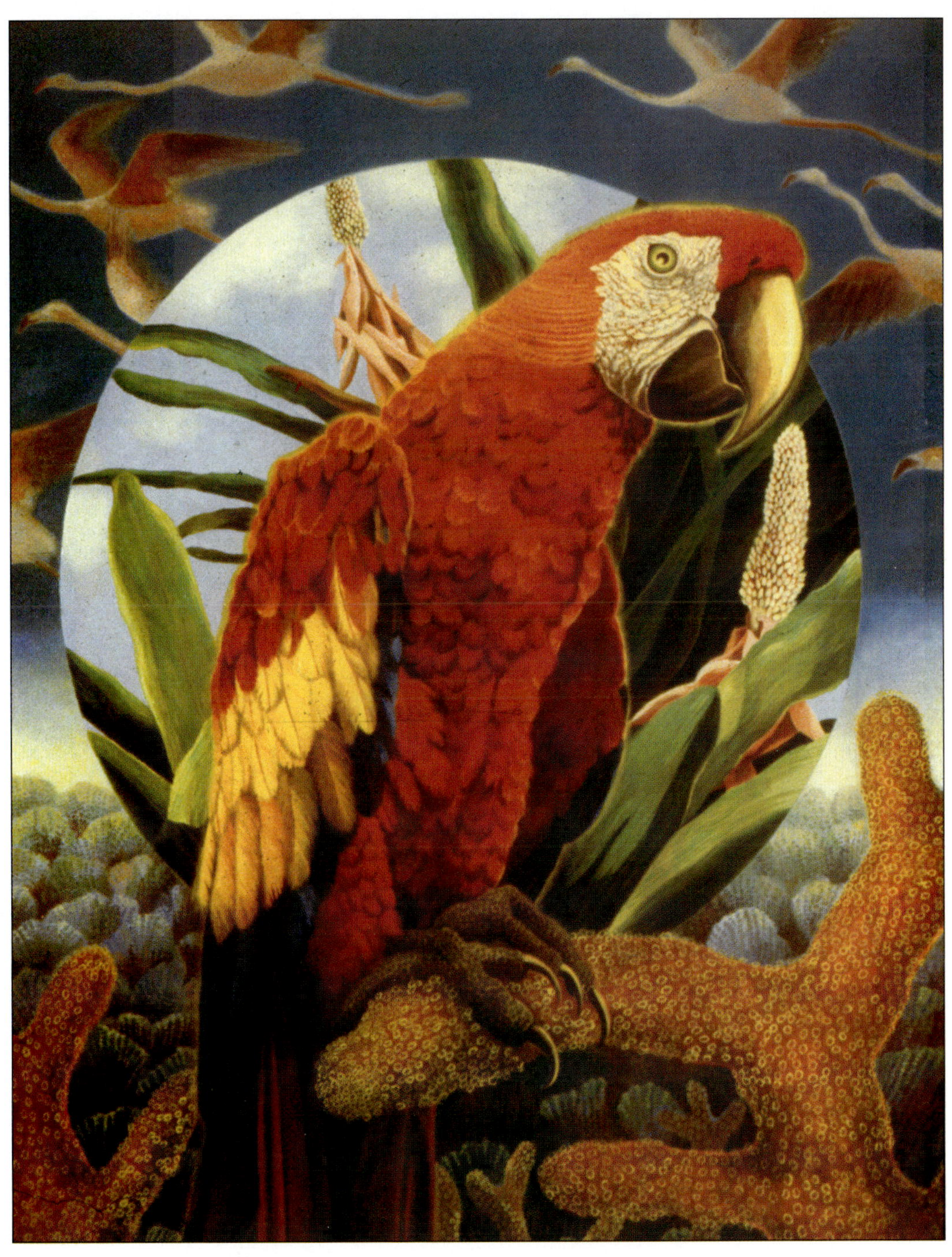

**15. Kali Series: Tao** © Kyra Belán, 1985
Oil painting, 50" x 40".
Bass Museum of Art, Miami Beach, FL.

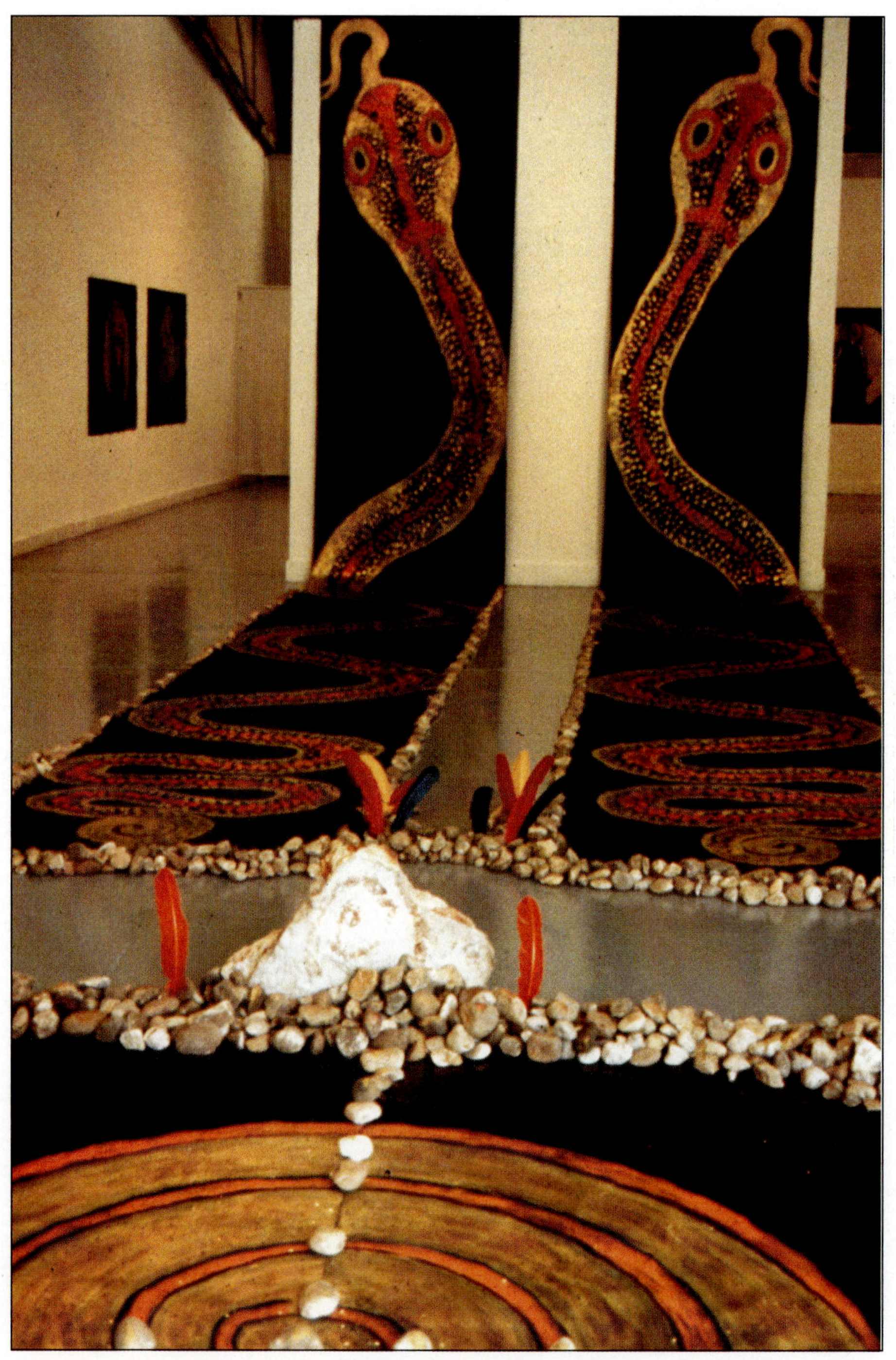

**16. Mother Earth, Mother God: Magic Circle XXIII**



Detail of environmental installation.

The 621 Gallery, Tallahassee, FL.

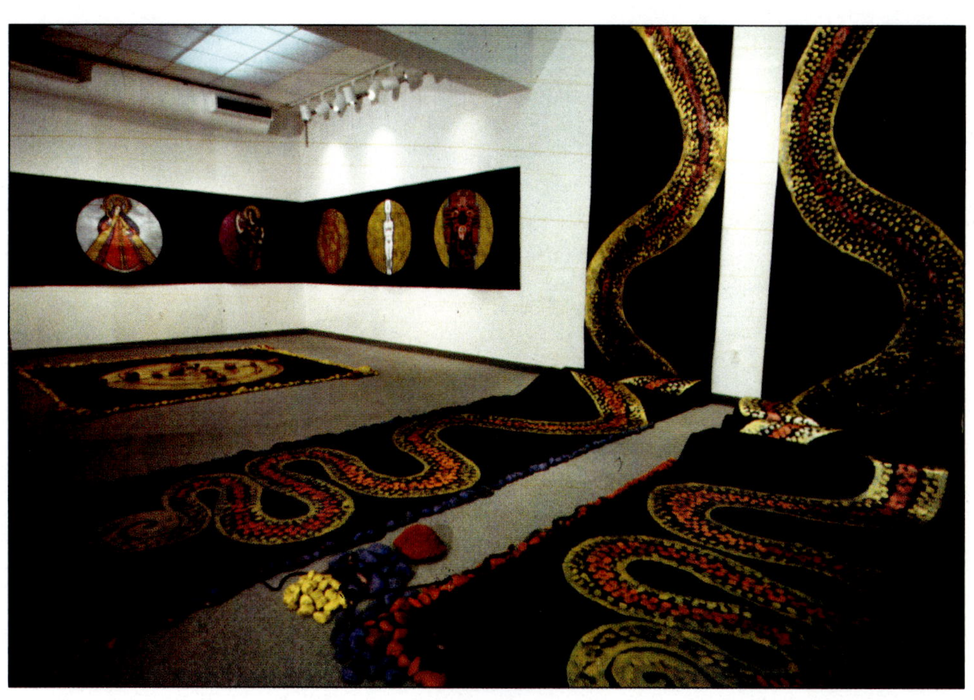

**17. Mother Earth, Changing Woman: Magic Circle XXIV**



Detail of site specific installation.

The Art Gallery, Broward Community College, Pembroke Pines, FL.

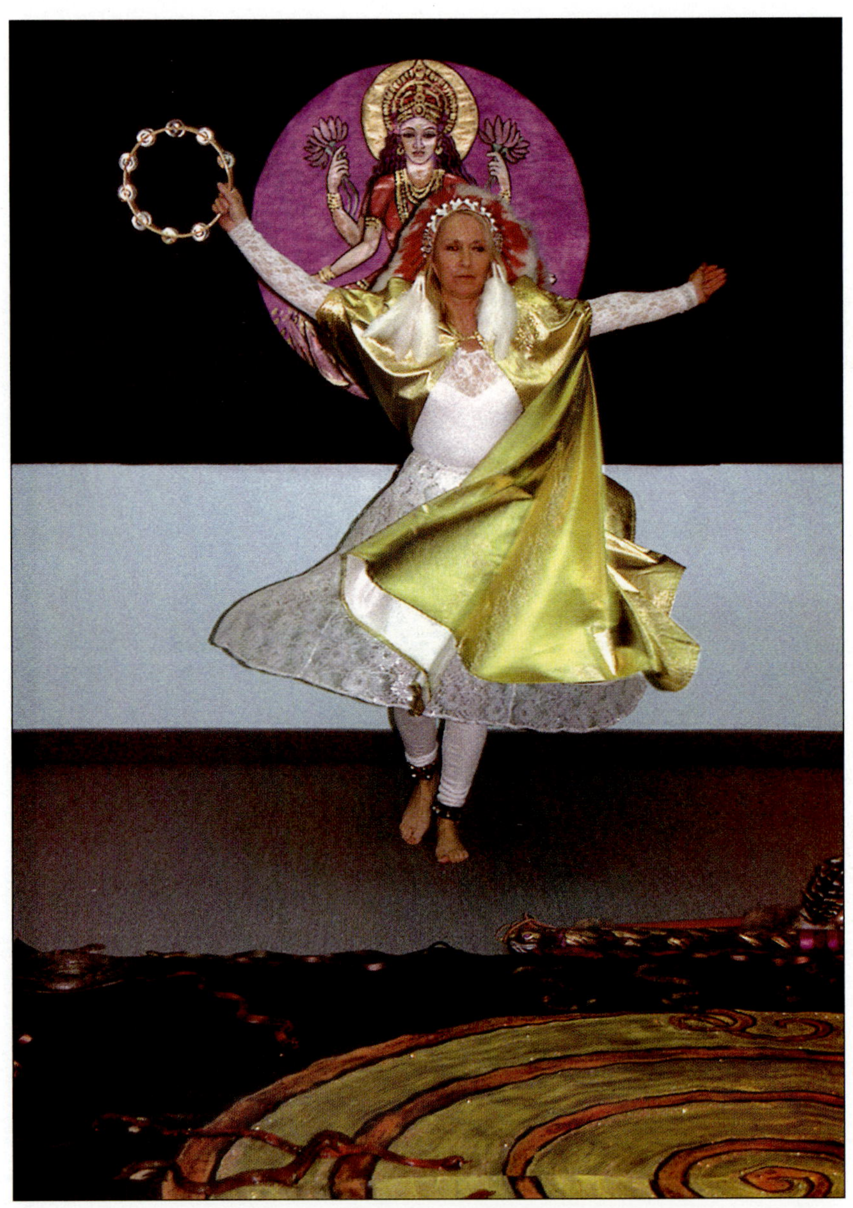

**18. Goddess Lakshmi: Magic Circle XXV**

© Kyra Belán, 1994

Artist in performance, detail of environmental installation.

Yoga Vedanta Science and Arts Center, Ft. Lauderdale, FL.

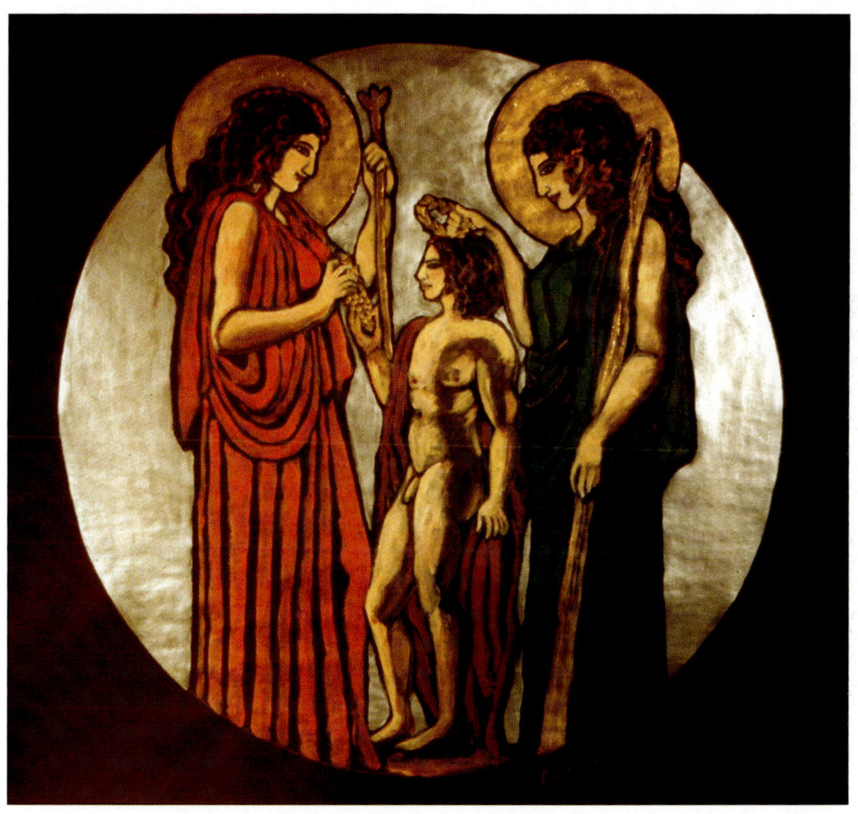

**19. Magic Circle Series:**
**Mother God Demeter and Daughter God Persephone**

Inspired by the Ancient Greek sculpture, “Great Eleusian Relief,” temple of Demeter and Persephone at Eleusis, Greece, c. 450 BCE
It is currently located at the National Museum, Athens, Greece.
Acrylic on paper, module, 52" x 73".

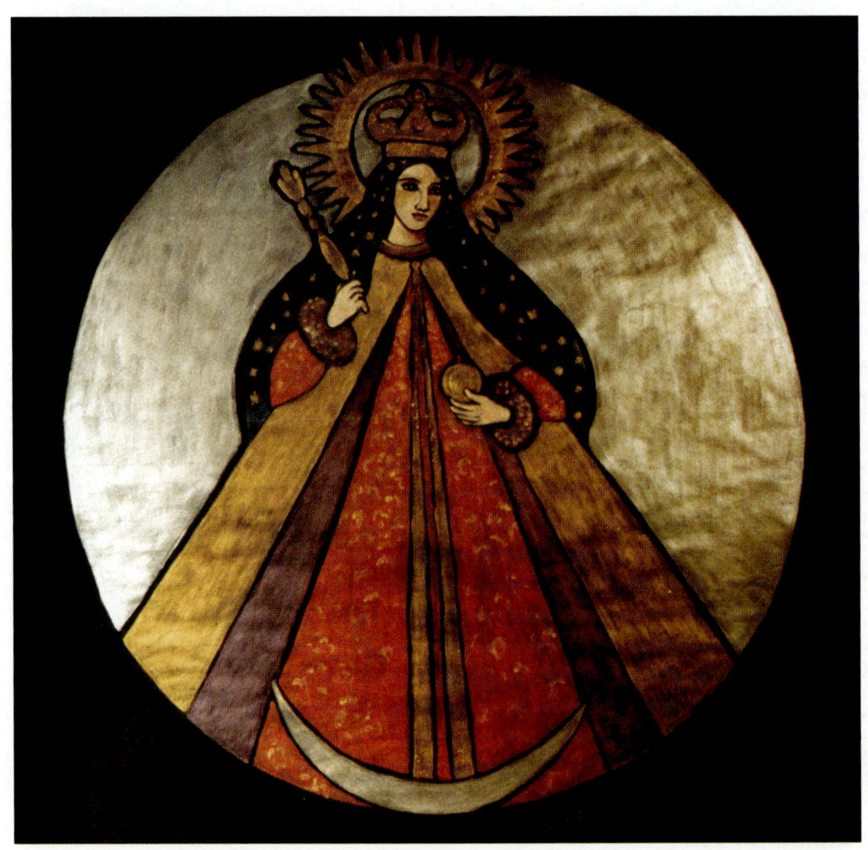

**20. Magic Circle Series: Nuestra Señora de Salud**



Inspired by numerous images of Seventeenth Century
Baroque art of South America
Acrylic on paper, module, 52" x 73".

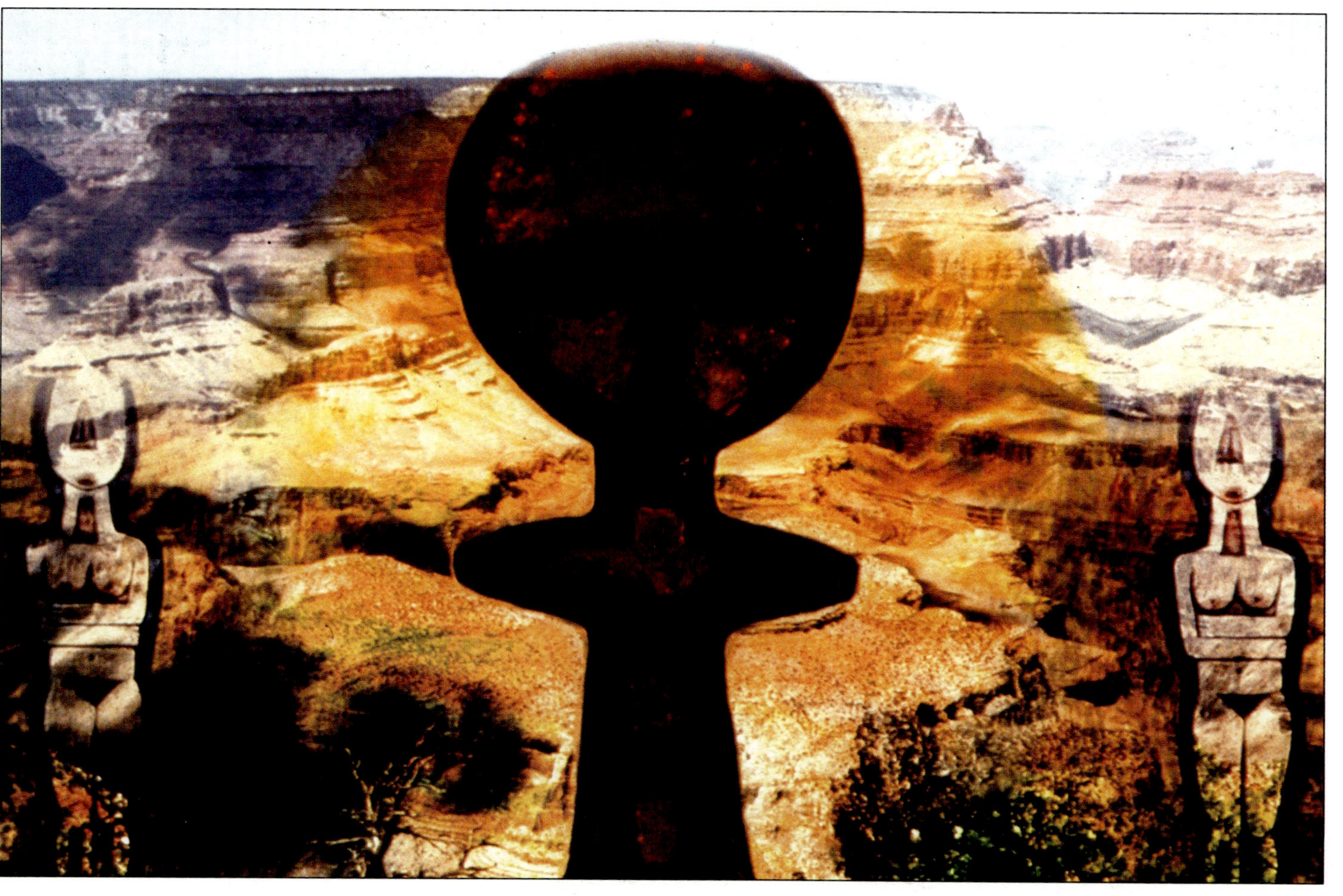

**21. Spirit Circle Series: Grand Canyon Akua Ba**
© Kyra Belán, 2000
Digital art on paper, 24" X 36"

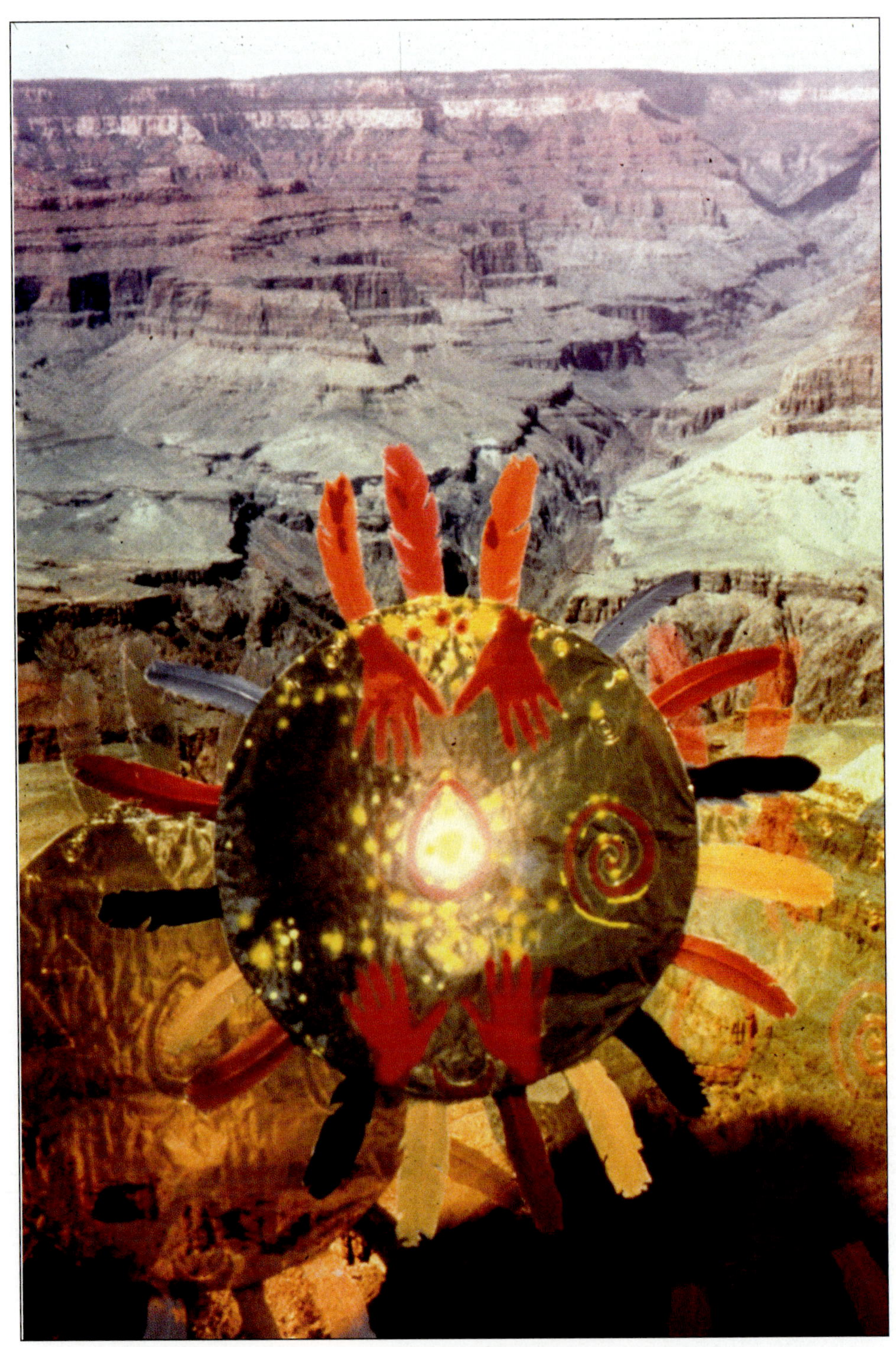

**22. Spirit Circle Series: Grand Canyon Shield**
© Kyra Belán, 1999
Digital art on canvas, 43" X 29"

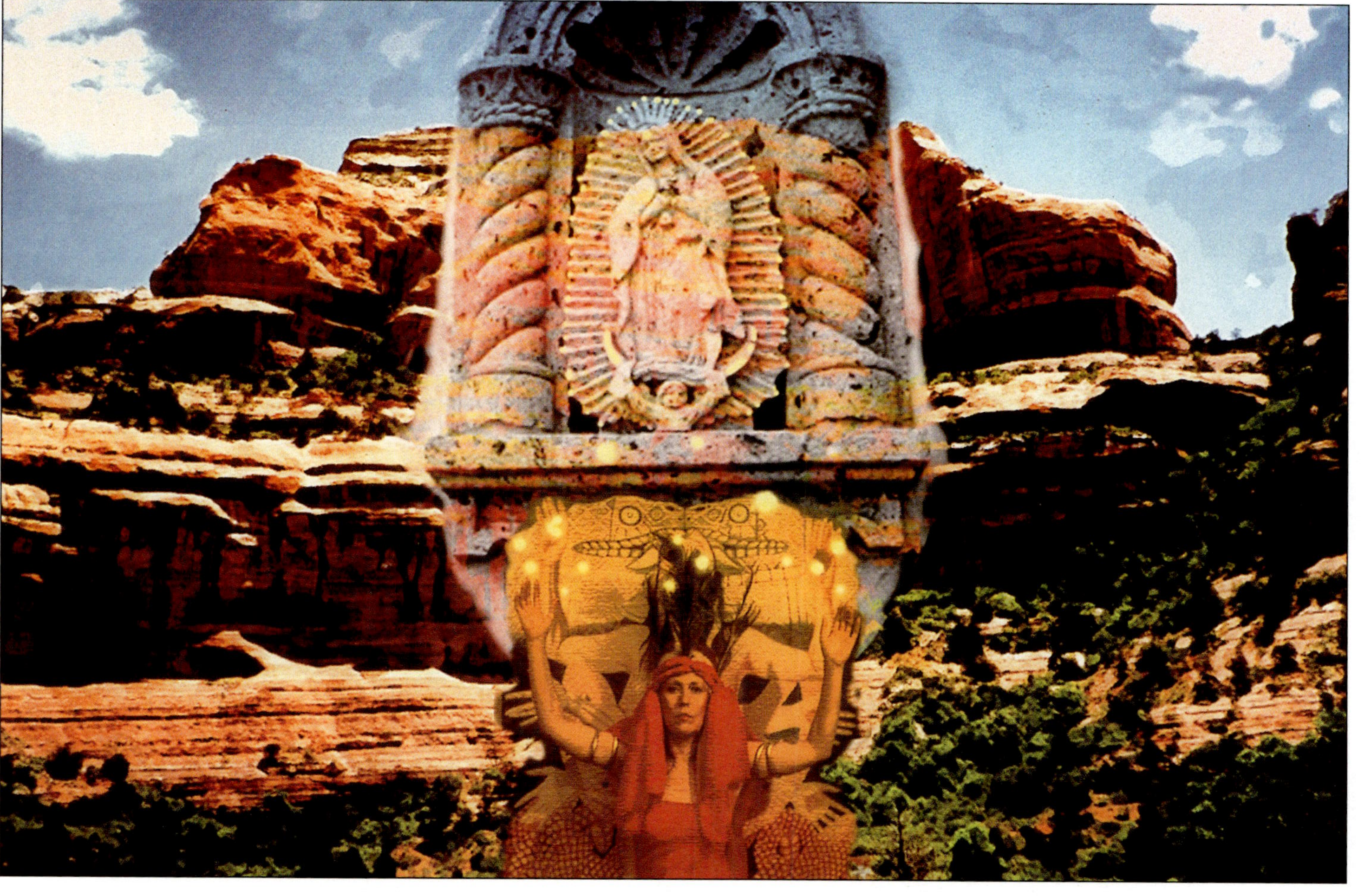

**23. Spirit Circle Series: Our Lady of Red Rocks**
© Kyra Belán, 1999
Digital art on canvas, 28" X 42"

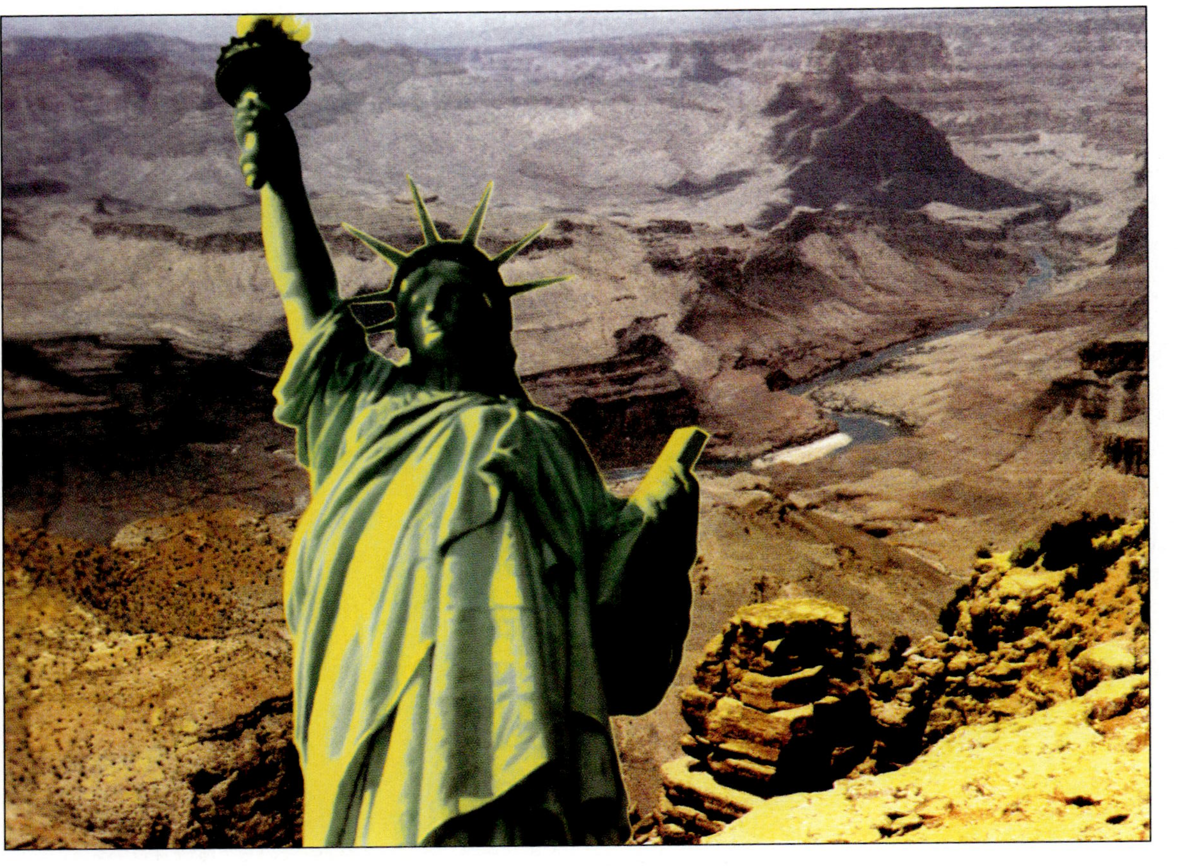

**24. Lady Liberty III**
© Kyra Belán 2004
Digital art on canvas

# *About the Artist/Author*

Artist, author, mythologist, and art historian, Dr. Kyra Belán graduated from Arizona State University with a B.F.A. in fine arts, and from Florida State University with a M.F.A. in visual arts. Her Ed.D., from Florida International University, is in higher education and art history. Dr. Belán has had over 40 solo art exhibitions and has participated in over 75 group exhibitions. She has received numerous awards, including the Southeastern College Art Conference's Award for Outstanding Artistic Achievement (2005), the Florida Arts Council's Individual Artist Fellowship, and her artworks are found in numerous public and private collections. Author of several articles published in journals, Dr. Belán has co-authored a book, *Dorothy Gillespie*, Radford University Press, 1998. She has written a novel, *Lucid Future*, Aegina Press, 1999, and a book titled *Madonnas: From Medieval to Modern*, Parkstone Press, 2001 (translated to French and German); and *The Virgin in Art: From Medieval to Modern*, Barnes & Noble Press, 2005. Currently, Dr. Belán is professor of art and art history at Broward Community College, Pembroke Pines, Florida.